Anthropology
and
Contemporary
Human Problems

Anthropology and Contemporary Human Problems

John H. Bodley
Washington State University

Cummings Publishing Company
Menlo Park, California · Reading, Massachusetts
London · Amsterdam · Don Mills, Ontario · Sydney

ACKNOWLEDGMENTS   My students and colleagues at Washington State University contributed many useful ideas and criticisms to this book, and much of the material in the first six chapters was critically reviewed by my Anthropology and World Problems class during the fall semester, 1974. Linda Jovanivich provided material on the Green Revolution, and I also drew freely on data supplied by Barry Hicks on the future; the typology of futurists in Chapter 9 is modified from a scheme he developed. Portions of the manuscript were read by Barry Hicks, Bob Kiste, John Nelson, Dan Stark, and my wife, Kathleen Bodley.

Cummings Publishing Company, Inc.
2727 Sand Hill Road
Menlo Park, California 94025

about the book

This book is intended to supplement introductory courses in anthropology. The purpose is to bring into focus the value of the cross-cultural, evolutionary, and cross-disciplinary perspectives that are unique to anthropology and to explain how these perspectives are applicable to a more profound understanding of large-scale complex problems of contemporary industrialized societies.

The book is a treatment of and a call for more anthropological research into the problems of overconsumption, adaptation to environment, resource depletion, hunger and starvation, overpopulation, violence, and war. Anthropologists have dealt with these issues in many different ways, in many different times, and in many different cultures. This book attempts to relate these anthropological insights to the contemporary world.

To evaluate objectively one's own culture is a most difficult task, yet it is a necessary one if long-range and effective measures are to be developed to insure human survival. Anthropology, of all the disciplines, should be centrally involved with this concern, and has been to a large degree, as is evidenced by current research and numerous case studies used in this book to advance the general thesis.

preface

In many respects the present work is a continuation of my earlier work, *Victims of Progress,* which dealt with the destruction of primitive cultures by our expanding industrial civilization. In *Anthropology and Contemporary Human Problems,* it is argued that many of our most serious difficulties are inherent in the basic cultural patterns of our civilization, and indeed in civilization itself. Primitive cultures are designed along fundamentally different lines and therefore managed to solve most of the problems which now seem about to overwhelm us. The contrasts between these two major types of culture —primitive and civilized—are so great that they must be virtually incompatible, and with the appearance of civilization the eventual disappearance of primitive cultures became almost inevitable. What we are now seeing is perhaps the final irony of cultural evolution— the latecomer, industrial civilization, has suddenly arisen as a clear dominant and a brilliant short-run success. We have eliminated the earlier primitive cultures, which were proven long-run successes, and there are now clear indications that civilization has accumulated enough internal problems to be self-terminating. We seem about to become victims of our own evolutionary progress. To avoid such an outcome, it is imperative that we view our contemporary problems in as wide a context as possible. We must go back and re-examine primitive cultures and compare their solutions to basic human problems with our own solutions. Perhaps this is anthropology's most critical purpose.

This book is not an exhaustive treatment of all modern problems. Instead, I have surveyed some of our most serious problem areas and have attempted to place them in an anthropological perspective. The reader must be cautioned that much of the data drawn from the archaeological and ethnographic record is fragmentary and open to more than one interpretation. I have tried to be objective and have indicated in several places where serious doubts are present. My own bias, that primitive cultures were generally well adapted to their environments and were in many other ways "superior," has undoubtedly colored my interpretation of the facts, but such a bias has proven a useful heuristic device.

This work could be subtitled *A Critique of Civilization*, like Stanley Diamond's *In Search of the Primitive*, from which I have drawn great inspiration. To criticize one's own culture is a difficult task and opens one to charges of hypocrisy and misunderstanding. If it is hypocritical to enjoy the benefits of civilization while still recognizing its shortcomings and working toward their solution, then I am guilty of hypocrisy. It must be clear that I am calling into question some of the most basic features of our culture. While for convenience many of my examples are drawn from the United States, I do not wish to single out any particular nation for special criticism. I also disavow any political-economic ideology and am emphatically not calling for a capitalist, socialist, Marxist, or communist solution. Perhaps my greatest frustration in writing this book is that while it emphasizes how profound the cultural changes must be if real solutions are to be found, how the necessary changes can be implemented and precisely what form they should take are open questions.

contents

1

anthropological perspectives on contemporary human problems

A knowledge of anthropology enables us to look with greater freedom at the problems confronting our civilization. (Boas 1928:preface)

Cultural evolution, through processes that many would label *progress,* has brought man to major turning points many times: the adoption of upright posture, early man's first use of tools, the development of language, culture as an adaptive strategy, food sharing, food production, social stratification, urbanization, state organization, and now industrialization. All of these changes have been decisive ones—crucial developments with critical implications for the future. However, industrialization is a *crisis* in the true medical sense. If for a moment we consider civilization a disease, then at this point the patient will either recover or die—as a species and as a cultural type.

Nature and Scope of the Problems

What we face is a *global* crisis. The entire species is in jeopardy; more is at stake now than merely the existence of isolated tribes or nations. A further complication is that we face not one, but *multiple* crises in many areas; and as they multiply, we may be confronted suddenly with an overwhelming "crisis of crises" (Platt 1969). The pace of culture change is now so rapid that new, unforeseen problems, each of crisis proportions, appear even before the earlier problems have been adequately identified. In effect, crises are now bigger (i.e., they bring greater potential for disaster), there are more of them, and they are arising more rapidly than ever before.

   We are undergoing an accelerating rate of culture change that strains our ability to adapt, and threatens to leave us in the vulnerable condition that Alvin Toffler (1971) aptly labels "future shock." This pace of culture change is apparent when the ages of the major archaeological periods are compared. The Paleolithic period lasted perhaps half a million years, possibly much longer, during which man remained basically a tribally organized hunter-gatherer. The transition through the Mesolithic into food producing and to the brink of urbanism in the Neolithic required perhaps 5,000 years, while nearly 5,000 years more were required to reach the beginnings of industrialization. The industrial era is now barely 200 years old (0.0004 percent of the age of the Paleolithic), and futurists are already proclaiming the arrival of the "postindustrial" era. As Toffler (1971:14) and others point out, much of our material culture has only been with us over the past 60 years or so—the space of one lifetime. Many of the most significant technological innovations, including antibiotics, TV, computers, nuclear energy, mass-produced organic compounds, and jet propulsion, have arrived within the past 25 years. The present generation is experiencing the most profound changes man has ever seen. While earlier crises were certainly "revolutionary" in their long-run impact, they occurred so slowly that they were imperceptible to the individuals involved, and their outcomes would not have been obvious for hundreds or even thousands of years. Cultural institutions were able gradually to adjust, but today we are often totally unprepared to deal with the unexpected impact of such rapid change.

Not only has the *pace* of change increased, but its *scope* has dramatically widened. The early evolution of man was not a global crisis. Man has only occupied all of both hemispheres for perhaps 15,000 years, barely 0.03 percent of his existence. The Neolithic "crisis" was passed independently in several areas, and was an event of basically local significance but with long-run implications. Even as recently as 150 years ago, perhaps 50 million politically autonomous primitive people still occupied vast areas of the world and were only marginally affected by either nation-states or the Industrial Revolution. Now, however, industrialization has become a global process that has destroyed or transformed all previous cultural adaptations and has given man the power not only to bring about his own extinction as a species, but also to speed the extinction of many other species and to alter basic biological and geological processes as well. If industrial man were to disappear overnight, he would leave an impoverished planet; but the extinction of man during the Paleolithic era would have been of no more global significance than the passing of the woolly mammoth. Even "local" crises now occur simultaneously throughout the world. The *human* impact of the present crisis is also far greater in scope than that of any previous crisis, because far more people are alive now than at any time in the past (the average population during the Paleolithic was approximately 0.001 percent of its present level) (Deevy 1960, Coale 1974).

Crisis Levels
We are presently confronted with crises on at least three levels: global, national, and personal. At the global level the biosphere's capacity to absorb human insults is being seriously strained, world resources are rapidly shrinking, and devastating armed conflicts threaten. Individual nation-states must meet these crises while at the same time they confront a multitude of domestic threats in the form of political instabilities and social and economic distress. Many nations are now hard-pressed in their efforts merely to continue satisfying minimal human needs for food, shelter, health, and education, and seem totally incapable of meeting rising demands for increased levels of material consumption. Individuals may temporarily ignore certain global and even national-level crises; but at the personal level, we are now being confronted with health, family, and value crises of unprecedented frequency, scope, and complexity. Whatever level we consider, our cultural means of individual and collective survival seem to be falling behind in their ability to cope with crisis.

Crisis Intensity

Whether we have 10 years or more like 20 to 30, unless we systematically find new large-scale solutions, we are in the gravest danger of destroying our society, our world, and ourselves in any of a number of different ways well before the end of this century. (Platt 1969)

Recently, an attempt to evaluate the intensities of current crises was published in *Science* by John Platt (1969), in an effort to establish priorities for a massive mobilization of scientists to deal effectively with the most critical world and national problems. In Platt's analysis, crises were cataloged by probable time of arrival into three categories spread over the next 50 years and into eight grades by probable intensity or degree of effect (see Table 1). The most dangerous crisis in terms of both imminence and intensity is, of course, the potential for total annihilation due to nuclear or radiological-chemical-biological warfare. Second-order crises, with the potential for massive destruction if not the immediate end of modern civilization, are famines, ecological catastrophes, failure of economic development, local wars, and the gap between rich and poor. Since this analysis was published in 1969, several of these second-order crises have actually already arrived. Third-order crises will mean widespread, nearly intolerable tensions and may well contribute to first- and second-order crises. Lower intensity crises may bring distress to millions of people, but do not threaten civilization immediately, or else they are likely to be distant enough in time that we can prepare for them at our leisure, as it were. The ice caps may indeed begin to melt (or expand) at a rapid rate within 30 to 50 years, but if we don't make it through the next 20 years for other reasons, we may never face such a "remote" crisis.

Crisis Awareness and Response

There is a question in the air, more sensed than seen, like the invisible approach of a distant storm. . . . "Is there hope for man?"

[The] question asks . . . whether we do not foresee in the human prospect a deterioration of things, even an impending catastrophe of fearful dimensions. (Heilbroner 1974:13)

TABLE 1. Classification of problems and crises by estimated time and intensity (World).

grade	estimated crisis intensity (number affected × degree of effect)	estimated time to crisis*		
		1 to 5 years	5 to 20 years	20 to 50 years
1.	10^{10} Total annihilation	Nuclear or RCBW escalation	Nuclear or RCBW escalation	(Solved or dead)
2.	10^9 Great destruction or change (physical, biological, or political)	(Too soon)	Famines Ecological balance Development failures Local wars Rich-poor gap	Economic structure and political theory Population and ecological balance Patterns of living Universal education Communications-integration Management of world Integrative philosophy
3.	10^8 Widespread almost unbearable tension	Administrative management Need for participation Group and racial conflict Poverty—rising expectations Environmental degradation	Poverty Pollution Racial wars Political rigidity Strong dictatorships	?

4.	10^7	Large-scale distress	Transportation Diseases Loss of old cultures	Housing Education Independence of big powers Communications gap	?
5.	10^6	Tension producing responsive change	Regional organization Water supplies		?
6.		Other problems—important, but adequately researched	Technical development design Intelligent monetary design		
7.		Exaggerated dangers and hopes			Eugenics Melting of ice caps
8.		Noncrisis problems being "overstudied"	Man in space Most basic science		

*If no major effort is made at anticipatory solution.

Industrialization has intensified many preexisting problems and has touched off a variety of new crises. Qualitatively unique social problems, international political problems, and now an environmental crisis have all suddenly materialized in rapid succession over the past 150 years and have widened to include the entire globe. Cultures perceive and respond to crisis in many different ways; but in view of the pace and scope of the present "multiple crisis," our capacity to adjust is clearly in doubt. As industrial civilization has progressed into its crisis, many individuals and institutions have sounded the alarm, the initial negative feedback mechanisms have been activated, but corrective response has been painfullly inadequate.

Certainly the earliest and most bitter resisters of progress have been the primitive peoples who have become forced participants, but they have not been alone or unsupported in their resistance. During the height of colonial expansion in the late 19th and early 20th centuries, a very active group of British anti-imperialists (Porter 1968) condemned the entire colonial adventure which was then feeding progress, and called for reduced industrial output. These scattered protests, however, were easily swept aside.

The first major industrialization crises to be widely perceived were the enormous social upheavals touched off by drastic economic transformation—the factory system in particular. These changes proved profoundly disruptive of the social order and spawned an almost instant outpouring of social criticism, dire predictions, and outright resistance. On the eve of the Industrial Revolution in England, the Luddites attempted to halt the entire process by attacking the new machines directly; and by the mid-19th century, Karl Marx and others predicted the collapse of at least one form of industrial civilization because of its "inherent contradictions." Many of these more obvious difficulties were partially met with belated laws setting minimum wages, providing social welfare, prescribing work conditions, allowing workers to organize, and attempting to regulate corporate economic power. The belatedness of such efforts is apparent in the fact that in the United States, there were no laws prohibiting child labor in mines and factories until after 1900.

At the level of international political organization, the potential for destructive military conflict, thanks to the new industrial tools of war and the new demands for resources, met with equally slow response, even though many individuals perceived the threats. Immediately after World War I, in which nearly 13 million soldiers were killed, there were tentative efforts to regulate international conflict, but it was not until World War II brought perhaps 30 million civilian and military deaths that more effective international regulatory organizations were established.

Industrial man's impact on the environment has been a more subtle crisis, and its full potential for catastrophe has only recently become widely recognized. The general feeling that a rapidly evolving technology could overcome any environmental limitations seems to have blinded most scientists, economists, and government planners to the need for accommodating to the world's physical boundaries until those limits were undeniably obvious. In the United States a group of scientists representing the American Association for the Advancement of Science petitioned Congress as early as 1873 for resource conservation measures; but the first forest reserve was not even established until 1891, nearly 20 years later; (Gustafson, Ries, Guise, and Hamilton 1939:7) and it was not until "Earth Day," 1970, almost a century later, that Americans generally began to acknowledge that industrial progress might not be fully compatible with nature.

The general pattern that is apparent so far in the response of modern nations to crises is for a considerable delay from the time that the factors that will lead to a crisis are set in motion until anyone perceives the potential problem, further delay until the problem is *widely* perceived, and still further delay until corrective action is taken. For example, DDT was "discovered" in 1934, was first used as an insecticide in 1943, was killing birds by the late 1950s and fish by the early 1960s, appeared as a contaminant of milk in 1963, but was not even partially banned until 1972. In this case, nearly 30 years' lag time was required before a biologically disastrous technology was regulated, even though its harmful aspects had been apparent to many scientists for some two decades. Unfortunately, DDT is still being applied on a vast scale throughout the "underdeveloped" world, and the potential for global damage is still enormous. For a cultural type that seems to value changes so highly, and which has indeed achieved a very high rate of change, such a correspondingly slow capacity for adjustment to obviously detrimental change seems incredibly maladaptive.

This poor response to crisis lends support to those who hold out such gloomy prospects for human survival. Aside from religious transformative movements that have periodically predicted the end of all things, it has only been in recent decades that a significant percentage of the members of any culture have ever had reason seriously to question the fate of mankind. This increasing doubt about the future is itself an important cultural fact which serves to highlight the gravity of the present crisis.

Anthropology's Contribution

> I hope to demonstrate that a clear understanding of the principles of anthropology illuminates the social processes of our times and may show us, if we are ready to listen to its teachings, what to do and what to avoid. (Boas 1928: 11)

We have defined the general nature of the world crisis and suggested some of the possible dangers and difficulties inherent in the slow response that is occurring—now it must be argued that anthropology has something important to say to these issues.

The problems facing us are unmistakable but complex, and acceptable solutions are still neither obvious nor easily implemented. In recent years, there has been an enormous outpouring of crisis-related literature. Specialists in many disciplines have attacked isolated problems; unfortunately, however, overall results have been limited. For example, far more has been written on pollution alone over the past five years than any single reader could master in a life-time, yet pollution remains a problem of crisis proportions. Such apparent ineffectiveness, in spite of intense activity, is partly due to a redundancy and extreme specialization in research effort, and the complexity and interrelatedness of underlying causes, but perhaps more importantly, to a lack of genuine overview on the part of the problem solvers. It is time to divert at least some of our research energies away from the minutiae of diverse problems and to focus on their broader context. What has been missing is *perspective*—a combination of detachment, a predilection for viewing the total picture in the widest spatial-temporal frame, and a clear recognition of the interrelatedness of social, cultural, biological, and psychological factors. Anthropology appears to be a discipline that is uniquely qualified to offer just such an overview. An anthropological overview may not provide all the answers we seek, nor even many easily acceptable solutions, but it can show us how we got where we are and suggest how we might get out.

In a sense, anthropology has been remarkably "preadapted" to serve a sort of early-warning, equilibrium feedback function for cultures such as our own that are obviously slipping out of balance. From its first establishment as a professional discipline, anthropology has been defined in terms of its holistic, cross-cultural, and evolutionary approaches. These methodological specialties provide the very perspectives that now are most needed. Each of these viewpoints offers special advantages in the present crisis and deserves to be discussed individually.

The Holistic Approach of Anthropology

Anthropology calls itself *the study of man* and is clearly the broadest in scope and most generalizing of the disciplines. With a little organizational shuffle, virtually every other social science, the humanities, and portions of the physical sciences could easily be accommodated as subdisciplines of anthropology. Anthropologists ordinarily receive general training in—or they may be concerned with—the biological, cultural, social, and psychological aspects of man, while they may *specialize* in any of these subfields. Those researchers emphasizing the sociocultural areas must constantly deal with the interaction of economic, social, and ideological systems, and must place these systems in relation to the natural environment. Only this kind of overview can hope to place the present problems in their full context.

The holistic approach leads naturally to the broad kinds of questions that must be asked if the modern crisis is to be adequately understood. For example, only an anthropologist might be expected to examine the psychobiological limits of man's ability to adapt to a rapidly changing culture, or to explore systematically the interrelationships between symbolic religious systems and a culture's adaptation to nature. This freedom to jump readily between subsystems and to follow research leads even across disciplinary barriers is a marvelously adaptive quality in a time when solutions must be found rapidly. In anthropology, the *research problem* is what often determines one's subdisciplinary orientation. Specialist expertise and methodology are problem-solving tools, not ends in themselves. In many other disciplines the opposite situation seems to be too often true.

If it is true, as ecologist Barry Commoner (1971) persuasively argues, that *overspecialization* is one of the primary reasons for our lack of response to crises, then any discipline that is willing to lower its disciplinary boundaries should offer special advantages. Clearly, the recent formation of interdisciplinary environmental science programs, where the problem defines the specialties, is a hopeful move in the right direction. Anthropologists should fit comfortably into such programs.

The Cross-Cultural Approach
No approach to our present crises can hope to be successful if it restricts itself to a single culture or even to a single culture type. We cannot be certain that the problems we see are unique to industrial civilization or to specific subtypes of industrial civilization; but more

importantly, other cultures may well have successfully avoided certain problems that we now find insurmountable.

Cross-cultural research also has certain other advantages. It requires a degree of objectivity and detachment that is often difficult to achieve when one deals with his own culture. Relationships may stand out far more clearly in an exotic culture merely because they occur in an unfamiliar setting, and an outside observer may be more willing to draw conclusions that might conflict with comfortable patterns of thought. The fieldwork experience itself also encourages a researcher to view his own culture through an outsider's eyes.

The Evolutionary Approach

Biological and cultural evolution affords a remarkable time perspective on our present condition. Without such a viewpoint, we would lack any clear picture of our own origins. In its broadest sense, evolution implies change; and evolutionary change is what brought man as a species from the tribe, to the state, and finally to industrial civilization. It should be clear that understanding this process of change will be a vital step toward directing our own fate.

The Concept of Primitive Culture

> My contention, then, is that the term *primitive* has content in anthropology; that it cannot be evaded; and that the attempt to explore its implications remains our central task, precisely because we are so civilized, and that anthropology can remain one of the most instrumental and useful, though it may often seem the most remote and eccentric, of disciplines. (Diamond 1968:104)

Anthropology's eclectic combination of methodological specialties finds its sharpest focus in the concept of *primitive culture*. This concept has traditionally been the area of research interest with which anthropologists have been most widely identified. Indeed, many anthropologists consider *primitive* to be *the* central concept in anthropology, and would define the exploration of its implications as our primary purpose. As Stanley Diamond, one of the leading exponents of this view, expresses it: "*Primitive* is, I believe, the critical term in anthropology, the word around which the field revolves" (1968:99).

Primitive means primary or original; and as anthropologists most often use the term, it refers to the human condition in nonstate cultures. Given the fact that no men have lived in states for more than the past 0.01 percent of human existence, and that at least a third of the 110 billion people who have ever lived, including those now living, have lived in primitive cultures, then with some justification primitive man may define the most basic human condition.

Perhaps the most striking and relevant generalizations that anthropology has revealed concerning primitive cultures is that they are totally different from our own culture and that, in a very real sense, they are the only *proven* cultural systems that man has ever known. They have existed for at least half a million years—maybe two million—and have successfully satisfied basic human needs without the aid of cities or states and without high levels of energy consumption or elaborate technology. In fact, primitive cultures represent an almost total contrast in adaptive strategy and basic cultural design to our own unproven cultural experiment. We can certainly learn a great deal about the nature of present world crises by carefully comparing our own situation with related aspects of primitive culture. That will be one of this book's primary objectives.

The Uniqueness of Primitive Cultures

Authentically primitive and maximally civilized traits are, I believe, as antithetical as it is possible for cultural attributes to become within the limits of an established human condition. (Diamond 1968:110–111)

Several significant contrasts are immediately apparent when the socioeconomic organizations of primitive and industrial cultures are compared. Primitive societies are quite small in scale, with densities of seldom more than one person per square kilometer, and maximum total population sizes of seldom over a thousand people divided into basically self-sufficient, kinship-based bands or villages of from 25 to a few hundred people. In comparison, industrial societies consist of millions of people organized into highly interdependent nation-states. This contrast in scale undoubtedly contributes to the obvious differences in degree of stratification and the corresponding differences in distribution of wealth, power, and opportunity between the different social systems. Within primitive cultures, status is normally a matter of sex, age, and personal qualities; and there is generally free access for all individuals to natural resources, food, and shelter. Historically, social stratification and inequality first become apparent with chiefdom-level societies; but even here, differential status does not deprive individuals of basic necessities. However, in an industrial culture, social stratification and inequality are developed to a high degree, and all individuals do not necessarily have free access to the same opportunities. On the basis of these differences, it might be assumed that personal and social problems related to inequality, such as poverty, powerlessness, and alienation, are not characteristic of primitive cultures, but they may be intrinsic aspects of industrial civilization.

Extreme contrasts also exist between primitive and industrial forms of economic organization, and these differences have obvious implications for the differential impact of these two cultural systems on the environment. Most significant here is the fact that primitive economies are locally self-sufficient, subsistence-based systems characterized by reciprocal exchanges and built-in limits to growth. Industrial economies are extremely specialized systems in which local areas generally do not consume the products they produce, and in which market exchanges occur where individual profit is the primary motive.

Writers on cultural evolution (Morgan 1878, White 1959, Redfield 1953, Service 1962) have emphasized the contrasts between primitive cultures and civilization outlined here, and have stressed the *qualitative* transformation that has occurred with the development of civilization. It seems clear that in their general configurations, at least, primitive and civilized cultures lie at opposite and incompatible poles. Primitive cultures are so unique that they can only minimally interact with states and still retain their full identity. There is no way for a primitive culture successfully to participate in an industrial system without first surrendering local self-reliance for dependence on the world market economy and de-emphasizing kinship to allow the profit system to operate freely. These changes will open the door to wealth inequality and social stratification, and a chain reaction of further changes that will mean the complete transformation of the original primitive culture.

Dropping the Concept of Primitive Culture

Unfortunately, anthropology's potential for relevance is being undermined by a growing number of anthropologists who have come to deny the uniqueness of primitive cultures and reject the notion that they have any special bearing on today's problems. Their position clearly must be challenged.

For many years, primitive peoples occupied the undisputed central position as anthropology's unique subject matter; but as it became apparent that these peoples were rapidly being transformed and exterminated, anthropology began to broaden its scope to include "complex" societies, and many researchers became absorbed in the promotion of economic development. At the same time, some anthropologists began to deny that primitive peoples could be distinguished from modern societies on the basis of any special unique characteristics, until finally even the term *primitive* was rejected as a derogatory, confusing, and therefore meaningless concept.

The fact that the term *primitive* has been used in a variety of careless and ill-defined ways has unfortunately been used as the principal reason for discarding both the term itself and the possible significance of the underlying concepts. It has been pointed out, for example, that peoples with highly developed civilizations, such as the Inca, have mistakenly been called primitive along with the relatively simple Eskimo; and because few anthropologists had carefully assessed the contrasts between primitive cultures and civilization, it was easy to assume that there really were no significant differences between them.

Obvious differences that could not be ignored were considered to be merely quantitative, and primitive cultures came to be characterized in strictly negative terms. In comparison with more "advanced" cultures, they were described as being merely *smaller* in scale, *less complex, simpler* in technology and as having *less control* over their environments than modern civilization. The possibility that these differences might actually constitute major qualitative contrasts, and might also offer critical adaptive advantages, was not widely recognized by anthropologists. Instead, many anthropologists became caught up in the prevailing euphoria over industrial progress and emphasized the inadequacies that were thought to accompany the quantitative "deficiencies" in primitive cultures, and generally concluded that civilization would be a sure improvement for them. It also seemed certain that such simple cultures would actually have little to offer an advanced, complex culture.

Some anthropologists have objected that the term *primitive* is offensive when applied to any contemporary society because it implies a lack of history, stagnation, and backwardness. Assuming falsely that the concept of stability in primitive culture means no change of any kind, they point out that all cultures change and all have long histories. What they neglect to note is that while primitive cultures did in fact undergo continual change, they still retained their basically unique structure and tended toward a balance with their resource base.

There has also been an implicit ethnocentrism in the argument that the term *primitive* is derogatory merely because it applies to cultural qualities that are truly different from those characteristic of industrial cultures. In fact, it may well be that the members of any primitive culture are not at all offended by their own unique qualities. Unless we wish to assume that our present form of civilization is the standard of normalcy by which all cultures are to be judged, there should be no feeling that the term *primitive* is at all derogatory; and actually, many scholars speak of primitive qualities with undisguised admiration.

Unfortunately, however, as the term *primitive* came under increasing criticism in the anthropological literature, it began to take on a derogatory connotation in many people's minds, and soon began to appear with apologies or quotation marks; and various substitute terms, suggesting the inevitability of progress, such as *preliterate, preindustrial,* or *precivilized,* were proposed. The real question of the uniqueness of primitive cultures was lost sight of in the debate over terminology, and it was finally declared that "primitive" was "not a legitimate concept deserving a single term" (Tax 1960). Perhaps most incredibly, some anthropologists began to consider the very *concept* primitive to be an obstacle to the progress of anthropology: "[W]hatever the reason, the continued use of and preoccupation with the concept 'primitive' (through such efforts as redefinition or substitution), will hamper the further progress of our science." (Hsu 1964:169–178) Predictably, there were soon demands that the term be completely abolished from use by the profession; as one anthropologist bluntly put it: "The word *primitive* should be dropped from the vocabulary of anthropology" (Southall 1970).

Dropping the concept *primitive* may well have helped anthropology progress as a discipline, and it may seem to be a purely academic matter. But it has also had implications for the welfare and even the survival of primitive peoples, and it clearly limits our perspectives on the present crisis.

The Dangerous Spirit of Rousseau

The rejection by anthropologists of the concept *primitive* was accompanied by a strong reaction against any "romantic" or "sentimental" emphasis on the positive qualities of "vanishing" cultures. For many years an anthropologist who acknowledged any particular admiration or respect for primitive cultures, or who compared civilization unfavorably with a tribal people and suggested that we might learn from them, was likely to be accused of "Rousseauan Romanticism."

In general, Romanticism seems to rank alongside ethnocentrism as the weakness to be most avoided by scientific anthropologists, and apologies are in order whenever primitive peoples are described in a favorable light. Edward Sapir (1964:96–97), for example, tells us that a sensitive ethnologist who has had firsthand field experience with a primitive society simply cannot help but admire the "well-rounded life" that the average member of that society leads. Even Ruth Benedict felt compelled to point out in her famous book, *Patterns of Culture*, that she is not using primitive case materials with any intention of "poeticizing the simpler peoples," and explicitly rejects as "romantic Utopianism" the possibility that primitives have qualities that we might profitably consider as alternatives to our own "maladies":   "But it is not in a return to ideals preserved for us by primitive peoples that our society will heal itself of its maladies. The romantic Utopianism that reaches out toward the simpler primitive, attractive as it sometimes may be, is as often, in ethnological study, a hindrance as a help," (Benedict 1959: 31–32)

Even more recent writers who actually have pointed out some specific advantages of primitive cultures are still apologizing. When Carleton S. Coon (1971:10) praises hunting peoples for having lived harmoniously with their environments, he hastens to add that he is not trying to follow Jean Jacques Rousseau's tradition by drawing a "glowing picture of the noble savage"; instead, he is interested in basic questions such as our own survival. In a similar manner, when physical anthropologist James V. Neel recently suggested a number of important principles, derived from research among primitive Brazilian and Venezuelan Indians, that modern society might follow to improve the genetic quality of its population, he was careful to include the disclaimer: "These suggestions do not stem from any romanticism concerning the noble savage." (1970)

Romanticism: Why Not?

In a television interview (Charbonnier 1969: 21–37) in which the famous French anthropologist Claude Levi-Strauss was asked to discuss the fundamental contrasts between primitive societies and civilization, he emphasized that primitive societies are like clocks in that they strive for stability, unanimity, and equality, while modern society could be compared to a steam engine because its hierarchical structure assumes a built-in disharmony and antagonism. The interviewer was amazed at this apparent violation of a familiar anthropological taboo, and incredulously said to the great man: "I seem to detect an echo of Rousseau's ideas in what you are saying."

Levi-Strauss responded simply: "Why not?"

This seems a fair question. Exploring the contrasts between civilization and primitive cultures is certainly a legitimate and even critical activity for anthropologists, whether or not it is considered Romanticism. Actually, the term *Romanticism* is somewhat misleading when applied to the kind of emphasis on primitive culture we are concerned with here. By definition, *Romanticism* can mean a preoccupation with the picturesque and imaginary or unreal. Certainly, primitive cultures are often picturesque and even exotic when compared to our own, but they are *real*. Their exotic qualities have never been presented as a reason for *not* studying primitive cultures; and in fact, studying such qualities has often been thought to be anthropology's principal reason for being. Of course, an overidentification

with primitives resulting in unreal data on exotic cultures, could justifiably be labeled Romanticism, but Rousseau himself has not often
been accused of that. Instead, at least one authority observes that
Rousseau "simply admires them [primitives] for qualities which they
admittedly possess." (Fairchild 1928:133)

Overall, the validity of the specific ethnographic qualities we
are attributing to primitives has never been seriously challenged by
careful field research. What in fact the "Romanticist anthropologists"
seem to be doing is critically investigating primitive cultures, finding
them in many respects superior to our own, and expressing regrets
that we have destroyed these cultures instead of learning from them.
This kind of Romanticism is clear in Coon's confession of admiration
for primitive hunters: "I respect and admire them. . . . they led
full and satisfactory lives, and it will do us no harm to reflect on the
advantages of some of their age-old ways of dealing with nature and
with each other." (Coon 1971:xix)

But why should there be such concern over this apparently in-
nocuous kind of Romanticism? It is evident that the possibility that
overinvolvement with primitives may bias ethnographic data is not
the principal fear; rather, the real danger is that Romanticism
threatens the preeminent position of applied anthropologists in the
culture modification—economic development field, and even more
serious is the danger that an anthropology overidentified with primitives will disappear with them.

In spite of their general reluctance to engage in "Romanticism,"
it is fortunate that at least some anthropologists have explored these
areas and reached some startling conclusions. For example, the work
of Neel, the physical anthropologist referred to earlier, sheds interesting light on the problem of how well individual potential may be
achieved in primitive society. After an eight-year, interdisciplinary,
team-conducted field study of some of the most isolated Amazonian
Indians, Neel concluded: "It is a sobering thought that the relatively
egalitarian structures of most primitive societies, plus the absence of
large individual differences in material wealth seems to ensure that,
within the culturally imposed boundaries, each individual in primi-

tive society leads a life (and enjoys reproductive success) more in accord with his innate capabilities than in our present democracy." (Neel 1970)

At this point, it would be appropriate to examine some of the qualities that other "Romanticist" anthropologists consider to be characteristic of primitive societies.

The Original Affluent Society

In 1965, 75 anthropologists assembled at Chicago* to examine the latest research findings on the world's last remaining primitive hunting peoples who were expected soon to become extinct. What resulted (Lee and DeVore 1968) was a new description of life in these simplest of ethnographically known societies, showing their existence to be stable, satisfying, and ecologically sound, and not at all "solitary, poore, nasty, brutish, and short," as Thomas Hobbes had proclaimed. It was learned, for example, that even remnant hunters such as the Bushmen, who survived in extreme and marginal environments, were not eking out a precarious existence, constantly on the edge of famine, as was thought; instead, they devoted only a few hours a week to subsistence and suffered no seasonal scarcity. When uncontaminated by outsiders, primitive hunters seemed to enjoy good health and long lives, while they had the good sense to maintain their wants at levels that could be fully and continuously satisfied without jeopardizing their environment. One researcher even suggested that this was, after all, the original "affluent society."

Most significantly, when the discussions ended, it was concluded that the hunting way of life, which had dominated perhaps 99 percent of man's cultural life span, had been "the most successful

---

*The Wenner Gren sponsored symposium on "Man the Hunter."

and persistent adaptation man has ever achieved" (Sahlins 1968); in comparison, newly arrived industrial civilization was in a precarious situation with the "exceedingly complex and unstable ecological conditions" it had created. At least one distinguished participant even felt that we should study why hunters were so successful, and that our civilization might actually learn something from them. These were remarkable conclusions to come from members of a profession which was vigorously disassociating itself from its long-exclusive identification with primitive peoples and which rigorously avoided any hint of Romanticism whenever it studied these so-called preliterate or preindustrial peoples. Hard ethnographic facts were forcing anthropologists to reconsider Rousseau's position.

Our Primitive Superiors

Rousseau was perhaps one of the earliest modern observers to comment on the success of primitive cultures, when in the 18th century, at the very beginning of the Industrial Revolution, he observed that the period of human history dominated by primitive cultures "must have been the happiest and most durable of epochs. The more we reflect on it, the more we shall find that this state was the least subject to revolutions, and altogether the very best man could experience. . . . all subsequent advances have been apparently so many steps towards the perfection of the individual, but in reality towards the decrepitude of the species." (Rousseau in Fairchild 1928)

A few widely known anthropologists have unabashedly followed Rousseau in this assessment of primitive cultures. Leslie A. White, for example, called nonagricultural, hunting societies "the most satisfying kind of social environment that man has ever lived in," and further elaborated: "[T]heir social systems . . . were unquestionably more congenial to the human primate's nature, and more compatible with his psychic needs and aspirations than any other of the cultures subsequent to the Agricultural Revolution, including our own society today." (White 1959:277–278)

Numerous other writers have also praised primitive cultures for successfully satisfying basic human needs. The evidence for this apparent success of primitive culture seems undeniable, especially when one considers the many thousands of years they have endured, their generally slow and conservative patterns of change, and the reluctance of surviving primitive peoples to abandon their life-styles.

2

adaptation, primitive culture, and the environmental crisis

Nor are those cultures that we might consider higher in general evolutionary standing necessarily more perfectly adapted to their environments than lower. Many great civilizations have fallen in the last 2,000 years, even in the midst of material plenty, while the Eskimos tenaciously maintained themselves in an incomparably more difficult habitat. The race is not to the swift, nor the battle to the strong. (Sahlins 1960: 26–27)

Many general conclusions emerge from the cultural ecological data that anthropologists have compiled over the years that are of direct relevance to our own environmental situation. Perhaps the most important conclusion to be drawn is that primitive cultures did indeed tend to mesh harmoniously with their environments. If man had never "advanced" beyond the hunting stage, it is unlikely that he would have ever initiated an environmental crisis. Even primitive food producers have been far more successful at avoiding environmental problems than most state-level cultures. Primitive cultures are clearly more stable and better suited to long-run survival than any more highly evolved cultures. These facts challenge many widely accepted interpretations of such basic anthropological concepts as cultural evolution and adaptation, and raise important questions concerning our own ability to survive.

Cultural Evolution and Adaptation

Among the widely held misconceptions regarding cultural evolution and adaptation is the view that evolutionary progress has meant greater security, greater freedom from environmental limitations, and greater efficiency of energy use. In many minds, higher levels of evolutionary development have also been equated with greater adaptive success. If theories of cultural evolution are to be harmonized with what is known about the obvious ability of primitive cultures to avoid environmental catastrophes, then these theories and their interpretations must be examined more closely.

The principal pioneer of modern cultural evolutionary theory, Leslie A. White (1949), defined evolutionary progress largely in terms of increasing per capita utilization of energy. A culture that consumed more energy per capita was simply more highly evolved. Other writers (Sahlins and Service 1960) have elaborated on this theory, arguing that two kinds of cultural evolution can be distinguished, *general* and *specific*. General evolution is concerned with levels of evolutionary progress, the more "advanced" forms that interested White. These higher forms are defined in terms of energy consumption, organizational complexity, and the ability to exploit a wider range of environments and to replace cultures at "lower" levels. Specific evolution means *adaptation to local environments*, and it is clear that cultures at low levels of evolutionary progress, as defined above, may be far more *efficient* in terms of energy input-output ratios, and far more stable and successfully adapted to their environments, than more "advanced" cultures. Cultural progress, in terms of general evolution, actually reduces security, diversity, and energy efficiency, and dramatically *increases* the likelihood of environmental crisis. Furthermore, it increases the work load of individuals.

Many of these points seem to have been missed by those anthropologists who have been particularly impressed with the material accomplishments of industrial civilization, and who have not paid close attention to the differences between general and specific evolution. For example, in a recent attempt to describe general levels of cultural evolution in terms of adaptation, Yehudi Cohen (1974:45–68) states that at each stage (hunting-gathering, cultivation, industrialism), man becomes better adapted for survival, more secure, freer from his environment, and more energy-efficient. In Cohen's view, cultural evolution has been achieved because man has sought to gain mastery over nature, and it has been inhibited in certain areas through man's ignorance of basic technologies. Recent research on such critical evolutionary advances as food production and state organizations suggests that the role of invention and discovery has been greatly overemphasized. It is more likely that such changes were gradually forced upon reluctant people as a result of unintended demographic imbalances. In this sense, "mastery over nature" has not been something eagerly sought by inventive minds; rather, people have been compelled to accept certain burdens and assume new adaptive risks by the grim need to readjust to altered circumstances.

Progress may indeed open more habitat types to exploitation by a given culture type, but this is not escaping the limits of nature, and it may prove highly maladaptive. Cohen devotes considerable attention to the "freedom from environmental limitations" concept and reaches some surprisingly shortsighted conclusions that directly conflict with more realistic assessments of the adaptive shortcomings of industrial culture. He argues, for example, that increasing mastery over nature leads to an increasingly secure food supply, and points to supermarkets and the ability to eat fresh fruit out of season as great triumphs over nature. Strawberries at Christmastime are, in this regard, "perhaps one of man's greatest achievements. . . ." However, if viewed in wider perspective, supermarkets and Christmas strawberries are incredibly wasteful of resources, and they are likely to be short-lived institutions as industrial civilization reaches the limits of its global environment.

Many writers confidently measure the "higher" adaptive success of industrial culture in terms of its apparent reproductive success and because of its ability to displace and destroy "lower," "less effective" cultures. What such assessments overlook is the time factor. As Sahlins points out in the quotation introducing this chapter, real adaptive success can only be measured in terms of survival—over the long run. If we insist on considering short-term reproductive success, or proliferation of people, an indication of adaptive achievement, then perhaps a new "law" of cultural evolution can be formulated: *Culture evolves as the global biomass becomes increasingly converted to the human sector.*

Certainly, a clear trend in cultural evolution to date has been toward a remarkable increase in the human sector of the global biomass (man, and domestic plants and animals) and a corresponding reduction in the earth's natural biomass. This reduction in the nonhuman sector is necessary because of the simple ecological fact that a fixed amount of solar energy fuels the planet's primary producers (green plants); consequently, there are absolute limits to how many consumers can exist (biologist Isaac Asimov [1971] places the actual limit of consumers at about two million million tons of biomass). As human consumers increase, natural consumers must decrease. The ultimate pinnacle of evolutionary achievement, then, should be the point when every gram of living material on earth has been transferred to the human sector and man's every natural "competitor" has been eliminated. At present rates of progress, it is estimated (Asimov 1971) that we may reach such a point by A.D. 2436.

Nature and Scope of the Environmental Crisis

In its most basic sense, the environmental crisis is a deterioration of environmental quality with a corresponding reduction in carrying capacity, due to human intervention in natural processes. At the present time, we are clearly running up against basic limits to the earth's ability to supply the resources that we consume and to absorb our industrial by-products. Later chapters will treat the specific environmental problems of food, energy, population, and resources in more detail; but first, it may be useful to consider the general implications of man's intervention in the biosphere.

The environmental crisis is not new; it has developed as general cultural evolution has given man greater ability to influence nature and has increased population and per capita consumption rates. Primitive hunters have contributed to the creation of grasslands; pastoral nomads have overgrazed their lands; peasant farmers have caused deforestation and erosion. From archaeological evidence, it is clear that primitive cultures and early civilization have at times faced their own local environmental crises as imbalances occurred, and have been forced to abandon certain regions or drastically alter their cultures. However, the scope and quality of the changes that global industrialization has set in motion over the past 200 years make these earlier problems seem quite insignificant. We now have the potential for disrupting basic life support processes and may already be inadvertently reducing our own prospects for survival. The following examples should make this point clear.

Death of the Tropical Rain Forest

In a recent article in *Scientific American,* Paul W. Richards, the world's leading authority on tropical rain forests, very calmly and objectively, with only a slight trace of bitterness, made the following announcement: "It appears likely that all of the world's tropical rain forests, with the exception of a few small, conserved relics, will be destroyed in the next 20 to 30 years. This destruction will inevitably have important consequences for life on the earth, although the nature and magnitude of these consequences cannot be foreseen with precision." (Richards 1973)

He remarked that this will be a "major event in the earth's history" and that it will irreversibly alter the course of biological evolution. The tropical rain forests have existed continuously for more than 60 million years and have been the source of most of the plants and animals, including man, that have moved out from them to pioneer the more difficult temperate zones. The rain forest is the most stable and complex ecosystem in the world and is characterized by a diversity of species that is unsurpassed by any other natural community. For all of its richness in plants and animals, the rain forest is remarkably poor in soil nutrients. Critical nutrients are stored largely in living plants, not in the soil, and are then quickly and efficiently recycled when plants die.

In the Amazon rain forest, the largest uninterrupted tract of tropical rain forest, scattered populations of primitive farmers, hunters, and fishermen have lived successfully for several thousand years by relying on shifting cultivation. Their adaptation rested on their ability to maintain fallow periods of sufficient length to allow regrowth of the primary forest before a new garden was opened. In recent years, outsiders have attempted to introduce permanent agricultural development schemes and have permanently destroyed the forest, leaving rain-leached, impoverished, rock-hard soils and scrub thorn forests in their place. As populations expand and governments look to the tropical forests for new lands to open to colonization, this destruction is accelerating throughout the tropical world.

It has sometimes been predicted that the clearing of these forests will lead to serious depletion of the global oxygen supply, but Richards feels that this is unlikely. He is not so certain, however, that their removal will not upset global climate patterns. In his estimation the destruction of the rain forest will clearly be a major loss for mankind in terms of potential human experience and scientific knowledge.

Death of the Oceans

> The end of the ocean came late in the summer of 1979, and it came even more rapidly than the biologists had expected. There had been signs for more than a decade, commencing with the discovery in 1968 that DDT slows down photosynthesis in marine plant life. It was announced in a short paper in the technical journal, *Science,* but to ecologists it smacked of doomsday. (Ehrlich 1969)

Perhaps the most serious environmental crisis, which has already been predicted by biologists and oceanographers is the death of the oceans. The above quotation is from a fictional scenario of such an event. In this case, it is assumed that pesticide pollution and overfishing will simplify the marine ecosystem to such an extent that toxic forms of marine plankton suddenly will expand, killing all other forms of marine life. There are many other possibilities. Oil pollution from spills, offshore drilling, and dumping may in itself become serious enough to kill off all marine plankton, particularly because oil on water concentrates chlorinated hydrocarbon residues.

Whatever the cause, the death of the ocean will be a far greater "event" in earth history than the destruction of the tropical rain forest. Marine phytoplankton supplies approximately 70 percent of the atmosphere's free oxygen—their destruction would almost certainly mean the disappearance of most higher life forms on the planet. Such an ecocatastrophe is now clearly within our capability, and indeed seems to be shaping up, "if present trends continue."

Since Ehrlich published his scenario in 1969, increasing data have been compiled emphasizing the extent of the damage that has already occurred. The richest fisheries in the world, off the coast of Peru, suddenly plunged in 1972 and 1973 to less than 25 percent of their 1970 peak production figures (Ehrlich predicted their end by 1975). Several other fisheries have already been eliminated; the great whales have been systematically exterminated; coastal marine ecosystems have already been seriously disrupted or destroyed by overuse, dumping, unintended pollution, and "reclamation" projects. Even the mid-ocean has become a cesspool of plastic and oil. The Baltic Sea is already in serious danger from pollution. The danger is unmistakable.

Environmental Crisis and Culture Change

Many times in the past, cultural systems out of balance with their environmental foundations have had massive culture change forced upon them. In fact, culturally initiated environmental change, or any changes in the balance of population to the resource base, will be an almost certain precursor of change in that culture toward the reestablishment of a balance, and there is no reason to believe that the fate of industrial civilization will be any different.

In Europe, following the arrival of Neolithic shifting cultivators, the limits of their subsistence adaptation were reached within a few thousand years. Forest fallow periods were shortened as population pressure increased, while domestic grazing animals further inhibited the regeneration of forest. Eventually, permanent open country and heath lands appeared over large areas of what had formerly been a vast expanse of virtually unbroken forest which hunting peoples had kept intact for tens of thousands of years (Clark 1952). As a result of this environmental crisis, shifting cultivation became all but impossible; the natural fertility of the forest soils was being exhausted; and a period of population movement, warfare, and dramatic culture change ensued. When conditions finally stabilized, it was at a higher population density and with an entirely different social and ecological basis. This is not the place to attempt an analysis of exactly how this imbalance in Neolithic Europe occurred. The important point is that it did occur, it was an imbalance, and it precipitated an environmental crisis and culture change in response.

Numerous other examples of similar environmental crises can be cited. There is clear evidence that agricultural practices in ancient Mesopotamia, where irrigation favored the gradual accumulation of salts in the soil, were contributing factors in the fall of Sumerian civilization after 2000 B.C. (Jacobsen and Adams 1958). In the New World, there is also increasing evidence that the "mysterious" sudden collapse of the classic Mayan civilization in Yucatan after A.D. 790 was at least partly a result of increasing demographic pressures on a limited resource base to the point that some kind of "environmental crisis" either occurred or was developing (Wiley and Shimkin 1971). Detailed archaeological data are available to document the collapse of a stratified, chiefdom-level culture on Marajó Island at the mouth of the Amazon River just prior to the arrival of Europeans, again as a result of overwhelming pressures on a limited resource base (Meggers and Evans 1957).

Such collapses and transformations must have occurred many times, and would seem to be the inevitable fate of any expansive, disequilibrium culture. However, on the basis of present anthropological data, it can be stated that, in general hunter-gatherers are very unlikely to accelerate their population and consumption rates to the point that environmental deterioration and a reduced carrying capacity result. Primitive food producers, with a similar economic organization, have somewhat more difficulty, but still tend to enjoy environmental equilibrium. Social stratification, inequality, urbanization, and state organization, however, set in motion a system that is almost inherently unstable. When expansive market systems and industrialization are added, disequilibrium is assured, and environmental problems become a certainty. The most critical difference now, however, is that the disequilibrium culture is a global culture, and we are seeing a global environmental crisis unfolding. The pre-dictable transformation or collapse of industrial culture will, like the passing of the tropical rain forest, be a "major event in earth history."

Global Disequilibrium: "The Limits to Growth"

We can thus say with some confidence that, under the assumption of no major change in the present system, population and industrial growth will certainly stop within the next century, at the latest. (Meadows 1972:126)

The basic behavior mode of the world system is exponential growth of population and capital, followed by collapse. . . . this behavior mode occurs if we assume no change in the present system or if we assume any number of technological changes in the system. (Meadows 1972:142)

On the very eve of the Industrial Revolution, in 1798, Thomas R. Malthus, a British economist, warned of population's potential for exponential growth and pointed out that, if unchecked, population would outstrip the ability of a country or the world to produce food. He revised and refined his basic argument several times in the face of a barrage of criticism that held that there was no such tendency, or that the potential of the earth was virtually limitless. Many critics, particularly economists and social planners, argued that population growth was essential for industrial growth, and that together these would assure continued happiness and prosperity for man. This growth concept has certainly been a central theme in the world view of industrial civilization; and perpetual expansion, whether in population or consumption, has in fact been the distinguishing fea-ture of industrial economic systems. Malthus was not alone in his pessimism over growth. Other early economists, including Adam Smith and David Ricardo, also felt that continual economic growth would not be possible forever because of ultimate limits and inevitable diminishing returns from a dwindling resource base. Any stabilization of the industrial economic system was thought to be so far in the future that no one need worry about planning for it. Only in recent years have significant numbers of scientists begun to doubt that continual growth can be sustained by a finite planet long into the foreseeable future.

In 1864, an American scholar, George P. Marsh, published a massive indictment of the deterioration of the natural environments of Europe and America that had already occurred due to human intervention, and boldly warned that a "shattered" earth and the extinction of the species might result from further human "crimes" against nature.

Over the next 100 years, after these early warnings, the hazards of constant growth in a finite world were largely ignored, thanks to the dramatic achievements of science and technology in increasing production. Few people seemed to worry that a sudden switch to nonrenewable new energy sources (coal and oil), and the imperialist expansion into Africa and Asia, might only increase the disequilibrium and temporarily delay a stabilization, while greatly raising the cost of readjustment and heightening the potential dangers.

By 1954, as the great effort for global economic development gained momentum, the combined problems of population growth, industrial expansion, and the limitations of the world to support such developments were posed as serious threats to the future survival of man in a provocative book by Harrison Brown entitled *The Challenge of Man's Future*. Brown suggested that the most likely outcome to expect would be the irreversible collapse of industrial civilization due to its own instabilities and the destruction of its resource base through inadequately regulated exploitation. The only other likely outcome that Brown could imagine which would permit the limited survival of industrial civilization would be through careful planning and rigid restriction of individual freedom by authoritarian governments. In effect, new mechanisms of social integration would need to evolve. Similar pessimism and warnings have been raised recently by

Robert L. Heilbroner (1974), an economist who a short time earlier was an optimistic champion of worldwide industrialization.

The most ambitious and authoritative attempt to examine the probable implications of the present instability of industrial civilization is *The Limits to Growth* study (Meadows et. al.) published in 1972. This study is the result of some two years of research by a 17-man international team of experts working with a complex computer model of the "global system" devised by Jay Forrester of the Massachusetts Institute of Technology. Starting from certain basic assumptions about the interrelatedness of population, agricultural production, resource depletion, industrial production, and pollution, the team set out to estimate how these factors might interact to set limits on the future expansion of industrial civilization (See Figure 1). The results of this research were surprising to many people and distressing to everyone. No matter how the variables were manipulated, (i.e., by technological solutions, assuming twice as many natural resources, solving the problem of pollution, and so on), the system collapses before A.D. 2100 because of basic environmental limits. Figure 2 illustrates how a collapse might occur if present trends continue. Stabilizing population extends the system somewhat, but collapse still occurs because resources are exhausted. According to these projections, the only feasible solution for maintaining industrial civilization as a viable adaptation is to stabilize both population and industrial production as quickly as possible.

The M.I.T. *Limits to Growth* study has prompted severe criticism from technological optimists, who imply that the long-run limitations are still far in the future and at present undefinable. The world model has been criticized as imprecise and too complex for wide understanding, and oversimplified. It has been suggested by such critics that it might be dangerous to attempt to bring economic growth to a halt, and those desiring stability are accused of being elitists who only wish to maintain the status quo in their favor. For their part, the critics have yet to present more adequate models or to show convincingly that present economic systems and values, and future technologies will deal with the problems that both pessimists and optimists agree already exist.

If the basic trends and the relationships between trends shown in the world model are valid, then perhaps it is time for anthropologists seriously to reconsider their own position on the question of economic growth. Certainly, anthropologists have been actively engaged in the promotion of economic development throughout the world. Now, perhaps, many will wish to explore the relationship between such growth and the increasing environmental crisis and the instabilities of our present industrial adaptation. Anthropologists may well want to join the rising debate over how industrial growth might end and how a transition to a steady-state economy might be achieved.

At this point, it will be useful to examine some of the explanations that have been offered for our present environmental difficulties, before moving to the perspectives that can be gained from primitive cultures.

"Roots" of the Environmental Crisis

Whether or not the environmental crisis will lead to a collapse of industrial civilization within the lifetime of many persons now living, as some scholars believe, its basic causes are still best understood as an imbalance between pressures on the environment and the environment's ability to meet them. Resources are being consumed

FIGURE 1   The Global System.   The entire world model is represented on the following page by a flow diagram in formal System Dynamics notation. Levels, or physical quantities that can be measured directly, are indicated by rectangles, rates that influence those levels by valves, and auxiliary variables that influence the rate equations by circles. Time delays are indicated by sections within rectangles. Real flows of people, goods, money, etc. are shown by solid arrows and causal relationships by broken arrows. Clouds represent sources or sinks that are not important to the model behavior. (Source: Donella H. Meadows et al., *The Limits to Growth* (New York: Universe Books, 1972), pp. 102–103.)

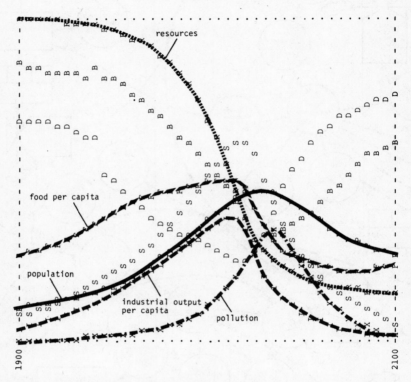

FIGURE 2   World Model, Standard Run. The "standard" world model run assumes no major change in the physical, economic, or social relationships that have historically governed the development of the world system. All variables plotted here follow historical values from 1900 to 1970. Food, industrial output, and population grow exponentially until the rapidly diminishing resource base forces a slowdown in industrial growth. Because of natural delays in the system, both population and pollution continue to increase for some time after the peak of industrialization. Population growth is finally halted by a rise in the death rate due to decreased food and medical services. (Source: Donnella H. Meadows et al., *The Limits to Growth* (New York: Universe Books, 1972), p. 124.)

at a rate greater than they are being produced by natural biological or geological processes, and wastes are being created that do not fit natural cycles. This imbalance may conveniently be considered a problem of *overconsumption* in order to emphasize that more is involved than an absolute increase in population. Overconsumption may be defined as consumption in a given area that exceeds the rates at which natural resources are produced by natural processes, to such an extent that the long-run stability of the culture involved is threatened. Every culture certainly has the potential for overconsumption, and this potential could be realized by a simple increase in population over the carrying capacity of a given region. However, this overconsumption seldom occurs in primitive cultures because negative feedback systems are activated to reduce population. Unusual increases in per capita consumption rates could also initiate overconsumption; but again such an outcome is normally prevented by negative feedback mechanisms. Unfortunately, industrial civilization has short-circuited the normal cultural feedback mechanisms which prevent overconsumption in at least four critical ways:

1. Dependence on nonrenewable resources
2. Dependence on imports
3. Urbanization
4. Institutionalized inequality

Perhaps the most critical turning point in the development of industrial civilization was its shift away from renewable resources to overwhelming dependence on stored fossil fuels, which have become substitutes for both solar energy and natural products such as fibers. These resources have been "banked" in the earth over millions of years and, in fact, represent stored solar energy; yet they are now being used to support temporarily a tremendous overgrowth of consumption far beyond what could ever be supported by local renewable resources. The danger in this case is that by the time these stored resources have become significantly depleted, we shall have "overshot" our renewable resource base to such an extent that collapse will be assured. A culture relying largely on local renewable resources would feel an impending shortage much sooner and could make corrective adjustments either by intensifying its productive technology or, more wisely, by reducing its population or consumption, or both.

A second critical way in which industrial civilization has temporarily escaped an inevitable balancing with resource limitations has been through its enormous reliance on extraterritorial resources—i.e., imports. Intercultural trade or exchanges of resources are perhaps universals, but it is unusual to find cultures totally dependent on such exchanges for survival. In the past, energy sources have probably never been imported; and trade was often limited to ritual items, or it may have served as a special means of maintaining peaceful intercultural relations. Reliance on imported resources to support otherwise unsupportable growth and consumption is an obvious source of instability and carries the same danger of overshoot and collapse as does reliance on stored nonrenewable resources.

Urbanization creates a similar problem because urban populations must be supported by internal "imports" from rural areas. The urban consumers are far removed from their resources and are unlikely to become immediately aware of impending shortages or of any other environmental impact of their consumption patterns.

Institutionalized inequality is normally defined by differential consumption patterns and serves to promote overconsumption while diverting much of its adverse impact onto "lower" classes who must first pay the real costs. Again, this process merely serves to divert and thereby delay the mechanisms that would otherwise maintain consumption within environmental limits.

In addition to overconsumption, industrial civilization has greatly increased the probability that it will cause environmental crises by disrupting natural cycles and simplifying ecosystems on a vast scale. Natural cycles have been disrupted by the introduction of new synthetic materials (such as plastics) which, as we have seen, have been used to support overconsumption artificially, but which also cannot be readily broken down by the environment to their constituent parts for reuse. Furthermore, even "natural" wastes have been created and concentrated in ways that have blocked their effective recycling or that have made them biologically destructive. In this regard, we have consistently violated what ecologist Barry Commoner has called the basic "laws" of ecology (1971). Simplification of ecosystems is best exemplified by the industrial factory farm, in which an attempt is made to exclude all but one or two "desirable" species. This process greatly lowers the biological productivity and stability of an ecosystem, and can only be maintained at enormous cost in imported energy, and by increased use of pesticides and synthetic fertilizers, which in turn deplete nonrenewable resources and disrupt natural cycles.

Thus, our present environmental crisis is the direct result of overconsumption, disruption of natural cycles, and simplification of ecosystems. Since all cultures seem to have the potential for degrading their environments by such means, it remains to be explained why states—and industrial states in particular—have been the culprits in this regard, while primitive cultures have done only minimal damage. Many writers point out a single basic cause such as misuse of technology, overpopulation, or misplaced values, and emphasize it almost to the exclusion of other factors. Their arguments run as follows: If we can simply develop better technology, achieve zero population growth, or invent a new value system, our environmental problems will be over. The population and technology arguments will be examined later, but for now the values argument may profitably be examined.

Ideological Roots

Much of the recent discussion of the need for a value change stems from an article published by historian Lynn White, Jr., in 1967.* The

---

*See also Anderson 1969.

author points out that religion promotes certain attitudes toward nature which are in turn reflected in ecological processes. Christianity is held responsible for our present crisis because in Genesis, God gave man dominion over nature, thereby initiating our victorious battle with nature. On the other hand, it is argued that primitive animism, which makes man part of nature, prevents such a battle and avoids the crisis. This viewpoint has much to recommend it, and it does emphasize important differences between primitive religions and Christianity; however, it confuses *association* with *causation* and may divert attention from the more fundamental changes that are needed. Anthropologists generally see religion in a *support* role, helping to maintain socioeconomic systems rather than directly causing them. Religious ideologies *reflect* economic adaptations and are more likely to change with them rather than vice versa. White concludes that: "Since the roots of our trouble are so largely religious, the remedy must also be essentially religious. . . ." This might be going at the problem backwards. More direct results could be achieved through a socioeconomic reorganization, and then religious ideology would swing in line.

Herders, Self-Interest, and Tragic Commons

Biologist Garrett Hardin (1968) sees the environmental crisis as a failure to define maximum good and considers it to be the inevitable outgrowth of individuals seeking their own self-interest in combination with a failure of appeals to conscience and social responsibility. He calls for mutually agreed-upon coercive restraints to maintain population and pollution within safe limits and suggests that these problems, strictly speaking, have no technical solutions. Like Lynn White, Jr., he feels that a change in values is required, but adds the important additional qualifications that political regulations must be strengthened.

It is clearly not possible to optimize both population and consumption, because limiting consumption will allow a larger population, and vice versa. Cultures must, in effect, define "maximum good" and then adjust population levels in conformity with the ability of specific environments to supply that "good" on a sustainable basis. Hardin correctly sees the solution of this problem, either implicitly or explicitly, as critical to the stability and survival of any cultural group, but fails to recognize that the problem has already been solved by primitive cultures without direct coercion. Regarding maximum good, Hardin asks: "Has any cultural group solved this practical problem at the present time, even on an intuitive level? One simple fact proves that none has: there is no prosperous population in the world today that has, and has had for some time, a growth rate of zero." (Hardin 1968)

This of course overlooks the fact, discussed in Chapter 1, that primitive cultures have maintained their stability by defining maximum good at easily satisfied levels, and in their own terms have achieved both "affluence" and environmental balance. At the same time, they have done so without the coercive restraints that Hardin feels will be needed to control the dangers of the pursuit of self-interest.

The example Hardin uses to illustrate why the pursuit of self-interest in the exploitation of a "commons" or public resource will not work is misleading because it fails to consider anthropological data. He assumes that a traditional herding society is kept in balance with its resources only because of warfares, poaching, and disease, which prevent individual herders from expanding their herds. When these controls are eliminated, Hardin supposes that individual herdsmen will continue to add extra animals to their own herds even beyond the point at which environmental damage results from overgrazing, because they will receive full advantage for each additional animal, while the costs of overgrazing will be shared by all herders. Each herdsman is thus caught in a conflict between social responsibility and personal self-interest, and only coercive force would make it obviously in his best interest to refrain from expanding his herd.

Anthropological research has shown that the actual situation in traditional herding societies is quite different, however. There is seldom any conflict between individual self-interest and social responsibility. Where self-sufficient individual households or small household groups must depend on herd animals for their primary subsistence, maximum herd size is determined by the number of animals a given herder can safely handle, quality of pasture, and daily grazing requirements of the animals, in addition to sociopolitical considerations. A large herd of large animals in an area of poor pastures would quickly become impractical, because the herd would need to move so rapidly to get enough to eat that productivity would decline (Spooner 1973). Overgrazing is encouraged when outside energy sources are introduced, making it possible to concentrate animals by drilling wells and hauling feed, and when animals are raised for the market rather than for direct subsistence. Many such developments have been promoted by governments interested in increasing the productivity of pastoral nomads, and have often included settlement schemes. Unfortunately, the result has often been serious overgrazing as traditional negative feedback mechanisms have been subverted. Only then does self-interest come into conflict with social responsibility.

Primitive Cultures and the Environment

Perhaps the roots of the environmental crisis will stand out more clearly if we examine some of the general ways in which primitive cultures have maintained such a successful adaptation. It appears that primitive cultures are characterized by traits that minimize maladaptive environmental disturbances; in contrast, industrial civilization is characterized by a notable absence of built-in cultural checks on environmental disturbances commensurate with its ability to create them.

I should not wish to minimize the fact that primitive cultures have sometimes seriously disturbed their local environments. It is quite clear that man has always been a significant force for environmental modification, but there can be no doubt that primitive cultures achieved a far stabler environmental adaptation than that presently assumed by industrial civilization.

The narrow range of environments that primitive cultures exploit is one of the most striking features of their adaptation when compared with an "industrial" adaptation. This is an aspect of the "import" factor discussed earlier. If too wide a range is exploited, a culture may escape the ecological constraints of a given local environment and become unresponsive to natural equilibrium mechanisms to the extent that it may ignore its own detrimental impact on that environment. Industrial nations are dependent on resources from throughout the world and may bring overwhelming external forces to bear on particular local environments, while in the short run they remain immune to whatever damage they may cause. For example, at the present time the Amazon rain forest ecosystem is being systematically destroyed by remote forces ultimately deriving from the industrial capitals of the world, while the primitive cultures occupying the area remain dependent on their local environments and respond immediately to detrimental changes within them (Meggers 1971).*

Environmental modifications occurring as a result of the intervention of primitive cultures in general appear to be much more gradual and more akin to "natural" environmental processes than the modifications caused by industrial civilization, which are often extremely rapid and qualitatively unusual. Industrial civilization introduces completely new environmental pollutants that disrupt natural biochemical processes. At the same time, ecosystems modified by industrial civilization become much simpler, less efficient,

---

*Rappaport (1971) makes the same point using a New Guinea example.

and more unstable than those affected by primitive cultures. Such differences sometimes result directly from contrasting subsistence systems. For example, the ecological advantages of primitive swiddens over intensive monocrop systems in tropical areas have frequently been noted (Rappaport 1971, Geertz 1963). In their crop diversity and organization, swidden plots structurally recreate the rain forest ecosystem, and thereby utilize solar energy with great efficiency and minimize the hazards of pests and disease. This point is discussed more fully in Chapter 4.

It is obvious that most experts on economic development do not understand the significance of these differences, because they usually argue that primitive, "pretechnological" cultures have little knowledge of their environment and no control over it. Yet the data of cultural ecology indicate that primitive cultures actually possess deep and highly practical knowledge of their environments based on intimate experience accumulated over many generations. The notion that primitive cultures have no control over their environment is based on a misunderstanding of what constitutes control. If "control" were understood to mean a stable and predictable exploitation of the environment, then primitive cultures may well have exercised greater real environmental control. The basic difference here seems to be that while industrial culture prides itself on its apparent ability to defy nature and struggles constantly to subdue it to its own ends, primitive cultures are designed to work within the natural limits of their environments. In this regard, long centuries of success would suggest that the primitive approach to control is far more knowledgeable.

Primitive Economics

Given the critical role that economics must play in any culture, some of the most important contrasts between primitive and industrial cultures should be expected here. Unfortunately, attempts by earlier anthropologists to describe primitive economic systems as if they merely represented simplified cash economies have resulted in widespread misunderstanding of such systems. In the older anthropological literature, it is not uncommon to find such inappropriate terms as *investment* and *interest* applied to primitive ceremonial exchanges, a bow and arrow called *capital,* and a shell necklace labeled *money.* At least one major textbook on primitive economics (Herskovitz 1952) attempted to follow classical economic analysis throughout, assuming, in spite of obvious difficulties, that primitive systems merely display modern economic institutions in a blurred and generalized fashion. Such interpretations have only served to obscure both the significant accomplishments and the unique qualities of primitive economic systems.

While primitive economies are often correctly described as cashless, subsistence-based, and simple in technology, these obvious contrasts alone do not explain their achievements. More important are the built-in limits to economic growth that characterize primitive cultures, and the fact that they explicitly recognize their dependency on the natural environment. In this respect, one of the key concepts in primitive economics is *limited good,* described by George Foster (1969:83) as the assumption that "*all* desired things in life . . . exist in finite and unexpandable quantities." Primitive man made this principle central to his economic system, while industrial man operates his economy on the diametrically opposed principle of *unlimited good,* which assumes that "with each passing generation people on average will have more of the good things of life." Within a primitive economy, several specific attributes, such as wealth-leveling devices, absolute property ceilings, fixed wants (Henry 1963), and the complementarity of production and needs, all center on the principle of limited good and contribute directly toward the maintenance of a basically stable, no-growth economy.

In a primitive society, wants are not considered open to infinite expansion, and the economy is designed to fill existing wants by producing exactly what is culturally recognized as a need. Wealth inequalities are often considered direct threats to the stability of a primitive community, and individual overacquisitiveness may be countered with public censure, expulsion, or charges of witchcraft. At the same time, individuals may obtain prestige through generosity, while the redistribution or destruction of excess goods is accomplished through kinship and ceremonial obligations, feasting, and gambling. In contrast, our economy operates on the assumption that wants must be continually expanded. Specific mechanisms, such as advertising agencies, are employed to increase wants, while individual acquisitiveness and increased consumption gain prestige.

Many anthropologists seem to miss the significance of growth-curbing mechanisms in primitive economies, and instead mistakenly represent as cultural universals the unlimited acquisitiveness characteristic of our economic system and the parallel inability to satisfy all of society's wants: "We have seen that the scarcity of goods in the face of the wants of a given people at a given time is a universal fact of human experience; that no economy has been discovered wherein enough goods are produced in enough variety to satisfy all the wants of all the members of any society." (Herskovits 1952:17)

Cultural devices to curb wants in primitive societies are also sometimes attributed to unavoidable circumstances, such as the fact that any accumulation of unessential goods would merely be an undesirable and impossible burden for nomadic peoples. This explanation may be partly valid in some instances, but it does not apply to primitive sedentary villages where limits on property accumulation are just as widespread. To explain their apparently self-imposed limits to economic growth, such villagers often simply state that property must not be allowed to threaten their basically egalitarian social systems. This is a significant point, for primitive economies with their careful limits on material wealth do in fact occur with egalitarian societies. In contrast, fundamentally non-egalitarian societies are characteristic of market systems. Clearly, if we want to understand the stability of primitive economies, we must look to other explanations.

Some economic development writers suggest that the only reason primitive societies curb their wants is because their technologies cannot fill them, the implication being that more productive techniques would free man's innate capacity for unlimited wants: "[Men] in every culture harbor unexpressed wishes to have more in order to be more. Once it becomes evident to them that it is possible to desire more, they will, by and large want more." (Goulet 1971:76)

Indeed, anthropologists have sometimes dramatically over-emphasized the supposed technological deficiencies of primitive economies.* Primitive systems have been described as if they were barely able to meet subsistence needs, and it has been assumed that primitive peoples faced a daily threat of starvation which forced them to devote virtually all their waking moments to the food quest. This traditional view remained almost unchallenged until careful studies of productivity and time-energy expenditure in primitive societies revealed that even the most technologically simple peoples were able to satisfy all their subsistence requirements with relatively little effort.** It has been shown, in fact, that many of these societies could have produced far more food if they had been so inclined; instead, they preferred to spend their time at other activities, such as socializing and leisure. It was discovered that hunters such as the Bushmen (Lee 1968) and certain Australian aborigines (McCarthy and McArthur 1960), who were thought to be among those groups closest to the starvation level, put in on the average no more than a 20-hour workweek getting food. Other researchers (Rappaport 1971, Carneiro 1960) have shown that primitive farming systems offer a reliable subsistence base that may actually be more efficient than the "factory farm" techniques replacing them.

---

*For example: Nash (1966:22), Dalton (1971:27), Levin and Potapov (1964: 488–499), Herskovitz (1952:16).
**Much of this data has been reviewed by Sahlins (1972).

On the basis of this kind of evidence, it can now be assumed that primitive cultures did not deliberately curb their wants and operate stable economies merely because they were incapable of either producing or desiring more, or because circumstances automatically prevented the accumulation of goods. Rather, it would appear that such systems survived and proliferated because of their greater long-run adaptive value.

Nature in Primitive Ideology

Numerous anthropologists have emphasized the fundamental contrasts in values, religion, and world view existing between primitive and industrial cultures in relation to the natural environment.* The most remarkable general difference is that primitive ideological systems often express man's dependence on nature and tend to place nature in a revered, sacred category. As Lynn White, Jr., and others have noted, the notion of a constant struggle to conquer nature, which is so characteristic of industrial civilization, where it is supported by biblical injunction, is notably absent in primitive cultures. Indeed, primitive man generally considers himself to be part of nature and may name himself after animals, impute souls to plants and animals, acknowledge ritual kinship with certain species, conduct rituals designed to help propagate particularly valued species, and offer ritual apologies when animals must be killed. Animals also abound in primitive origin myths; and at death, one's soul is often believed to be transformed into an animal. Careful research has shown that many of these seemingly irrational beliefs may actually contribute directly to the stability of primitive cultures by contributing to the regulation of both population size and levels of resource consumption. Population growth, for example, is curbed by beliefs

---

*See for example Spoehr (1956) and Gutkind (1956).

calling for sexual abstinence, abortion, infanticide, and ritual warfare, while various taboos may control the exploitation of specific food resources. In highland New Guinea, it has been shown that ceremonial cycles help maintain a balance between the human population, pig herds, and the natural environment (see Chapter 6, Rappaport 1968). Other writers (Bartlett 1956) have pointed out that sacred groves in many parts of the world have maintained forest remnants and reduced soil erosion; while under Christian influence, the forests have been chopped down, with unfortunate results. It is significant that these belief systems often disintegrate under the impact of industrial civilization, and are replaced by other beliefs that accelerate environmental disequilibrium.

The Desana Equilibrium Model

The case of the Desana Indians of the Colombian Amazon will now be examined in order to illustrate, in reference to a specific example, how the unique characteristics of primitive cultures operate to maintain a balance with the resource base, and to show how this balance may be disturbed by industrial civilization. The Desana are a primitive society of some 1,000 hunters and manioc farmers living in the Vaupés region of Colombia. According to the in-depth research of Colombian anthropologist Gerardo Reichel-Dolmatoff (1971), their culture "has formulated a series of very strict norms in order to assure the maintenance of a biotic equilibrium."

Perhaps the most exciting aspect of Desana culture is that its norms are explicitly based on such fundamental ecological principles as the energy cycle and the interdependence of life forms. The Desana assume that the fertility of both man and animals is dependent on the same finite circuit of recycling solar energy, and it is recognized that uncontrolled human population growth would unbalance the entire energy system through overhunting. Various cultural mechanisms are employed to prevent disequilibrium, including contraceptive herbs, used to support the stated norm of no more than two to three children per family, and a variety of sexual taboos and specific ritual observances that limit the frequency of hunting. It is understood that the availability of game animals is under the control of a supernatural being, the "keeper of game," who can restrict the supply or cause illness if the norms regulating hunting and sexual activity are not observed. A key role is played by the shaman, who must mediate between the demands of society for meat and the limited resources available. In order to carry out this duty, he communicates with the "keeper of game" by using hallucinogenic drugs and attempts to gain his favor while keeping the hunters informed of his demands.

The entire Desana culture is supported by its creation myth and is constantly reinforced by daily ritual activities, by periodic ceremonies, and, more importantly, by its obvious success. The system is designed to operate indefinitely into the future, and archaeological evidence indicates that the Amazon tropical forest cultural adaptation, which the Desana represent, has already existed for at least 4,000 years (Lathrap 1970). Unfortunately, however, missionaries are now seeking to replace Desana beliefs with opposing Christian beliefs, and settlers are arriving to "share" Desana resources. These outside pressures have already begun to upset the delicate balances Desana culture evolved.

Primitive Conservation in the Pacific

This chapter may be concluded with a description by anthropologist George P. Murdock of the condition of the high tropical islands of the Pacific after long years of undisturbed occupation by primitive cultures:

There was no destruction of forests by reckless lumbering with resultant reduction in water retention. There was no wholesale replacement of natural cover by cultivated crops such as occurs with modern sugar or copra plantations or intensive rice cultivation. There was no pollution of streams or coastal waters by sewage or chemical plants; no flooding of valleys by artificial lakes constructed for irrigation or hydroelectric power; no ruining of land surfaces through strip mining or slag piles; no massive earth removal for roads or air strips. There was no extensive soil erosion initiated by careless plowing or by overgrazing. The indigenous pig does not compare with the goat or the sheep as a conservationist's nightmare. (Murdock 1963)

3

natural resources
and the culture of consumption

The biosphere with industrial man suddenly added is like a balanced aquarium into which large animals are introduced. Consumption temporarily exceeds production, the balance is upset, the products of respiration accumulate, and the fuels for consumption become scarcer and scarcer until production is sufficiently accelerated and respiration is balanced. In some experimental systems balance is achieved only after the large consumers which originally started the imbalance are dead. Will this happen to man? (Odum 1971:18)

In the previous chapter, two specific aspects of the environmental crisis—resource depletion and pollution—were related to over-consumption. The present chapter will explore further the problem of overconsumption, because it appears to be the critical defining feature of industrial culture in contrast with primitive culture, and because it is the feature which most contributes to the present insta-bility of the industrial adaptation. Here, we shall be concerned spe-cifically with how industrial cultures extract and utilize energy and other natural resources in comparison with patterns typical of primi-tive cultures, and how these patterns relate to the environmental crisis.

Energy and Culture: Basic Considerations

It becomes the primary function of culture, therefore, to harness and control energy so that it may be put to work in man's service. . . . The functioning of culture as a whole therefore rests upon and is determined by the amount of energy harnessed and by the way in which it is put to work. (White 1949:367–368)

[C]ulture evolves as the amount of energy harnessed per capita per year is increased, or as the efficiency of the instrumental means of putting the energy to work is increased. (White 1949:368–369)

Anthropologist Leslie A. White has elaborated a theory of the evolu-tion of culture based largely on energy utilization. In his view, cul-ture is an extrasomatic, superorganic mechanism for harnessing energy. The earliest human cultures necessarily remained at a very low level of evolution as long as they were restricted to their own energy and minimal use of wind, rain, and fire. The additional con-trol of solar energy through domesticated plants and animals re-leased vast amounts of energy and made possible higher levels of social complexity, greater productivity per unit of area, and greater population density. These developments culminated with the appearance of state organization.

Since White developed this evolutionary scheme in 1949, other researchers have shown that the theory is quite misleading. In fact, up until the use of fossil fuel energy sources, *per capita* use has not increased significantly—manpower has remained the basic source of mechanical energy. The real difference was that domestication permitted larger populations, and thus larger *total energy* was available for building culture (Sahlins 1972:5–6). That state organization can arise without domestication, or with only minimal use of domesticates, is demonstrated by the evolution of civilization in Peru by 1000 B.C. on a marine fishing base (Mosely 1975).

White feels that the full potential for cultural evolutionary advance on the basis of agriculture alone was realized before the Christian Era, and that further advance into industrial civilization was only made possible by the *fuel revolution,* his term for the utilization of fossil fuels. With the discovery of nuclear energy, White felt, culture was poised on the verge of a major new energy revolution which could lead to even higher levels of evolutionary progress. Brazilian anthropologist Darcy Ribeiro (1968) confidently applied the term *thermonuclear revolution* to this new era, but it is not at all certain that culture will survive such a revolution.

It is certainly reasonable and useful to describe general evolutionary progress in terms of energy utilization; but if we are concerned with the environmental crisis and with achieving a successful and sustainable cultural adaptation, then a classification of cultures which considers not only the rate at which energy resources are consumed—but also the rate at which they are being depleted may be far more meaningful. The global energy sources which are most significant for human utilization may be divided into three categories:

1. Solar radiation
2. Fossil fuels
3. Nuclear energy

Solar radiation can be considered a steady "income" source of energy which may be renewed daily or annually and may be converted by green plants through photosynthesis into usable forms of energy, or through the movement of water and wind; or some of this energy may be concentrated and converted directly to heat for human use. Only a very small, relatively constant quantity of energy can ever be available through these sources, and because of the Second Law of Thermodynamics, the amount of energy available for use is constantly reduced at each conversion. Fossil fuels supply solar energy that has been trapped by green plants and stored in the earth through incomplete oxidation over the past 600 million years, and represent only a minute fraction of the globe's annual energy budget. The process of fossil fuel formation is presumably still under way but at a rate too slow in human terms for this energy source to be considered anything other than nonrenewable. Any use of this stored energy must then be considered a withdrawal from a steadily dwindling stock. Nuclear energy can be released from its storage within the atomic structure; but the most easily utilized radioactive fuels are in limited supply, and all controlled releases of nuclear energy require enormous inputs of energy to be safely maintained and to deal with the waste heat and radioactive materials produced. Nuclear energy also must be converted to electrical energy and thus seems an unlikely replacement for all present uses of fossil fuels in industrial civilization.

In terms of energy use, cultures may easily be divided into "high-energy cultures" and "low-energy cultures," and these categories have immediate implications for both evolutionary progress and adaptive success. The quantitative differences between high- and low-energy cultures can be seen easily in terms of their per capita levels of energy consumption. Prior to the fuel revolution, it has been estimated, no state-organized cultures utilized more than 26,000 kilocalories per capita daily, while primitive nonstate hunters and farmers utilized between 4,000 and 12,000 kilocalories per capita daily (see Figure 3). These cultures might all qualify as low-energy cultures, and might theoretically be stable adaptations. In contrast, early industrial cultures utilizing fossil fuels consumed ap-

FIGURE 3 Daily Consumption of Energy per Capita for Six Stages in Human Development. Daily Consumption of energy per capita was calculated by the author for six stages in human development (and with an accuracy that decreases with antiquity). Primitive man (East Africa about 1,000,000 years ago) without the use of fire had only the energy of the food he ate. Hunting man (Europe about 100,000 years ago) had more food and also burned wood for heat and cooking. Primitive agricultural man (Fertile Crescent in 5000 B.C.) was growing crops and had gained animal energy. Advanced agricultural man (northwestern Europe in A.D. 1400) had some coal for heating, some water power and wind power and animal transport. Industrial man (in England in 1875) had the steam engine. In 1970 technological man (in the U.S.) consumed 230,000 kilocalories per day, much of it in form of electricity *(hatched area)*. Food is divided into plant foods *(far left)* and animal foods (or foods fed to animals). (Source: Earl Cook, "The Flow of Energy in an Industrial Society," *Scientific American*, Vol. 224, No. 3 (1971), p. 136.)

proximately 70,000 kilocalories per capita daily, and Americans by 1970 had elevated the rate to 230,000 (Cook 1971). These high-energy industrial cultures clearly represent a qualitative difference in energy consumption that merits a special terminological distinction.

It can be seen that given the apparently immutable laws of thermodynamics and the physical limitations of the global energy budget, any culture that taps renewable solar energy sources must necessarily remain a low-energy culture relative to those drawing on stored, depletable sources. Theoretically, low-energy cultures could exist another five billion years until the sun burns out, while high-energy cultures must be transformed to low-energy cultures when their depleted energy stores are burned up, or perhaps be destroyed by the waste heat they unavoidably produce through energy conversion. High-energy cultures thus have life spans that can easily be predicted for comparison with the five-billion-year life expectancy of low-energy cultures. Estimates for the depletion of fossil fuels vary slightly, depending on accepted rates of utilization and the total reserves estimated, but the general magnitude of the figures is clear. One of the most pessimistic estimates, that recently presented by *The Limits to Growth* study (Meadows et. al. 1972), suggests that at present exponential rates of consumption, known reserves of oil will be gone in 20 years, natural gas in 22 years, and coal in 111 years (see Figure 4 for another estimate for oil depletion). If we assume that oil and natural gas are indeed depleted so quickly, then a switch to full reliance on coal would greatly accelerate its depletion. The most optimistic estimates would give us perhaps 100 years' worth of oil and 500 or 600 years' worth of coal. High-grade uranium ores needed to support our present nuclear fission technology will be in very short supply within 20 years, and a switch to vastly more costly and unproven systems such as "breeder" and fusion reactors will be urgently needed if a high-energy culture is to be sustained.* Even if this

---

*There has been a tremendous outpouring of energy-related works in recent years. I have drawn primarily on the 1969 *Committee on Resources and Man* study sponsored by the National Academy of Sciences, the *Scientific American* special issue for Sept. 1971, and the collected papers in Finkel (1974).

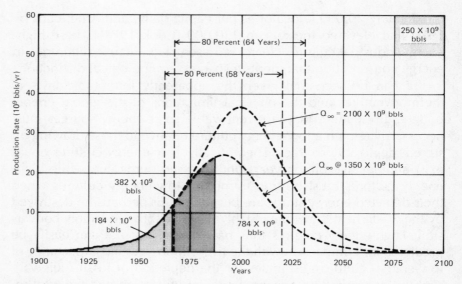

FIGURE 4   Complete Cycles of World Crude Oil Production.   (Source: Hubert, p. 196)

transition is successfully achieved, continued progress appears un-likely because even at the present rate of increases in energy utiliza-tion it is estimated that waste heat may adversely alter world climate within 30 to 50 years. Within 200 years of a mere 5 percent annual increase in world energy production, the heat produced would equal that received from the sun, and all life on earth would cease to exist (Luten 1974). Long before such a "Sun Day" could possibly arrive, however, the polar ice caps would melt, flooding out most of the world's urban centers, and enormous adverse changes in world vege-tation would occur.

   Thus a continually expanding high-energy culture will be self-terminating, and its maximum life expectancy can be no more than a few hundred years. Furthermore, it is doubtful that relatively high levels of energy utilization can be stabilized at safely sustainable levels with nuclear technology, because of its unknown risks, and because of the uncertainty that unstable high-energy cultures will evolve the social mechanisms needed to achieve such a transition, and finally because of the operation of Justus von Liebig's Law of the Minimum.

More than energy alone is necessary to sustain a high-energy culture—because if that energy is used to produce what Leslie A. White calls "human need-serving goods and services," other raw materials must be consumed. Liebig's law states that an organism's growth and survival will be limited by the essential material that is present in the lowest quantity. If this law is applied to cultures, and if we assume that specifiable annual quantities of iron, copper, and aluminum are essential for the continued existence of a high-energy industrial culture, then its life expectancy may be even shorter than its potential energy base would permit. *The Limits to Growth* study indicates that at present exponential use rates, presently exploitable world iron ore reserves will be extinguished within 173 years, aluminum within 55 years, and copper within 48 years. The availability of mineral resources may be extended by recycling and more costly exploitation technologies; but their quantity will inevitably diminish through use, and any culture entirely dependent upon them will not outlast the shortest lived critical mineral resource. While it is not possible to estimate precisely the life expectancy of a high-energy culture, it can confidently be stated that it will never be as successful as low-energy cultures, which might have enjoyed a five-billion-year existence if they had not been destroyed by high-energy cultures. Evolutionary progress beyond low-energy cultures may thus only be possible through self-limiting overconsumption that will initiate environmental crises and ultimately destroy a culture's ability to adapt.

The Culture of Consumption Defined

Industrial civilization has developed into something totally unique in the evolution of culture—a *culture of consumption* (Bodley 1975:4–5), a culture whose major economic, social, and ideological systems are geared to nonsustainable levels of resource consumption and to continual, ever-higher elevation of those levels on a per capita basis. This is *overconsumption,* not only in terms of reduced cultural viability, but also in a strictly biological sense, as ecologist Howard Odum explains:

> In the industrial system with man living off a fuel, he manages all his affairs with industrial machinery, all parts of which are metabolically consumers. . . . The system of man has consumption in excess of production. The products of respiration—carbon dioxide, metabolic water, and mineralized inorganic wastes—are discharged in rates in excess of their incorporation into organic matter by photosynthesis. If the industrialized urban system were enclosed in a chamber with only the air above it at the time, it would quickly exhaust its oxygen, be stifled with waste, and destroy itself since it does not have the recycling pattern of the agrarian system. (Odum 1971:17)

Odum estimates that on a global scale, "human industries add about a 5 percent excess of consumption over production."

Growth through increased consumption is so much a part of our present economy that most economists find it difficult to imagine any other state, even though perpetual growth is only possible in an infinite environment. Some writers (Boulding 1966) have characterized the present economy of growth as a "frontier" or "cowboy" economy, meaning that it is the type of economic system that might be appropriate to a particular period of expansion into a new environment, but it becomes inappropriate when that historical period has passed and further expansion threatens to become destructive. A more descriptive term might be simply "consumption economy"; the important point is that such a system is defined by a continual increase in "throughput," i.e., production and consumption measured in terms of gross national product. There is little account made of the unintended by-products of the process. Waste, depletion, pollution, and various indirect social costs or "externalities" do not immediately detract from GNP and may actually be a positive aspect of it. For example, accidents and diseases caused by the production and consumption process contribute to economic growth because further output of goods and services must deal with them. Adverse side effects of growth will be certain to make growth self-limiting in the long run; but because of the investment process, a consumption economy is focused only on the immediate future and disregards impacts even 25 or 50 years into the future.

Perpetual economic growth is firmly entrenched in the culture of consumption and has become a solution to maintaining a grossly stratified, nonegalitarian social system. Disruptive dissatisfaction among the lowest classes due to poverty and unemployment can be prevented without the most wealthy sacrificing their positions if the total volume of wealth can be steadily increased. In this way the poor gradually become "wealthy" while their relative position remains constant. The same principle operates at the world level. "Poor" nations might be prevented from warring against rich nations if certain minimal levels of economic growth can be maintained.

In the ideological system of the culture of consumption, predictably, the primary focus seems to be on increasing consumption, although this is defined as "progress" or "economic growth." An elaborate mythology of unquestioned "truths" supports the economic system and helps convince individual members of the consumption culture that they are well served by the system. Unfortunately, however, many of these cultural myths can be easily shattered by careful examination. For example, higher standards of living or improved quality of life need not be a necessary correlate of progress measured in terms of ever-increasing per capita consumption of energy. Cross-national surveys (Mazur and Rosa 1974) suggest that only up to a certain point do increases in energy use correspond with rises in commonly accepted measures of quality of life in industrial cultures, such as health care, education, and "cultural" activities. Very high energy levels may be part of evolutionary progress, but they make little contribution to improving the quality of life. There are even indications that very high energy use rates are related to such negative qualities as high suicide and divorce rates, but the causal relationships have not been fully explored.

It is also firmly believed that the ever-increasing output of household appliance consumer goods has meant a steady reduction in housework and an increase in leisure time. Consumer appliances thus become principal indicators of a high standard of living. Anthropological research among primitive hunters, however, has shown that they worked far less at household tasks, and indeed less at all subsistence pursuits, than any modern populations. Aboriginal Australian women, for example, were found to devote an average of approximately 20 hours per week to collecting and preparing food (McCarthy and McArthur 1960), while women in rural America in the 1920's, without the benefit of laborsaving appliances, devoted approximately 52 hours a week to their housework (Vanek 1974). Some 50 years later, contrary to all expectations, urban, nonworking women were putting in 55 hours a week at their housework, in spite of all their new "laborsaving" dishwashers, washing machines, vacuum cleaners, and electric mixers. This actual *increase* in work time shows how illusory the idea of an increased standard of living may be when judged according to the consumption culture's traditionally accepted measures. Some of this increased work load is probably due in part to the fact that more time is now required for such consumption-related tasks as shopping and caring for an increased volume of clothing. The economic value of a woman's household work is also so poorly defined that women may feel compelled to make their contribution more conspicuous.

The relationship between a culture of consumption and the natural environment can be seen more clearly through the examination of specific examples. The following sections will deal primarily with the United States in an effort to illustrate special principles that may be valid for all consumption cultures and that clearly show how serious environmental crises may be precipitated by over-consumption.

Resource Consumption in America

The United States is without question the leading example of a culture of consumption. Within a few decades, it has suddenly become the world's major consumer of nonrenewable resources on both an absolute and a per capita basis. Estimates vary widely, but it appears that by 1970, while their population constituted only about 6 percent of the world total, Americans consumed some 40 percent of the world's total annual production, and 35 percent of the world's energy (Cook 1971). The historic pattern of this consumption illustrates important trends that may be generally characteristic of consumption cultures.

High and rapidly increasing rates of energy consumption have been made possible by switches from primary dependence on theoretically renewable "income" sources such as fuel wood to nonrenewable "capital stock" resources such as coal. In 1850, approximately 90 percent of America's energy was derived from fuel wood; but by 1890, over 50 percent was supplied by coal. By 1960, nearly 70 percent came from oil and natural gas, and optimists hope that in the near future nuclear energy will replace depleted fossil fuels (Landsberg 1964). In a mere 100 years, Americans have tripled their per capita use of energy and multiplied their total use 30 times. They have already made two major shifts in their basic energy sources, and now face shortages and further adjustments in the foreseeable future. Much of this increased use has been at enormous environmental cost due to air pollution from burning the fuels, and from disturbances caused by drilling and mining operations and accidents such as oil spills. As more easily exploited energy resources have become depleted, higher extraction costs have forced the United States to rely heavily on imported energy sources; the result has been increasing political uncertainties and economic instabilities due to high rates of inflation. In spite of all the adverse environmental effects, political and economic instabilities, and the unknown risks, the country's leading economic planners continue to assume that energy consumption must keep increasing, perhaps even doubling by the year 2000.

Certainly, a critical question to ask is how a culture of consumption responds to the impact of its own consumption on what must be an ever-dwindling resource base. Primitive cultures, as noted earlier, tend to respond quickly to adverse impacts on their resource base because they are immediately dependent on local resources. Industrial cultures, however, lack this instant responsiveness because of their complexity and specialization. They are especially vulnerable to overgrowth and collapse because of the rapidity with which they are expanding. More importantly, they lack substitute response mechanisms, and the market system seems to thrive on resource depletion. Governments have occasionally stockpiled certain critical resources as strategic reserves as a military preparedness measure; but in general, present political institutions and leaders seem quite unwilling or unable to prepare in advance for inevitable shortages. The only specialized mechanisms for anticipating critical resource shortages that industrial cultures have so far evolved are the teams of experts that have periodically taken stock of resources and advised governments of potential problems. Characteristically, however, these assessments have been surprisingly shortsighted and optimistic, or else their warnings have been simply disregarded. The consumption culture seems unable to imagine its own demise.

Taking Stock

> Our nation, looking toward a future of continuing economic
> progress, is well-advised to take stock of its natural resources.
> Industry can expand only so far as raw materials are available.
> (Dewhurst 1955:754)

After World War II, in 1949, the United Nations brought together in New York over 700 scientists from 50 nations to exchange information on world problems of conservation and resource utilization. In assessing the world mineral situation, H. L. Keenleyside, Canada's Deputy Minister of Mines and Resources, noted that between 1900 and 1949 more world mineral resources had been consumed than during all of man's previous existence. He felt that there were as yet no critical mineral shortages developing, but recognized future limitations: "Thus it is quite clear that the combination of an increasing population and rising standards of living will place a strain on our metal resources which will almost certainly in the end prove beyond the capacity of man and nature to supply." (Keenleyside 1950:38)

In order to postpone the inevitable, Keenleyside recommended increased exploration for minerals, improved extraction and processing technology, conservation, and substitution. Given increasing demands, his warning was clear: "[Unless] there is a fundamental change in the economic fabric of human society we will ultimately be faced with the exhaustion of many of our mineral resources."

In the United States, no comprehensive inventory of natural resources was ever undertaken until 1908. There were early moves toward conservation, but little concern that serious problems might arise. A major study published in 1947, entitled *America's Needs and Resources* (Dewhurst 1947), attempted to project national requirements for resources for 1960. It reported that no real resource exhaustion was likely within 20 years, although high-grade zinc, lead, and bauxite ores might be exhausted by that time and oil shortages might occur somewhat later. The report recognized that domestic mineral resources would ultimately be depleted; but it was felt that, given free access to foreign resources, an "expanding American economy" could be supported for "many decades to come." Curiously, the report suggested that even if imports were unavailable, there was no reason for believing that reliance on domestic resources would be a necessary barrier to continued economic growth.

Eight years later, the *America's Needs and Resources* study was updated with the publication of a new edition (Dewhurst 1955) which displayed a greater appreciation for the incredible consumption rates that Americans were developing, but this awareness was more than overshadowed by an even greater confidence in the country's ability to solve any problem. It was noted that, by 1950, Americans were consuming some 18 tons of raw materials per capita, and that the United States consumed as much of many important minerals as the rest of the world combined. In spite of these staggering facts, the authors of the report were certain that there would be no insurmountable problems that would limit further growth: "Despite man's seemingly devastating exploitation, he has merely scratched a small segment of this gigantic ball of resources on which he lives. Our power to use the materials in nature is growing rather than diminishing, through favorable technology and economic organization." (Dewhurst 1955:754–755)

While, perhaps, in 1955 we were only scratching the surface of the globe's resources, the suddenly increased extent of this scratching on the part of Americans is perhaps seen in greater perspective by the observation published in President Truman's *Resources for Freedom* study (United States, President's Materials Policy Commission 1952), which pointed out that just since 1914, American consumption of most minerals and fuels exceeded total world consumption for all previous time. Furthermore, other projections show how quickly this minor scratching could have a serious impact on a finite earth. In 1956, geochemist Harrison Brown calculated that a world population of 30 billion (which some experts feel would be the maximum conceivable human population and which might be reached at present rates by 2075), with nuclear breeder technology and the capability of extracting all needed mineral resources directly from ordinary rock and seawater, would literally eat up the continents. The crust of the earth would be skimmed off at the rate of 3.3 millimeters a year, or over three meters every thousand years.

In 1963 a third major assessment of American resources was published by the Resources for the Future corporation supported by the Ford Foundation. The 1,000-page report, entitled *Resources in America's Future* (Landsberg et al. 1963), attempted to project supply and demand for natural resources up to the year 2000. The authors of the study recognized the general difficulty of any such projections but felt they were essential for decision making. They recommended that such studies be conducted or updated every five years by a government agency, perhaps through computer simulation techniques. This study, like earlier assessments, could foresee no immediate critical general shortages. Although the authors felt that some specific problems might arise, they assumed that any problems would be solvable. New technology, world trade, and careful utilization would maintain continued high consumption rates. On the basis of careful projections, which considered the interrelatedness of population, technology, and "demand" levels, and assuming continued imports, no major wars or economic depressions, the RFF report concluded that within 40 years the United States would triple its annual consumption of energy, metals, and timber. Resource shortages would be no major handicap to progress. This optimistic view was quite in agreement with earlier studies on this point:

> On the whole, it seems clear that we shall not be hampered in meeting future needs by a shortage of raw materials. (Dewhurst 1955:939)

> Neither a long view of the past, nor current trends, nor our most careful estimates of future possibilities suggest any general running out of resources in this country during the remainder of this century. The possibilities of using lower grades of raw material, of substituting plentiful materials for scarce ones, of getting more use out of given amounts, of importing things from other countries, and of making multiple use of land and water resources seem to be sufficient guarantee against across-the-board shortage. (Landsberg 1964:13)

The RFF projections optimistically assumed continued technological advances, greater efficiency, and continued substitution of synthetics for natural materials. Without constant technological "advance," it is clear that the culture of consumption would rapidly be faced with what the RFF report called "inconvenient and perhaps critical material limitations." For example, it was estimated that 64 percent of the fibers consumed in the year 2000 would be synthetics drawn largely from fossil fuel stocks. The report noted that by 1952, western softwood forests were already being cut at over their replacement rate and warned that unless we wished to be extremely optimistic we could expect a continued depletion of western forests. Eastern hardwood forests would be "on the way to extinction" by the end of the century. Annual demand for forest products by 2000 was expected to be double the annual rate of forest growth now; and it seemed that short of technological miracles that would produce synthetic hybrid trees capable of growing twice as fast, only substitution of plastics and consumption of the world's tropical rain forests would support continued American "needs." Unfortunately, we see now that the tropical forests and the oil for the substitute plastics will quite likely both be gone by the year 2000. Presumably, if the culture of consumption does find itself still intact by 2000, we can hope for further miracles to carry us to 2050, and so on.

It is difficult to escape the conclusion that the consumption culture is fighting a losing battle to support a rising level of consumption which must ultimately be unsupportable. At any given moment the culture seems poised on the edge of total collapse but somehow manages to put forth greater effort to keep the system functioning a little longer through any means short of reduced consumption.

Shortly after publication of the RFF study, the National Academy of Sciences conducted its own two-year study, which took a much broader approach to the resources and consumption question. This work, entitled *Resources and Man,* was completed in 1968 and published in 1969. It was concerned with the entire globe and looked beyond the year 2000. The outlook was far more sober and raised serious questions about the long-range viability of an ever-expanding industrial culture. It warned that the earth's supply of oil may be gone in 70–80 years, coal in 200–300 years, and that in the not-distant future the high-energy cultures will only be supportable by nuclear breeder technology. Some authors even felt that there were serious possibilities that certain critical mineral shortages might arise before

2000. Mercury, tin, tungsten, and helium were minerals where true shortages were either already occurring or threatened. The report was also clear on one point—even given technological break-throughs, continued expansion in consumption rates cannot be supported indefinitely. The report holds out the hope that if population and consumption can be stabilized at reasonable levels, industrial society may last for centuries or millennia.

The most recent report from the National Academy of Sciences, entitled *Mineral Resources and the Environment* and published in 1975, carries the most pessimistic warning of all: "Man faces the prospect of a series of shocks of varying severity as shortages occur in one material after another, with the first real shortages perhaps only a matter of a few years away. . . ." This report suggests that world oil supplies may be gone within 50 years and, for the first time ever, calls for a massive conservation program and an actual reduction in consumption:

> Because of the limits to natural resources as well as to means of
> alleviating these limits, it is recommended that the federal
> government proclaim and deliberately pursue a national policy of
> conservation of material, energy and environmental resources,
> informing the public and the private sectors fully about the needs
> and techniques for reducing energy consumption, the
> development of substitute materials, increasing the durability and
> maintainability of products, and reclamation and recycling.

Thus the world's leading culture of consumption has gone from just scratching the surface of world resources to almost quite literally the "bottom of the barrel" in a mere 20 years. Perhaps Americans deserve a special trophy for evolutionary progress.

The Economics of Resource Depletion

> Sooner or later, the market price will get high enough to choke off
> the demand entirely. At that moment production falls to

> zero. . . . the last ton produced will also be the last ton in the ground. The resource will be exhausted at the instant it has priced itself out of the market. The Age of Oil or Zinc or Whatever It Is will have come to an end. (Solow 1974:3)

The culture of consumption has clearly developed within the framework of an economic system that advances systematically from one resource to another, supported by theoretical assumptions that deny that "real" scarcity or limits to further growth can exist. We have already seen how industrial society has moved rapidly through several alternative energy sources as they become depleted or inadequate. This process occurs with different grades of ore and virtually every other depletable resource from whales to timber, and represents the predictable operation of market principles in combination with continuing technological advances.

To orthodox economists, the simple solution to the obvious incompatability between an ever-expanding economy and a finite world is to "redefine" *resource*. When, for example, as was the case in the whaling industry in the 1940's (Payne 1968), blue whales were being exterminated, then fin whales may be declared a replacement resource, and then Sei whales, and then sperm whales. When the whales run out, we can save the whaling industry by converting it into a krill-catching industry. Krill are an Antarctic shrimp formerly eaten by whales.

Theoretical support for such a process of self-perpetuating depletion and never-ending technical progress has been clearly spelled out by economists Harold Barnett and Chandler Morse in their influential study *Scarcity and Growth: The Economics of Natural Resource Availability,* published in 1963 for the Resources for the Future Corporation. The primary objective of the *Scarcity and Growth* study seems to be to disprove the notion of the classical economists such as Thomas R. Malthus, David Ricardo, and John Stuart Mill that resource scarcity will halt economic growth. Such an outcome, according to Barnett and Morse, would only be possible in a world without progress, and is quite unrealistic in today's world. What they are saying, of course, is that progress will end when progress ends, but they cannot conceive of such a contingency: "The notion of an absolute limit to natural resource availability is untenable when the definition of resources changes drastically and unpredictably over time." (Barnett and Morse 1963:7)

In other words, today trees and whales, tomorrow plastic and granite. According to these enthusiastic consumption economists, depletion of resources will make way for economic alternatives of equal or even *superior* qualities and at reduced cost. Industrial technology is now virtually "turning the tables on nature, making her subservient to man." Whatever resource scarcity may exist is always *relative,* never absolute, and substitution always solves it. Resource limits cannot be defined in economic terms, so the argument goes, and therefore they must not exist. Attempting to conserve resources now might actually reduce the "heritage" of future generations because it could preclude future technological advances. The authors mistakenly assume that primitive cultures failed to expand their economic systems because they neglected to control their populations and were too ignorant to redefine their resources technologically.

Barnett and Morse represent the superoptimistic orthodox view. The process of relative scarcity and substitution they describe typifies the operation of the consumption economy thus far, but there is no solid evidence that it will be able to continue operating this way or that it would even be desirable for it to do so. Some unorthodox economists have recently characterized these theories as pure "growthmania," simply absurd, and contrary to the Second Law of Thermodynamics. It has been pointed out that the assumptions of Barnett and Morse were based largely on trends in the mining industry between 1870 and 1957, and that they ignored clear cases of increased costs and diminishing returns. New theories of a steady-state economy are beginning to emerge.

The Consumption Culture's Environmental Cost: Western Coal

Any culture that continues to accelerate consumption in a fixed environment will eventually be forced into making trade-offs between environmental quality and a continuation of its consumption pattern. The fossil fuel base of the present consumption culture in the United States is now seriously threatened as domestic sources of petroleum and natural gas have fallen short of domestic consumption in recent years. Nuclear technology, a short time ago hailed as a source of unlimited energy, is an unlikely solution because it is proving far more costly and hazardous than previously supposed. Instead, the nation is now preparing to strip the coal reserves of the western states in an effort to meet the ever-expanding energy "needs" of the country. When the proposed federal coal-leasing program is initiated, vast areas of the West, which were left in almost pristine condition after supporting primitive Indian cultures for perhaps 20,000 years, will be deliberately devastated on a massive scale to perpetuate the culture of consumption for a few short years.

The 1974 *Draft Environmental Impact Statement* (United States, Department of the Interior), dealing with the coal-leasing program and written by the Bureau of Land Management, makes the rationale for the coal stripping clear, and concisely summarizes the costs. The entire procedure is a remarkable example of the extremity to which overconsumption can drive a culture. The fundamental assumption underlying the proposed stripping program is simply that economic growth cannot be sustained without it: "We assume the first principal demand pressure for coal development will be from the physical and economic inability of the United States to obtain sufficient oil supplies to meet the demand generated by normal growth rates of the national economy." (BLM Part I:8).

"Normal growth rates" means that over the next 25 years the population will increase by less than 50 percent, but total energy

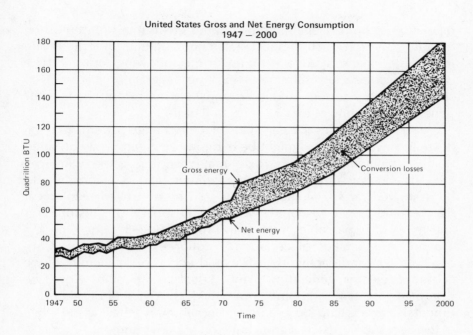

FIGURE 5   United States Energy Consumption. (Source: United States, De-
partment of the Interior, Bureau of Land Management, *Draft Environmental Impact
Statement: Proposed Federal Coal Leasing Program* (2 vols.; Washington, D.C.: U.S.
Government Printing Office, 1974), Vol. 1, Part 1, p. 26.)

consumption will nearly double (see Figure 5). If we are having
difficulties meeting our energy needs now, it should be no surprise
that, if present total consumption is more than doubled by the year
2000, it will be at an enormous cost.

Strip mining coal involves simply removing all the overlying surface material, placing it to one side, and extracting the coal. Federal

regulations require "rehabilitation" of the site, but this term must be broadly interpreted. The impact statement carefully understates the immediate effects of surface mines in the following terms: "The operation completely eliminates existing vegetation, disrupts soil structure, alters current land uses, and to some extent changes the general topography of the area" (BLM Part III:33).

The report makes it clear that surface drainage patterns may be disrupted; water sources might be eliminated; streams may be silted in and contaminated with toxic materials; big game wintering grounds and migration routes, and wildlife habitat in general, would be destroyed; archaeological sites would be destroyed; geological features and scenic resources would be destroyed or "disrupted"; and miles of impassable "high walls" might be left. Where underground mining takes place, surface collapses might occur. Contamination by radioactive fly ash would occur in the vicinity of the coal-fired electric generating plants. Local communities would be disrupted by a temporary influx of outsiders. A variety of other detrimental impacts can be predicted. In summary, the "grand scale of the operation impacts significantly on the environment."

"Restoration" of stripped areas is expected to require from 20 to 30 years, but the statement is concerned only with the period before 1985. "More lengthy projections" are considered to be "impractical." The statement glibly notes, however, that: "Man cannot immediately restore natural biotic communities." Experience with strip mining in Appalachia indicates that the worst erosion and pollution problems may occur as much as 25 years after mining; in some cases, spoil piles are still eroding 65 years after the coal was extracted. Some researchers estimate that 800 to 3,000 years may be needed before toxic wastes will leach away (Spaulding and Ogden 1968). We know for certain that the leased areas will never be the same again, but the total cost is incalculable. What is most important for the culture of consumption is that the coal will be destroyed, too! It will again be time to look for another energy source to carry us to the next crisis.

Consumption Culture versus
Primitive Culture: Bougainville Copper

Overconsumption by the industrial nations not only destroys the physical environment, but it has also been the primary cause of the almost total destruction of primitive cultures over the past 150 years. Throughout the world, tribal cultures have been devastated along with their environments as the resources they controlled have become necessary components of industrial growth. This subject has been dealt with at length elsewhere (Bodley 1975); but here, a single example may be presented to illustrate how the consumption culture's need for a critical mineral resource can totally overwhelm small-scale cultures thousands of miles away.

Copper is one of industry's primary raw materials and is being consumed in such enormous quantities by the industrialized nations that if present trends continue the world's supply of ore will be exhausted within 20 to 50 years (Meadows et al. 1972, Table 4). Nearly 60 percent of the world's annual copper production is consumed by three of the most highly industrialized nations—the United States, Japan, and the Soviet Union. By itself, the United States consumes 33 percent of the world's total production—substantially more than it can produce. In fact, in 1968, Americans were consuming the equivalent of 15 pounds of copper per person per year, much of it in the form of copper electrical wiring. Even though copper ore has become progressively more difficult to find, and the quality of the ore is steadily decreasing, and even though production costs have steadily risen, there has been no effort to limit consumption (Lovering 1968). Instead, copper ore is being exploited for the short-run benefit of the richest industrial nations—wherever in the world it can be found and regardless of the impact on local populations and their environments.

In 1963 the Australian administration of the Trust Territory of New Guinea gave an Australian mining corporation, Conzinc Riotinto Australia, Ltd., permission to prospect for minerals in the center of Bougainville Island in an area occupied by subsistence-farming tribal peoples. Major deposits of copper ore were discovered, and a gigantic project was soon under way which was described a "perhaps one of the most ambitious mining ventures ever undertaken" (Mining Magazine 1971). When production began in 1972, some $400 million had been invested, and a company-owned town for 3,000 people had been established at the mine site, which was connected by a pipeline and a 16-mile highway to a specially constructed public port town for 8,000 people built on the coast.

The environment posed seemingly insurmountable problems for the engineers because of the island's rugged topography, loose soil, and heavy rainfall. Constant slumping made road building in the area "a major engineering achievement" requiring constant relocation and the excavation of some 13 million cubic yards of material. When conventional underground mining techniques proved economically unfeasible, the company burned off the tropical forest cover and resorted to open-pit, stripping techniques on an immense scale. The problem of disposing of the enormous quantity of tailings had not been solved when production was begun, and there was no discussion of the environmental impact of the project or possible plans for restoration of the region.

While the physical environment posed a serious enough problem for the successful development of the mine, the company encountered "social barriers" which were even more difficult to solve. From the time prospecting began, there were serious difficulties in securing the approval and goodwill of the local tribal population. As one report euphemistically explained, "the company encountered many difficulties in establishing its presence satisfactorily." (Ryan 1972) In the first place, under the existing tribal system of land tenure, no one had the right to transfer land to outsiders, and many people were very reluctant to accept any form of compensation or rent for *use* of their land because they feared they might thereby lose it completely (Dakeyne 1967). Not surprisingly, the company had a difficult time explaining to the indigenous people why it was necessary for them to move aside so that their homesites and gardens could be totally destroyed. In compensation, the Australian administration negotiated an agreement with the company in which the local people were to receive a rent of $2.00 an acre for their land, which they were to provide to meet the "reasonable needs" of the company. In exchange for their traditional homes, which were destroyed, the people were to receive "durable" buildings. Royalties would accrue to the administration to be used for the further "progress" of all the people in the territory, and various other inducements were offered to secure their cooperation, including employment opportunities, provision for resettlement, and opportunities to buy shares in the company.

The company reportedly (Ryan 1972) attempted to minimize the "inevitable" disturbances to the local people and, apparently making good use of applied anthropology, was bringing "experience, sound personnel and community management and enlightened policies" to bear on the problem of satisfactorily establishing its presence. Plans called for the integration of the people into the company's operation, and they were to feel that they would have some choice: "Policy seeks social integration which gives a local person some option on how fast he wants to go along this course." It is not clear what option was open to those who chose not to approve the "integration" course, but there was certainly no way for the people to resist the $400-million operation effectively. This lack of real choice was apparent when, during the company's negotiations for tribal land, it refused to halt construction because the company considered the expense involved in any work stoppage to be unacceptable. The people merely had to make the best of an unfortunate situation.

United Nations visiting missions to the area in 1968 and 1971 (United Nations, Trusteeship Council) found many local people disturbed over their treatment by the company and reported that violent disputes had occurred. However, the district police and the Australian administration sided with the company, and violent resistance was clearly not a solution. The UN mission acknowledged that "mistakes" had been made, but felt that the islanders were being presented with a unique opportunity to raise their living standards. From the company's view, the whole problem was due to the natives' strong emotional ties to their land, and the natives' misunderstanding and "difficulty in comprehending the project" due to their having been "quite sheltered from contact with a western-type industrial society." The local people realized perfectly well what was happening to them, but they were powerless to do anything about it.

Perhaps the most critical anthropological question to ask is: What cultural forces drive the present consumption patterns of the consumption culture? We *can* say that overconsumption is not an innate human trait; it *is* culturally determined. It is also clear that high rates of consumption, or a lack of cultural controls on consumption, relate to social stratification within a culture; but there are many stratified societies that have set limits to consumption. The presence of specialized institutions to increase consumption, such as advertising agencies, must play an especially critical role, but why do they exist? The only reasonable explanation seems to lie in the structure of the modern market economy itself—it is uniquely geared toward expanding consumption, but *why* this is so is still unclear. The following two chapters will explore further the problem of overconsumption by focusing on the food systems of primitive and industrial cultures.

4

world hunger and the evolution of food production

[The] power of obtaining an additional quantity of food from the earth by proper management and in a certain time, has the most remote relation imaginable to the power of keeping pace with an unrestricted increase of population. (Malthus 1807)

The battle to feed all of humanity is over. In the 1970's the world will undergo famines—hundreds of millions of people are going to starve to death. . . .(Ehrlich 1968)

Food is related to the environmental crisis in two obvious ways: Cultural patterns of food acquisition and consumption may contribute to environmental deterioration, while food supply is in turn threatened by increasing environmental deterioration and rising demands due to population increase and changing cultural preferences. The food system of industrial civilization deviates in several remarkable ways from the primitive food systems that have effectively satisfied human nutritional requirements for thousands of years, and these differences raise serious questions regarding the probable long-range effectiveness of the present system.

The Malthusian Dilemma

> The power of the earth to produce subsistence is certainly not unlimited, but it is strictly speaking indefinite; that is, its limits are not defined, and the time will probably never arrive when we shall be able to say that no further labour or ingenuity of man could make further additions to it. But the power of obtaining an additional quantity of food from the earth by proper management and in a certain time, has the most remote relation imaginable to the power of keeping pace with an unrestricted increase of population. (Malthus 1807)

British economist Thomas R. Malthus was certainly the most influential early writer to raise the fundamental question of the relationship between population growth and food production. Writing first in 1798, he argued that, if unchecked, human population had the natural capacity to expand at a geometrical or exponential rate, while, over the long run, food production could only be expected to increase at an arithmatical or *linear* rate. The capacity for population growth is largely an empirical question, and Malthus had data to support the view that a doubling every 25 years was possible. Reliable data on food production through time were unfortunately not

available, but Malthus merely assumed that there were in fact ultimate limits and that whatever those limits were, food production
could not long be expected to keep pace with a doubling population.
He felt that as population began to press on the subsistence base,
"misery," in the form of poverty, would tend to reduce population
growth, while greater efforts would be made to increase production
through opening new land and improved techniques until eventually
a balance would be restored. Malthus was convinced that these
principles were self-evident laws of nature.

　　To illustrate the operation of these "laws," he projected population and food production trends for Britain and the world, and
showed how quickly an exponentially growing population would
surpass a linearly expanding food production system. Many writers
have misunderstood him on this point. He did not make specific *predictions* for future demographic patterns, but merely tried to show
how unchecked population growth would compare with what he felt
were optimistic projections for increases in food production. Malthus
certainly did not anticipate the enormous population expansion that
has in fact occurred, but these later developments have actually mir-
rored very closely the models of unregulated growth that he constructed. Figures 6 and 7 graph the population and food production
curves for the world and for Britain that Malthus projected on the
basis of his theoretical maximum population growth (doubling every
25 years) and simple linear growth in food production. His starting
point of one billion people for the world is precisely the world estimate for 1800 presently accepted by many demographers; however,
at that time the world population was doubling only every 172 years.
By 1950, the doubling time had dropped to just over 80 years; it presently stands at less than 35 years—perilously close to the 25-year
doubling Malthus assumed. Thanks to recent technological developments and enormous subsidies of fossil fuels, over the past
25 years overall world food production has just kept pace with
population; but distributional problems have already created an unmistakable hunger gap, and it is not at all clear how much longer
food production can be successfully increased. In a general sense the

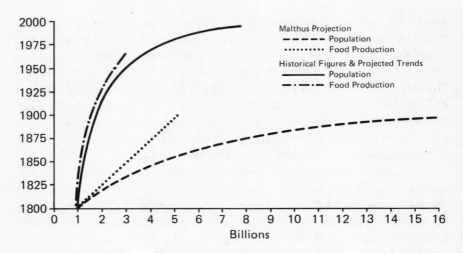

FIGURE 6   Population and Food Production (World).   The gap between world population and food is based on the estimate of 50 million hungry made by the editors of *Time* (Nov. 11, 1974, "The World Food Crisis," pp. 66–80). (Source: Data from Thomas R. Malthus, *An Essay on the Principle of Population* (New York and London: Macmillan Co., 1895).

world is now experiencing the very problem that Malthus projected, but it is happening 150 years later than his model indicated.

In Britain, over the past 175 years, the gap between food production and population growth has widened very much as might be expected given basic Malthusian assumptions, although both have grown much slower. At present, Britain is only producing about two thirds of its basic requirements in grain and meat, and makes up the deficiency through imports (Cooke 1970). This gap is about what Malthus would expect after 50 years of exponential population growth in Britain. He suggested that food production in England might keep pace with the first doubling of population during the first 25 years by opening up more land and offering "great encouragements" to agriculture, but he was certain that domestic production would be unable to cope with the second doubling. The second

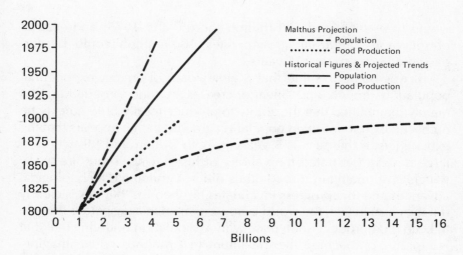

FIGURE 7 Population and Food Production (Britain). (Source: Data from Thomas R. Malthus, *An Essay on the Principle of Population* (New York and London: Macmillan Co., 1895).

doubling actually occurred shortly after 1900, some 50 years later than in the model, but food production still did not keep up with it. In fact, while total acreage has varied only slightly through time, British wheat production per acre required 150 years to achieve its first doubling and has now reached an apparent plateau well short of the second doubling. Significant advances beyond the first doubling were only possible through enormous applications of chemical fertilizers. In order to feed the *present* population, regardless of future growth, experts calculate that present levels of British grain and livestock production must be doubled immediately. While this increase may still be theoretically possible, it will require further vast inputs of fossil fuels and radical changes in food patterns. Extreme optimists suggest that Britain might actually support 100 million people if every technologically conceivable adjustment could be implemented (Cooke 1970). It is important to note that, given Malthusian population growth, Britain's population of 10 million in 1800 would have surpassed 100 million shortly after 1875; and even at present non-Malthusian growth rates, 100 million could be surpassed within a mere 125 years.

If it is borne in mind that Malthus did not *predict* exponential population growth and linear increases in food production, but merely maintained that the ability to produce food would quickly be outpaced by uncontrolled population growth, then it appears that the experience of the past 175 years in both Britain and the world at large has demonstrated the validity of his "laws." There are many writers who maintain that Malthus did not anticipate technological advances and that progress invalidates his theories, but this is clearly not the case. In fact, the world is now engaged in a desperate struggle to keep food production in pace with a population doubling rate that is rapidly approaching the maximum that Malthus could imagine, but did not expect. The "green revolution," the world food conferences, and the enormous food-aid programs are all part of the attempt to keep the two great powers, population and food production, in balance while avoiding the misery that must inevitably occur as the balance shifts in favor of population. Malthus is now being vindicated, not disproven.

Famine in the Modern World

[Despite] the enormous sums invested, the impressive technical progress we have made, and the extraordinary efforts by governments, by international bodies, and by scientific and technical communities—mankind has by and large failed in its supreme effort to feed adequately those billions of people *now* living on earth. Of these, at least one billion are undernourished, and the diets of an additional eight hundred million are deficient in one or several key nutrients. (Borgstrom 1967:xi)

Famine is not new. It has been, and continues to be, a chronic hazard of civilization. Famines of varying degrees and intensity were recorded in China at the rate of 1,828 over the 2,019 years up to 1911. Four million people may have died in China in 1920–21. Three million died in the Indian famine of 1769–70, two to four million in West Bengal in 1943. Five to 10 million may have died in Russian famines from 1918 to 1934. Famines have ravaged Europe many times, and even England counted more than 200 famines between A.D. 10 and A.D. 1846 (Ehrlich and Erlich 1972). Since Malthus outlined the dangers in 1798, Europe has moved to the brink of famine, and sometimes beyond, several times. By the middle of the 19th century a general food crisis was developing in Europe, but it was alleviated by emigration and food imports from the United States. The most notable problem during this period was the Irish "potato famine" of 1845–46. The introduction of the potato to Ireland permitted rapid population growth up to some eight million people by 1841; but a blight struck the monocrop, and more than a million people died and another million emigrated. The Irish population has since stabilized at half its preblight level. A second European food crisis developed early in this century but was averted when vast acreages in Australia, Argentina, and Canada were taken from aboriginal hunting peoples and put into production for the world market.

In 1905, Harvard geologist Nathaniel S. Shaler warned that the world was very near the limits of food production; he doubted that a threefold population expansion could be supported. World population then stood at well under two billion. Forty years later the United Nations declared that much of the world suffered from malnutrition and launched a major "freedom from hunger" campaign. In 1965, Georg Borgstrom, a food scientist with 20 years of experience, declared that the world had already failed in its effort to feed itself, and that hunger—"hunger rampant"—was now the great issue of our age. In 1967, William and Paul Paddock, brothers with long experience in tropical agriculture and national food systems in the underdeveloped world, published a major book in which they predicted that by 1975 United States grain surpluses would no longer be able to make up for world food shortages, and a period of disastrous famines would begin.

Recognizing the dangers, President Lyndon B. Johnson declared that the world food problem was "one of the foremost challenges of mankind today"; and in 1966, he directed his Science Advisory Committee to investigate the problem and look for solutions (United States, President's Science Advisory Committee 1967). The committee brought together 115 experts on all aspects of the problem from universities, industry, and government agencies. They worked for a year, with subpanels devoted to such topics as food supply, population, nutritional needs, plant and animal productivity, soils and climate, marketing, processing, and distribution. Finally, in 1967, the committee issued a three-volume, 1,200-page report, confirming all the dire predictions that had been made before. Their major conclusion was that: "The scale, severity, and duration of the world food problem are so great that a massive, long-range, innovative effort unprecedented in human history will be required to master it." (1967 Vol. 1:11)

The report dealt with the basic problem of the food crisis in the immediate future, the 20 years from 1965 to 1985, on the mistaken assumption, or at least the hope, that effective family planning programs would be initiated immediately and would stabilize the population by 1985. The panelists felt that if the food problem was solved by 1985, it would be manageable well into the future. By 1975, barely halfway to the 1985 safety target, we can see that the population problem has slight hope of being stabilized in the near future, and it appears that the predictions of *"Famine—1975!"* are being fulfilled. At the United Nations World Food Conference which met in Rome in November, 1974, it was reported that 460 million people were threatened with immediate famine and that 10 million would probably die before the year was out. In his latest book, biologist Paul Ehrlich (Erlich and Erlich 1974) states flatly that it is already too late for population programs to prevent famine, because the great famines are already under way. At the Rome food conference, one American agronomist was quoted as saying that unless something was done to provide better food security for the world, "we may be seeing the end of our civilization."

Measuring Hunger

There are several ways of determining the adequacy with which the world or any given region is meeting its nutritional needs. One obvious and apparently simple method is to estimate per capita calorie and protein requirements and to compare these figures with estimates of the availability or the actual consumption of nutrients. This is a very difficult method to work with, in fact, because it is not easy to establish a completely adequate basic nutritional standard for the world. In the first place, caloric requirements vary with age, sex, health status, body weight, quality of diet, physical activity, and climate. A world average might have little relevance in any particular area. Furthermore, low body weights in many countries, and their corresponding "adequate" levels of per capita caloric requirements, may be very misleading because these low weights may in turn be a result of nutritional deficiency in children which prevented the population from realizing its genetic growth potential. There may also be a large gap between calories available and calories consumed, because food may be lost in storage, shipping, and preparation—a further gap between calories consumed and calories absorbed. It is well known that intestinal parasite infestations, which are common in tropical countries, can divert a significant proportion of the calories an infected individual consumes. Other difficulties involve distinguishing between whether specific applications of caloric requirements are concerned with minimum, average, or optimum allowances, and how these are defined.

The United Nations Food and Agriculture Organization (1963) (FAO) has conducted three major world food surveys covering the periods 1934–38, 1948–52, and 1957–59, and more recently has prepared annual world food balance sheets. These data vary widely in quality and have serious limitations, but they remain one of the most useful assessments of the world food situation, and their conclusions merit careful consideration. The first survey, published in 1946, concluded that immediately prior to World War II, two thirds of the world had less than a desirable quantity of food available at the retail level. They fell below a 2,750 daily per capita calorie availability level, which was then considered a reasonable minimum figure, it being assumed that probably 10 percent of that amount would be lost before being actually consumed. The postwar survey found that even fewer calories were available per capita than previously; however, a slight adjustment in the calculated average caloric requirements made the gap between adequate and inadequate appear somewhat smaller. A serious decline in the proportion of animal protein in calorie-poor areas was also noted. The third survey, published in 1967, found that calorie availability was only slightly above prewar levels and that much of the increase occurred in the already industrialized nations, leaving the rest of the world relatively further behind. It was concluded that 10 to 15 percent of the world was undernourished in terms of caloric quantity, and as much as half of the world was qualitatively malnourished in terms of protein availability. Considering these figures at the world level, of course, conceals where the real famine problems lie, because nutrients are very inequitably distributed in the world at large and within individual countries. The third FAO food survey indicated that at least 20 percent of the population in underdeveloped countries was undernourished, and for 60 percent the diet was qualitatively inadequate.

The extent to which a somewhat different interpretation of the caloric adequacy of the diet can yield a different picture of the world food situation is clear when the estimates by the U.S. Department of Argiculture, also published in 1963, are compared with UN estimates. In this report, Lester R. Brown estimated that nearly 80 percent of the underdeveloped world population, or 56 percent of the population of the entire world, was below acceptable caloric levels. Ninety-two percent of Asia was found to be deficient! Some writers scoff at such figures and argue that much lower average per capita requirements are really adequate. Others feel that these estimates may even be too low.

While there may be honest dispute over the establishment of nutritional standards, there can be little dispute over certain other indicators of major world food problems. One particularly ominous change in the world food system occurred in the early 1950s, when the underdeveloped countries stopped exporting grain and became net importers (Brown 1963:76, Paddock and Paddock 1967:41–44). Many of these countries have become increasingly dependent on grain produced by the United States and Canada to make up periodic shortfalls or to supplement regular deficiencies. This is a total reversal of the prior situation when these same countries were grain exporters.

Perhaps the most directly meaningful indication of food shortage is the occurrence of deficiency diseases and deaths related to malnutrition. While deaths due to actual starvation are rarely recorded, it is certain that poor nutrition dramatically increases mortality rates from many other causes. It is well known, for example, that the elevated infant mortality rates in much of the world are to a considerable extent due to protein-calorie deficiency. Numerous studies have shown that infant deaths due to common childhood diseases that seldom are fatal in developed countries can be sharply reduced by provision of adequate diets. The most severe and most common protein-calorie deficiency diseases are kwashiorkor and marasmus, which largely affect children and involve a dramatic wasting-away of body tissue (Trowell 1954). Protein deficiency is also clearly linked to mental retardation and growth impairment in children (Montagu 1972). The extent of such health problems is impossible to estimate precisely because of inadequate surveys and varying interpretations of clinical symptoms. However, these conditions are clearly reflected in the fact that infant mortality rates in underdeveloped countries are often 30 to 40 times higher than the rates of developed countries. Growth retardation related to malnutrition has been called "almost universal" in poor countries, and some writers have placed malnutrition rates at as high as 70 percent in these countries.

Many of the symptoms of chronic food deficiency are probably so common in hungry areas that they have become accepted as "normal" conditions. Reduced physical activity and a general physiological slowdown are basic adaptations to starvation (Young and Scrimshaw 1971), but these symptoms may not be immediately obvious when they characterize entire populations or segments of populations.

Another indirect indication of food problems in specific areas is the price of foodstuffs in relation to income levels or the ability to purchase food. There is abundant evidence showing clear relationships between poverty and malnutrition. Below certain income levels, it may simply not be possible to obtain an adequate diet. This is generally the case in rural areas where formerly self-sufficient farmers with presumably adequate diets have been forced to replace traditional food crops with cash crops that do not generate enough income to allow them to purchase sufficient food (Gross and Underwood 1971). Urban populations must rely entirely on cash to provide their food. The President's Science Advisory Committee report presented data for India showing that in 1961–62, 20 percent of the population fell within income levels that allowed them to obtain on the average only about 80 percent of their caloric requirements and less than their needed protein. In 1958, in Maharashtra State, poor people at the lowest income levels were consuming only 58 percent of their caloric requirements and 64 percent of their protein needs, while those at the highest income levels received 131 percent and 148 percent, respectively. It is significant that estimates of malnutrition derived from income levels correspond quite closely to estimates based on total availability of nutrients in relation to total need such as those proposed by the FAO *Third World Food Survey*.

The Evolution of Food Systems

In a sense, the Malthusian dilemma—the problem of balancing the power of population with the power of food production—is the most basic adaptive test that any culture must successfully solve if it is long to survive. Anthropologists have devoted a large share of their research effort to examining subsistence systems in various cultures, and archaeologists in particular have focused on the evolution of food-producing systems as one of their primary research topics. The major findings of this research are of special relevance to a better understanding of today's world food crisis.

Much of the early theoretical literature on the evolution of food systems has been cluttered by a consistent tendency to view each change in subsistence as a hard-won major improvement that was only achieved through some brilliant invention. Furthermore, "advances" in food production have traditionally been considered prerequisites for increases in population and other forms of evolutionary progress. More recent research, particularly since 1960, has resulted in a complete reversal or a serious reappraisal of many of these theories.

It is not at all clear that a subsistence system based on domestication of plants and animals and settled farm life is such an obvious improvement over hunting and gathering. It is quite certain, however, that famines and general food insecurity are recurrent problems only in cultures that are dependent on *producing* their own food from domesticates. Hunters and gatherers generally have a convenient cushion against food shortages, even given the vagaries of weather, because their subsistence depends on collecting food from a diverse range of species drawn from complex and stable natural or only partially modified ecosystems. Hunters may easily switch and choose among a wide variety of wild foods in the event that specific food sources fail. Farmers, however, must rely on a few species grown in artificial, highly simplified, and relatively unstable ecosystems. Such systems are quite vulnerable to many kinds of disruption; and when crop failures occur, famine is almost certain to follow. Clear testimony to the greater security of hunting adaptations is afforded by the cases on record of farming populations joining neighboring hunting peoples in order to weather out droughts and by the common tendency of hunting populations to reject farming until it was absolutely forced upon them.* There are also cases of farmers who turned hunters when the right conditions presented themselves.

Not only is farming less *secure* than food collecting; it often involves longer, more monotonous work, and a loss of independence and mobility. In some cases, it has even meant a switch to nutritionally inferior foods. Given so many disadvantages, it seems remarkable that man ever bothered with domestication, and the origin of domestication has become one of the major theoretical debates in anthropology.

It has become increasingly apparent that domestication was not a sudden or unique technological discovery. At best, it was a long process of transformation that occurred independently in perhaps five or more major areas of the world. Theories that stress the "invention" aspect of the process are quite misleading, because there is no reason to believe that peoples with the accumulated knowledge of many thousands of years of plant collecting would not realize that plants grew from seeds and cuttings. There are also many examples of food gatherers who maintained trade contacts with food producers and were well acquainted with the basics of farm life but had no desire to emulate it.**

The most reasonable theories are those that assume some kind of disequilibrium between population and food production in specific areas that made greater productivity per square mile necessary.

The transition from hunting to farming has been intensively investigated in the Tehuacan Valley of central Mexico since 1961 by

---

*Woodburn (1968), for example, reports that the hunting and gathering Hadza are joined by their farming neighbors when famines occur.

**The Australian Aborigines maintained contacts with New Guinea agricultural peoples, but did not themselves take up farming.

archaeologist Richard S. MacNeish (1971). After several years of work and the examination of some 454 sites, a detailed culture history covering the period from 10,000 B.C. to A.D. 1520 has been reconstructed. This work reveals a gradual shift during the first 3,000 years from small nomadic bands depending primarily on extensive hunting of game to more careful scheduling of subsistence activities and a greater dependence on wild plant foods as gradual climatic changes brought environmental modifications that reduced the frequency of game. It appears that these changes set in motion another gradual process of sedentarization, increasing concentration of population, and increasing dependence on plant food. By approximately 4,000 B.C., 14 percent of subsistence was derived from cultivated plants; and by about 1000 B.C., they accounted for 40 percent.

In the Near East a very similar picture is beginning to emerge (Flannery 1969). In that area, somewhat prior to 20,000 B.C. and up to about 10,000 B.C., a gradual intensification in subsistence began, which represented a shift away from large game to a "broad spectrum" of wild foods. These wild foods included wild cereal grasses and small invertebrates, and the subsistence shift occurred together with the adoption of sedentary life. It has been suggested that this change was a consequence of local population disequilibriums in game-poor areas caused in turn by overflow population from the richest hunting zones. Unfortunately, it is not yet clear what caused the initial overpopulation in the optimum hunting areas. A later climatic shift toward a warmer and wetter period may have accelerated the process, however. Sedentariness may have encouraged further population growth by disrupting prior checks on fertility and may have led to increasing pressure on marginal areas, where full domestication and farming eventually became a necessity. The slowness of the transformation process is apparent when it is realized that early dry farming was not well established in the Near East until around 7,000 B.C. Thus, perhaps 10,000 years of gradually increasing population in very specific environmental zones caused an intensification in food collecting and ultimately forced people into domestication. The domestication process in that area was of course much more complex and probably would not have occurred at all without a series of intervening variables such as peculiarities of climate and soil conditions which suited dense stands of wild cereal grasses, and cultural "preadaptations" such as grinding stone technology and storage pits.

The early dry-farming technique in the Middle East afforded a subsistence system that was relatively insecure because total harvests of wheat might fluctuate widely, depending on weather conditions. Some of the domesticates even displaced wild foods of higher protein and caloric content. The only clear advantage of farming over hunting was that it supported a much denser population. Thus an initial "victory" was scored in the struggle to keep food production in line with an expanding population; but as we shall see, the ultimate costs were high. One immediate, undoubtedly unexpected side effect of the change was that cultivated grains quickly displaced wild legumes and grasses, which were greatly valued as wild foods but could not compete successfully with the domesticates. These desirable wild plants were replaced by relatively useless weeds such as ryegrass, and a major alteration of the native flora ensued. Early cultivators almost literally burned their bridges behind them and thus made a return to wild-plant gathering very unlikely. It is of course probable that the entire process took place so gradually that no one would have realized the full implications.

It has been suggested that in tropical areas, early moves toward domestication occurred within a framework of careful ecosystem manipulation in which mixed communities of desirable food plants replaced less useful species in what became small domestic garden plots in the immediate vicinity of households (Harris 1972). This may have occurred in a few specific zones of high biological productivity and seasonal variation in resource availability in connection with sedentarization. Fixed-plot horticulture was readily suited to sedentary living because the rich organic wastes that tended to accumulate about house sites provided an ideal environment, and such gardens could be easily tended and protected from competitors. As population density increased, it became necessary to increase productivity by opening larger gardens further from the house, but these new gardens had to be periodically moved because of the invasion of weeds, decline of soil fertility, and a variety of other reasons. The result was a new form of cultivation, commonly called swidden, slash-and-burn, or shifting cultivation, which proved to be a highly productive, very adaptive subsistence strategy. In this system a garden site is cleared in the forest with the aid of fire or axes; the slashings are burned, providing a dressing of fertile ashes and debris; and a garden is maintained for a year or two. A new garden is then opened elsewhere, and the old plot is allowed to return to forest. Such a pattern can greatly elevate the carrying capacity of a region over what could be supported by hunting and gathering; and as long as the fallow periods allow regrowth of the forest, the system can be quite stable.

Two distinct forms of shifting cultivation apparently evolved separately, each with quite different implications for ecological stability and cultural evolution. In the more humid zones, swidden systems based on vegetative reproduction of root crops such as yams and manioc developed; while in the drier zones the emphasis was on seed crops such as corn, beans, rice, and millet.

Root-crop gardens are characterized by greater species diversity, and the plants are usually arranged in a mixed pattern of overlapping layers that closely duplicates the structure of the unmodified tropical rain forest. The result is the creation of a fairly stable ecosystem and a dense leafy canopy that maximizes incoming solar radiation for photosynthesis, and minimizes potential erosion and leaching of nutrients from heavy rainfall. At the same time the crops utilized make only light demands on the soil. The primary disadvantage of this system is that the typical crops are usually poor sources of protein and heavy reliance is placed on wild fish and game.

Seed-crop gardens, in contrast, are not diverse; they do not form a protective canopy; they make greater demands on the soil, and are thus more vulnerable to soil erosion, depletion of nutrients, fluctuation in weather, and invasion of weeds and insects. These problems are compensated for by the fact that seed crops tend to be much richer in protein and thus open a wider range of habitats because there is less need to depend on animal protein. Cultures relying on seed-crop swidden cultivation, as a result of some of these differences, tend to expand more readily into new environments and have even replaced more stable root-crop cultivators in several cases.

The transformation from food-*collecting,* -hunting, and -gathering subsistence systems to food-*producing,* cultivating systems was without question an enormously significant event in the evolution of culture.* It can be viewed as an expansion of the subsistence base in response to population pressure, and in a sense represents the failure of the previously successful homeostatic control mechanisms of hunting societies, which may never be fully explained. Food production was not a necessary or even desirable improvement over food collecting. It was a major evolutionary advance, however, in that it was related to increased population density, which quickly meant new forms of social organization and higher levels of integration. It must be emphasized that this assessment of the process is a reversal of the more traditional view, which held that food production was "discovered" and then population grew. It is also quite likely, as we shall see, that the state itself had a hand in promoting further population growth and technological advance.

Food production has been widely acclaimed as a dramatic new source of energy and a laborsaving device which increased leisure and left man free to build culture. This does not seem to have been the case. Even with domesticated plants and animals, man still remained the basic source of mechanical energy until much later. What actually happened in the transformation was that more people worked longer hours than ever before to produce more food in a smaller area. Careful comparison of the inputs of labor and outputs of calories between contemporary hunters and shifting cultivators reveals that increases in efficiency with early farming were not significant enough to encourage hunters to adopt it for that reason

---

*Smith (1972) presents a general survey of the consequences of food production.

TABLE 2 Hours per one million calories in primitive hunting and shifting cultivating cultures

subsistence	culture	hours of labor
Hunting	Bushmen[a]	694
	Australians[b]	631
	Amahuaka[c]	795
	Miskito[d]	787
Shifting	Amahuaka[e]	603
cultivation	Tsembaga[f]	720

Sources: a) Lee 1969, b) McCarthy and McArthur 1960, c) Carneiro 1968, d) Nietschmann 1973, e) Carneiro 1968, f) Rappaport 1971.

alone.* Table 2, which presents the number of hours required to produce one million calories of food (enough to sustain an average person for one year)** for several different cultures, shows that some hunting cultures may even get by with a lighter total work load than some shifting cultivators. The comparison is more striking in Table 3, which compares the Bushmen and the Tsembaga of New Guinea, the two most traditional hunting and shifting cultivating cultures for which relatively complete data are now available. The Bushmen are hunter-gatherers in the harsh Kalahari desert of southern Africa; yet, even with their seemingly difficult environment, they work less hours per worker and are able to maintain a smaller percentage of their population in the work force than the shifting cultivators. The Tsembaga, while they work harder to maintain their gardens and domesticated animals, and occupy a much richer environment, are able to support a population a hundred times denser than that of the Bushmen. Clearly, the only gain is in population, and that gain is at a cost.

---

*Carneiro (1968) argues for precisely this viewpoint using data from the Amazon basin.

**A comparative figure used by Carneiro (1968).

TABLE 3 Labor, dependency ratio, and population density in hunting and shifting cultivating cultures

subsistence	culture	hours of labor per worker annually	workers per 100 persons	density per square kilometer
Hunting	Bushman[a]	805	61	0.25
Cultivating	Tsembaga[b]	820	70	25.00

Sources: a) Lee 1969, b) Rappaport 1971.

The Domestic Mode of Food Production

While in many cases there are obvious technological differences, food production in primitive cultures differs in other, very important respects from any food systems found in state-level cultures. Many of these critical differences have been outlined in a recent study by Marshall Sahlins, entitled *Stone Age Economics* (1972, chapters 2 and 3), and they are valid for both primitive hunters and cultivators. According to Sahlins, when food production is for local, household, or village domestic consumption, as in all primitive cultures, actual production tends to be far below the maximum that might be sustained, given the potential limitations of technology, labor force, and resources. The result of this *underproduction* is that the danger of a primitive culture ever exceeding the carrying capacity of its environment is greatly reduced, as is the likelihood of environmental deterioration and famine. On the other hand, as political advancement occurs, food production is accelerated, and so is the possibility of overshooting carrying capacities, and the attendant famine and environmental deterioration.

Underproduction is an important concept, but it must be approached with caution. It does present an obvious contrast with the *overconsumption* of industrial cultures; but before it can be established with certainty, some estimate of potential production or carrying capacity must be arrived at.

   Many estimates are available of the potential carrying capacity for specific shifting cultivators, derived from simple calculations of the amount of land needed to feed an individual per year, the length of time a garden was cropped, and the length of the fallow period. The Kuikuru in South America were found (Carneiro 1960) to be at a population density of only 7 percent of what their immediate locality would support in terms of garden produce, although the limited availability of fish and game as a protein source would be certain to reduce the total possible. Sahlins presents data from nine other traditional cultures practicing shifting cultivation in Africa, Asia, and New Guinea, showing that actual population densities ranged from as low as 8 percent of the carrying capacity to an average of 50 percent. In only one culture in the sample did local areas reach the full carrying capacity. Another study (Brown and Brookfield 1963) of 12 Chimbu subgroups in New Guinea found them ranging from 22 to 97 percent of maximum sustainable densities, and averaging just 64 percent of capacity. Precise figures on carrying capacity for hunters are more difficult to calculate, but J. B. Birdsell (1971) has suggested that Australian aborigines maintained themselves at an "optimum" carrying capacity which was 10 to 20 percent below the "maximum" capacity. Other researchers have frequently commented that hunters seem generally not to be exploiting their food resources to the maximum potential. Similar observations have been made for primitive pastoralists. The problem here, of course, is that it is difficult for a researcher at one point in time to estimate the extent of long-term fluctuation in the availability of resources. Cultures which do not store food must necessarily be restricted to the population that can be supported in the worst year.
   Another approach to underproduction, which avoids the problem of carrying capacity, is simply to assess the labor potential of a given culture and evaluate how hard the population is working at food production (Sahlins 1972). There is actually very wide cross-cultural variation in the length of the average working life span, the sexual division of labor, seasonal labor, and the output of individual households within a given culture. For example, it is not uncommon

for young adults to be uninvolved in food production, and primitive cultures may often retire adults far sooner than may be the case in politically advanced cultures. Young Bushman males may be 25 years of age before they are actively involved in subsistence activities, and older men may retire by 60. It is quite characteristic in primitive cultures generally for labor to be irregular and intermittent. Particular tasks are easily and frequently postponed for what might seem the most trivial excuses—because of the weather, for a nap, for visiting, for feasting, or for no reason at all. Among agriculturalists, and in some cases even among hunters, there may be seasonal slack periods when virtually no hunting or farming may be done. There are also wide tolerances of individual variation in work load; some persons do far more than their "share," while others consistently loaf. Even the concept "work" as opposed to "play" or "leisure" may not be an important distinction in all cultures. There seems little doubt that most primitive peoples could easily produce a "surplus" of food above their own immediate subsistence needs if they merely worked a little harder, put in a few more hours a week, or slightly reshuffled their labor force. The limitation on production, then, is not an inadequate technology or a scarcity of natural resources. It is the presence of a built-in cultural limit; or, phrased negatively, there is a cultural lack of incentive to raise production in primitive cultures where production is essentially for domestic use.

It is a striking and well-verified fact that many households in primitive cultures do not actually produce enough to feed themselves and must depend on the overproduction of the most ambitious households to provide their needs. This variation in household productivity may result from normal stages in the domestic cycle when households may be more vulnerable, from chance variation in dependency ratios; it may be caused by random variation in success at hunting or farming, misfortune, or simply because some households choose not to work as hard as others.

Sahlins argues that what makes "Stone Age" or primitive economies unique in comparison with "more advanced" economies is that in primitive economies the basic production unit, the dominant institution, is the household. This creates a qualitatively very remarkable kind of economy, and its operation can only be understood in its own terms. Most importantly, within this domestic mode of production lies a major key to the adaptive success of primitive subsistence systems.

The domestic mode of production is based on marriage and a sexual division of labor, a simple technology which is available to all, and where each household can perform all the technological functions itself. Individual households in a primitive culture are not economically autonomous, but the critical point is that the objective of production is domestic use. Food production goals are set by the individual food-consuming household. When the specific need— daily in the case of hunters, or annually in the case of garden planting—is met, then labor ceases. The system is not designed to produce a surplus above domestic needs. In a market economy, production is for exchange, for cash, for profit. There is no culturally recognized limit to production, because the need for wealth is infinitely expandable. The distinctive features of industrial food production will be examined below; but here, it may be noted that the contrasts between the primitive, domestic mode of production and the market mode of production are so great that much of the economic behavior of tribal peoples in contacts with market-oriented outsiders has been considered quite irrational. What has been interpreted as laziness or ignorance on the part of tribesmen is actually the operation of a very unique and very adaptive system of food production.

Equilibrium mechanisms within primitive cultures helping to maintain production at a low level relative to the maximum potential include the operation of "Chayanov's Rule." This basic labor principle was originally formulated by A. V. Chayanov (1966) in a study of Russian peasants. Chayanov noted that in larger households, where there were more workers, each worker worked less than did the average worker in smaller households. Sahlins rephrases the rule as follows: "Intensity of labor in a system of domestic production for use varies inversely with the relative working capacity of the producing unit." (Sahlins 1972:91)

Thus the potentially most productive households automatically tend to slack off, while individuals in smaller households must work harder. In effect, household production norms are culturally set at average levels, not at the highest attainable. The maintenance of living standards by some households at a level significantly above that attainable by the majority would lead to social disorder in the absence of more elaborate forms of political control.

The general egalitarianness of primitive cultures is an obvious element in the success of primitive subsistence systems. In the first place, all households enjoy free access to the natural resources needed for their subsistence. Various redistributive mechanisms may be initiated when serious local imbalances result due to random fluctuations in demography or subsistence success. A further stabilizing factor is that reciprocal pooling of food and redistribution along kinship networks assure a relatively uniform distribution of nutrients. As a result, everyone enjoys the same nutritional standard.

Technological Advances in Food Production

If population densities are to rise, food production must be intensified either by increased labor or by technological improvements. How this might occur in a primitive culture is an interesting theoretical problem, because, as we have seen, food production is relatively frozen by the shutoff factors inherent in the domestic mode of production, and population growth is normally minimized by the operation of the equilibrium mechanisms outlined in Chapter 6. In effect, there is normally no Malthusian dilemma in primitive cultures—the two forces are continuously kept in check. These facts place a new light on the traditional argument as to whether technological advances in food production cause population growth, or whether population growth itself causes advances in food production. The most basic determining factors would appear to lie in the actual arrangement of the social system. Primitive social systems are, as we have shown, structured to restrain both population and food production. They are, by definition, no-growth systems. Growth of either population or food production, or both, may however be deliberately promoted and even institutionalized within more complex social systems.

Within primitive cultures organized around the domestic mode of production, there is a constant struggle to balance the demands of the society at large, which extract food from individual households by means of kinship obligations, with the immediate self-interest of each isolated household. If growth of either population or food production is to occur, a social system must develop which will tap the "underdeveloped" resources and transform the domestic mode of production into something else. Political authority must overcome the natural tendency of individual households to set their own production goals and to maintain their economic autonomy over and against the interests of the larger society. The political order must establish a *public* economy. "Big-man" leadership systems, segmentary lineage and clan systems, and hierarchical chiefdoms all represent different sociopolitical strategies for mobilizing productivity above the cutoff point normally operating in the domestic mode of production, but still remaining within the limitations of a kin-based, nonstate social system.

It does seem to be the case that certain cultures respond to the ever-present tendency of population to expand by increasing food production and at the same time developing more complex forms of social organization. These three variables—population growth, intensification of subsistence, and increasing social complexity—are so interrelated that it is not always reasonable to assign priority to any one of them, although a number of recent theorists place primary emphasis on population growth as the basic determinant. It can be assumed that technological improvements which demand greater

intensification of labor will only come about in the presence of
population pressure. Conversely, they may be facilitated by the prior
existence of certain levels of sociopolitical organization. A complex
irrigation system, for example, could probably not be initiated in a
society that lacked effective supralocal forms of political control. For
their part, more complex forms of social organization may often
become necessary as disputes over access to resources begin to arise
in situations of increasing population pressure.

   Danish economist Ester Boserup (1965) argues that technological changes in primitive agriculture can all be viewed as
responses to population pressure. Her approach is very similar to that
of anthropologists in recent attempts to explain the transition from
hunting to farming. She assumes that the earliest, simplest farming
techniques, such as shifting cultivation, were more productive per
man-hour of labor than more advanced systems, but they were *less*
productive per unit of land. People would automatically prefer such
extensive methods; i.e., these methods simply required less work to
produce food than more intensive methods. There is indeed a clear
relationship between the frequency of cropping in a given unit of
land and the density of population. Denser populations require more
intensive land use. Fallow periods may well be shortened as a direct
response to an increase of population in local areas, and this
shortening of fallow periods or more intense land use will initiate
ecological changes which force the use of new technology. Under a
typical swidden or "forest fallow" system, a simple digging stick is all
that is required for planting in newly cleared, virtually weed-free
forest. However, when the fallow cycle is shortened because of the
need to increase food production in a limited area, then the
increasing appearance of weeds makes hoes necessary. Continued
shortening of fallow periods will lead to grasses which can be easily
cultivated with plows.

   From this viewpoint, advances in food production can be seen
as not simply brilliant inventions which in turn cause population
growth; rather, they were forced upon people by prior population
growth. It would make no sense at all for a shifting cultivator with
adequate forest resources to invent a plow, because it would simply

not fit his mode of land use and would not be an advantage. It must not be forgotten, however, that intensification in food production will of course reinforce the need for further intensification by supporting and amplifying the prior deviation from population equilibrium. This "deviation amplification" is a basic process of population growth, and population growth and subsistence intensification clearly constitutes a self-intensifying spiral.

As cultural evolution proceeds, the basic trend is for food production to become more and more intensive, for more food to be produced in a smaller and smaller area by a smaller and smaller percentage of the total population. In Mesopotamia, Kent V. Flannery (1969) estimates that probably 35 percent of modern-day Iran would have provided a favorable habitat for hunting cultures which were able to support 0.1 persons per square kilometer in the late Paleolithic period. Ten percent of Iran was suited for dry farming, and it supported one or two persons per square kilometer. Highly intensive irrigation agriculture is possible over only one percent of the total area of the country; but with it, up to six or more persons per square kilometer were supported even in ancient Mesopotamia. This level of productivity implies both state organization and a totally different kind of food system.

State-Level Food Systems

The most intensive food production systems can apparently only be supported by state-level political systems. State-level food systems contrast strongly with patterns characteristic of primitive cultures. Through political coercion, states are able to exact food production from local villages and households in the form of taxes or tribute far above the levels that would be required for local needs. Specific data on highly productive wet rice cultivators in China prior to the Communist government (cited Harris, M. 1971:203–217) shows that 84 percent of their crop was an "exported surplus" beyond their immediate subsistence needs. With increases of this magnitude, it is not surprising that states may often be much closer to the maximum carrying capacity of their environments than primitive cultures.

Other important cultural features of state-level food systems are that access to productive resources such as land and water may be allocated according to social class and status, and that significant segments of the population may not be involved in food production at all. This arrangement makes it quite likely that nutrients will no longer be equally distributed in the society—some social classes may indeed be hungry, while other classes are "overnourished." This combination of differential access to subsistence resources and inequitable distribution of nutrients by social class is, as we have seen, one of the basic correlates of hunger in the modern world.

Thus, there are three aspects of the food problem which might be considered adverse side effects of evolutionary progress. On the one hand, the adoption of agriculture creates an ecologically less stable food system which is inherently more prone to famine-causing fluctuation. Secondly, as a deviation amplification, technological advances in food production tend to reinforce an accelerating spiral of population and further subsistence intensification which must inevitably place greater strains on the ecosystem and increase the likelihood of further environmental deterioration, and results in an approach close to, if not beyond, the ultimate carrying capacity of the resource base. Finally, social stratification creates an imbalance in the availability of food to the population. It would appear from this analysis that many of the food problems that the world is now experiencing are merely predictable cultural evolution processes and intrinsic features of state-level organization. Many of these difficulties have been with us since the first appearance of agriculture around 10,000 years ago, but they were clearly intensified and enlarged by the evolution of states and urban civilization some 5,000 years ago. The fact that they are still unsolved suggests that these may be quite intractable problems that may well only be overcome through a drastic transformation process. This picture has been altered considerably over the past 200 years, however, by the emergence of the culture of consumption and its unique food system.

5

industrial food systems

If we insist on a high-energy food system, we should consider starting with coal, oil, garbage—or any other source of hydrocarbons—and producing in factories bacteria, fungi, and yeasts. These products could then be flavored and colored appropriately for cultural tastes. (Steinhart and Steinhart 1974:315)

The food systems of industrial nations represent an enormous advance in evolutionary progress and a proportionate loss in long-run adaptive success. The primary distinguishing feature of these systems is their fossil fuel energy subsidy, which permits very high crop yields for very low inputs of human energy. Other critical aspects are the extreme complexity of the production-consumption chain, and the tendency to increase the per capita energy and resource cost of food consumption through expanded dependence on synthetic and highly processed foods and inefficiently produced animal protein. These systems are not only far more costly in terms of per capita demands for energy and resources, but they are unquestionably more frail than primitive systems, they demand much more intensive ecosystem management, and they have greater potential for environmental deterioration. Perhaps, most critically, they can clearly not be sustained at present rates of increase or even at present levels unless they are radically restructured. It is also very doubtful that if such systems diffuse, they could be supported at all on a global basis, given present population levels. These are critical issues because the present strategy for solving the world food crisis not only ignores the fact that many of the problems are inherent features of state-level cultures based on intensive food production systems, but also makes the dangerous assumption that industrial food systems will feed the world if they can only be established everywhere.

Factory Food Production

If the nonhuman energy expended in the production, processing, distribution, storage, and preparation of food in America is ignored, the system may indeed appear to be very efficient. Anthropologist Marvin Harris (1971) has given the American food system highest

TABLE 4 Energy input-output efficiency in five food systems

culture	technology	calories produced per calorie expended
Bushman	hunting/gathering	9.6
Tsembaga (New Guinea)	shifting cultivation	18.0
	pig raising	2.1
	total	9.8
Genieri (Gambia)	hoe farming	11.2
China	irrigated wet rice	53.5
United States	factory farming	
	human labor	210.0
	nonhuman energy	0.13

Sources: Marvin Harris, *Culture, Man and Nature* (New York: Thomas Crowell Co., Inc., 1971), pp. 203–17; John S. Steinhart and Carol E. Steinhart, "Energy Use in the U. S. Food System," *Science,* Vol. 184 (1974), pp. 307–16.

ratings in "technoenvironmental advantage"* in comparison with the energy efficiency of hunters, shifting cultivators, hoe farmers, and wet rice growers. His figures are based on a simple estimate of the hours expended per farm worker, multiplied by a fixed rate of 150 calories expended per hour, and divided into the quantity of food calories produced in a given period of time. These calculations may be a reasonable approximation of energy input-output ratios for primitive farmers and hunters, but they are completely inadequate when they ignore the fossil fuel subsidy in the industrial food system. Table 4 presents the basic technoenvironmental efficiency rating of the five cultures evaluated by Harris, but adds a correction for the efficiency of the U.S. system by counting separately the nonhuman energy inputs from production to consumption. The surprising fact is that while American farm laborers may only expend one calorie of

---

*In his 1975 edition of *Culture, Man and Nature* (renamed *Culture, People and Nature*), Harris revises his efficiency rating for the U.S. food production system on the basis of the fossil fuel costs, following Steinhart and Steinhart (1974) and others.

human energy for every 210 food calories they produce, approximately eight calories of nonhuman energy, primarily in the form of fossil fuels, are also required for each calorie produced. It is apparent that the industrial food system is actually operating at an energy efficiency deficit.

Ecologist Howard T. Odum (1971) has brilliantly outlined the energy flow systems underlying subsistence patterns at different levels of cultural development using carefully designed cybernetic models. As a hunter and gatherer man was dependent for his subsistence on highly complex and stable ecosystems which were largely self-regulating, closed cybernetic systems. In a tropical rain forest, for example (see Figure 8), the diverse species of the forest do all the work of concentrating energy and nutrients and regulating their flow. Nutrients are largely stored in the living plants and animals and are quickly and efficiently recycled upon their death. Primitive shifting cultivators adjusted to the forest ecosystem by making use of the artificial energy pulse generated each time a forest plot was cut and burned (see Figure 9). This pulse temporarily eliminated competitor species and concentrated nutrients in order briefly to transfer the energy flow into food crops. Except for this minor intervention, the system continued to be basically self-regulating and immediately began to return to its starting point; that is, natural forest succession began at once. Thus, nature did most of the work, and as long as their power base remained restricted to local inputs of solar energy, primitive cultures were generally unable to harness enough power to seriously disrupt their supporting ecosystems.

When modern nations began to channel fossil fuel energy into their food systems, the picture was suddenly and radically changed. Odum describes the new fossil fuel food systems very neatly as follows:

> One of the results of industrialization based on the new concentrated energy sources was abundant food rolling out from huge fields which were sowed with machinery, tilled with tractors, and weeded and poisoned with chemicals. Epidemic

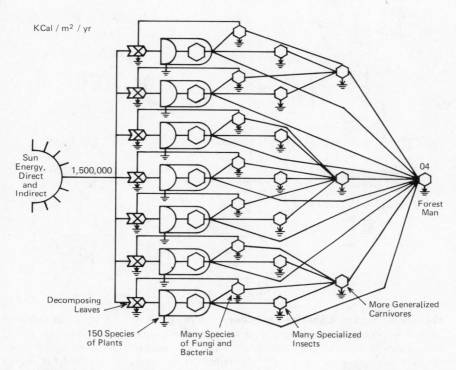

KCal / m² / yr

Sun Energy, Direct and Indirect

1,500,000

04

Forest Man

More Generalized Carnivores

Decomposing Leaves

150 Species of Plants

Many Species of Fungi and Bacteria

Many Specialized Insects

FIGURE 8   Man as a Hunter.   Network matrix supporting and stabilizing a tropical rain forest system. Man is a minor component, but he has integrating and control functions because of the convergence of pathways. (Source: Howard T. Odum, *Environment, Power, and Society* (New York: John Wiley & Sons, Inc., Inter-Science, 1971), p. 87.)

diseases were kept in check by great teams of scientists in distant experiment stations developing new and changing varieties to stay ahead of the evolution of disease adaptation. Soon a few people were supporting many, and most of the rural population left the little farms to fill the new industrial cities. (Odum 1971:115)

The greater crop yields which followed industrialization must not be considered simply the result of brilliant inventions, education,

FIGURE 9   Man as a Shifting Cultivator.   Energy diagram for shifting agriculture. Man serves as a switching timer, transferring the flow of energy into food crops made temporarily possible by the material and work accumulated during the long period of plant succession between short agricultural cycles. (Source: Howard T. Odum, *Environment, Power, and Society* (New York: John Wiley & Sons, Inc., Inter-Science, 1971), p. 113.)

determination, and great technological know-how. An enormous energy subsidy was essential. Factory farms do not achieve more efficient rates of photosynthesis and energy conversion. Actually, even some of the most productive factory farms, such as industrialized rice farms, convert only about 0.25 percent of incoming solar radiation into useful energy, while a tropical rain forest operates at 3.5 percent efficiency (Odum 1971). Larger per acre yields are possible on factory farms because fossil fuels replace the energy loop the natural ecosystem reserved for its own mechanisms of self-regulation (see Fig. 10). This system is simply a

FIGURE 10 Factory Farming with Fossil Fuels. Man in a system of industrialized, high-yield agriculture. Energetic inputs include flows of fossil fuels which replace the work formerly done by man, his animals, and the network of animals and plants in which he was formerly nursed. Work flows include the following: (1) mechanized and commercial preparation of seeding and planting, replacing the natural dispersion system; (2) fertilizer excesses which replace the mineral recycling system; (3) chemical and power weeding, replacing the woody maintenance of a shading system; (4) soil preparation and treatment to replace the forest soil-building processes; (5) insecticides which replace the system of chemical diversity and carnivores for preventing epidemic grazing and disease; (6) development of varieties which are capable of passing on the savings in work to net food storages. New varieties are developed as diseases appear, thus providing the genetic selection formerly arranged by the forest evolution and selection system. In this system 170 persons per square mile support 32 times this number in cities. The level of grain production in the United States is about 1000 kcal/(m²)(yr). The fuel subsidy is calculated using 10^4 kcal/dollar. If production yields $60/(acre)(yr) and if the costs are 90 percent of the gross, then $54/acre is the measure to use of materials and services from the industrialized culture. This becomes 54 × 10^4 kcal/acre or 135 kcal/(m²)(yr). (Source: Howard T. Odum, *Environment, Power, and Society* (New York: John Wiley & Sons, Inc., Inter-Science, 1971), p. 119.)

means of converting oil into food. In effect, as Odum phrases it, in a factory agricultural system, "fossil fuel supported works of man have eliminated the natural species and substituted industrial services for the services of those natural species, releasing the same basic production to yield." (Odum 1971:117)

A factory farm is actually an extremely costly, sloppy, and inefficient attempt to replace nature with a very simplified, artificially maintained and subsidized machine. Chemical fertilizers manufactured and transported with fossil fuels replace the tightly calibrated nutrient cycles of the natural ecosystem. More chemicals and machinery control the weeds that in a swidden system are merely part of the restart mechanism which are shaded out as the successional pattern they initiate proceeds. Plant geneticists working in laboratories replace the natural process of biological evolution based on natural selection and species diversity. The delicate natural balances which prevent consumer species from overgrazing are eliminated by heavy application of chemical poisons. Pollution and environmental deterioration are unintended direct by-products of industrial farming because the exotic nutrients and insecticides do not fit into natural ecosystem cycles but instead merely pile up in unexpected places to block these cycles. The massive use of chemical pesticides also has serious direct implications for public health, and has stirred widespread public concern and controversy on many occasions.

Much of the energy and manpower needed to support an industrial food system is disguised by statistics that focus on farm labor and yields per acre. Harris, in the estimate of the efficiency of U.S. food production cited earlier, used a figure of five million farm workers in 1964. New figures, presented in Table 5, prepared from data in the *Statistical Abstract of the U.S.*, suggest that in 1972 more than 11 million people were full-time workers in the food system, even with a reduction of 700,000 in the count of actual farm workers! The addition of 386,000 support workers in the manufacturing and marketing of farm machinery and chemicals,

TABLE 5 Labor in the U.S. food system, 1972 (in millions of workers)

Farm labor	4.3	million
Support sectors		
farm machine manufacturing	0.132	
agri-chemical manufacturing	0.052	
farm equipment sales	0.088	
agri-scientists	0.018	
Dept. of Agriculture	0.114	
Total, primary production	4.686	million
Food processing industry	1.700	
Food wholesalers	.537	
Eating and drinking places	2.684	
Retail grocers	1.400	
Total, processors and distributors	6.321	million
Food system total	11.007	million

Source: *The American Almanac,* 1974, Statistical Abstract of the United States, New York: Grosset and Dunlap, Inc.

agricultural sciences, and the federal Department of Agriculture brings the total number of workers in direct support of food production up to 4.6 million. Some writers have even estimated that as many as two support workers are needed for each farm worker (Pimentel 1973).

Factory Potatoes versus Swidden Sweet Potatoes

> Profit is the only reason for growing potatoes. (Knudson 1972:76)

The extent to which fossil fuel subsidized farming systems have artificially replaced the functions of the natural ecosystem, and the incredible energy and environmental costs of this change, stand out with remarkable clarity when the production of Irish potatoes on a typical American farm* is compared with the methods of raising sweet potatoes in traditional New Guinea swidden gardens (Rappaport 1971). Potatoes (Irish or sweet) occupy roughly the same position in each culture, in that they are quantitatively the most important single vegetable consumed and are unquestionably basic staples in the diet. In American culture, meat and potatoes make a meal complete.

On a factory farm in the United States, potatoes can be grown as a successful monocrop only with the help of vast energy inputs to maintain correct soil conditions, moisture, and nutrients, and to control weeds, epidemic diseases, and insect infestations. On the swidden sweet potato farm, all of these functions are carried out by the natural ecosystem, and by the diversity of the garden plantings, which imitates that natural system. No irrigation or fertilizer is required on swidden plots, but factory potato farmers must apply chemical fertilizer constantly and in many areas must irrigate to maintain their high yields. In areas where overhead sprinklers are used, special chemicals may be applied to the soil to prevent compaction and lost filtration caused by the perpetual mechanical rain (Hagood 1972). Weeds, insects, and diseases may be variously controlled before planting by chemical treatment of the tubers, by application of chemical herbicides and insecticides to the soil, and sometimes even by soil fumigation which kills virtually all soil organisms. There are specialized preemergence weed killers, and a wide variety of other herbicides and insecticides, which may be applied while the crop is growing. In some cases, special chemicals are sprayed on the crop to inhibit sprouting after harvest, or to intensify the red skin color of certain potatoes to increase their market value. It may be noted that part of this energy-expensive chemical program is carried out as a cosmetic treatment to prevent

---

*Talburt and Smith (1967) and various of the *Annual Proceedings of the Annual Washington Potato Conference.*

unsightly blemishes which may lower consumer acceptance but have little effect on increasing actual yields. Where potatoes are contracted to go into chips, the vines must be chemically killed weeks before harvesting in order to prevent starch buildup in the tubers, which causes an undesirable darkening in the finished potato chips.

The extent of some of this chemical maintenance may be seen in specific production statistics from Washington State, which was third in the nation for potato production in the late 1960s. In 1969, 60 percent of the potato acreage on farms devoted principally to that crop was chemically sprayed by airplane for insect control, and some farms required as many as five to nine separate treatments (United States Department of Commerce 1969). Only slightly fewer acres were treated chemically for disease control, and 40 percent were treated for weeds. In addition to the tractors and trucks normally required on farms, there were hundreds of specialized machines on Washington farms in 1967 to cut potato seed, and for use as potato harvesters, windrowers, diggers, and planters. In 1969, more than 36,000 tons of liquid and dry fertilizer were applied to 62,500 acres of potatoes—more than a thousand pounds per acre—and virtually the entire crop required both fertilizing and irrigation.

With this kind of treatment, it is not surprising that yields increased from a national average of 65 hundredweight per acre in 1920 to 380 hundredweight in Washington in 1969. In caloric terms, this means that approximately 10 million calories were being produced per acre. In comparison, New Guinea sweet potato farmers were producing approximately 5 million calories per acre with more than a dozen major crops combined. In addition to the direct energy subsidy from fossil fuels, Washington potato farmers were passing on other hidden costs, which makes full assessment of the costs impossible in the short term. For example, extensive irrigation already seems to be causing minor microclimatic alterations in the region; there is the danger that irrigation will also lead to soil salinization; heavy use of fertilizers and other chemicals will in time increasingly leach into rivers and underground water sources, killing susceptible species and overnourishing others; while intensively cultivated areas are more subject to wind erosion.

Energy Costs of the Distribution System

In a primitive culture, as we have seen, food is largely produced by the households that consume it. Only small quantities are normally distributed beyond individual households, and this distribution occurs within a framework of reciprocal sharing between close kinsmen. In stratified chiefdom-level societies, production and consumption still remain largely at the household level; but some foodstuffs may be concentrated by chiefs as tribute, to be partially redistributed at feasts or in times of crisis, and to support craft specialists for the production of sumptuary goods. With the evolution of the state and the appearance of urban centers, large quantities of food had to be transferred from the rural subsistence farmers or peasants to the cities to support the nonfood producers. This transfer has been variously effected through the payment of taxes, through the operations of special trader classes, or through well-developed market exchanges. Reliance only on solar-energy-powered agriculture apparently placed severe limitations on the extent to which the population of a given culture could be concentrated in cities, not only because of the restrictions that were placed on food production, but also because of the energy costs of transportation. With the tapping of fossil fuels and the rise of industrialized urban centers, which concentrated up to 95 percent of the population, the energy costs of the food distribution system have suddenly come to overshadow totally the costs of actual production.

Only a very rough estimate of the *total* energy costs of the present American food system are possible. John D. Steinhart and Carol E. Steinhart calculated recently that in 1970, eight to 12 calories were expended in the production, distribution, and consumption of a single calorie of food. This includes such energy costs as the manufacturing and operation of farm machinery, fertilizer, irrigation, food processing, packaging, transportation, and manufacturing of trucks, and both industrial and domestic cooking and refrigeration (see Table 6). Higher estimates would include the energy cost of shipping food by rail, ship, and air, disposal of food-related wastes, maintenance of buildings and equipment, a percentage of highway construction costs, agricultural research, and domestic use of private automobiles to move food from supermarket to home. Other estimates have placed the figure as high as 20 calories in for one calorie out, and this may be far more realistic.

According to Steinhart and Steinhart's conservative estimate, less than 25 percent of the total energy expended in the American food system actually went to support primary production on the farm; the other 75 percent plus went to processing, marketing, and domestic uses. Significantly, more manpower was also engaged in the food distribution network than on the farm, even if labor costs in the transportation system are disregarded (see Table 5). Clearly, the distribution component of the industrial food system is responsible for much of the enormous energy cost of the total system and for this reason deserves special investigation.

Many of the increased energy costs of the U.S. food system appear to be related solely to the marketing process. There has been little change in the actual quantity of calories and protein consumed by Americans per capita in recent decades, and there are obvious limits to expansion of these rates; but even so, the per capita costs of American food consumption doubled between 1940 and 1970. During this period the per capita energy costs of packaging increased 119 percent; and the overall per capita energy costs of processing, packaging, and transportation from factory to marketplace increased by 95 percent (Stewart and Stewart 1974).

There has been a dramatic switch in recent years toward the consumption of more energy-intensive food. By 1970, America's food was more transported and more expensively processed and

TABLE 6 Energy use in the United States food system in 10^{12} Kcal

component	1940	1947	1950	1954	1958	1960	1964	1968	1970
					On farm				
Fuel (direct use)	70.0	136.0	158.0	172.8	179.0	188.0	213.9	226.0	232.0
Electricity	0.7	32.0	32.9	40.0	44.0	46.1	50.0	57.3	63.8
Fertilizer	12.4	19.5	24.0	30.6	32.2	41.0	60.0	87.0	94.0
Agricultural steel	1.6	2.0	2.7	2.5	2.0	1.7	2.5	2.4	2.0
Farm machinery	9.0	34.7	30.0	29.5	50.2	52.0	60.0	75.0	80.0
Tractors	12.8	25.0	30.8	23.6	16.4	11.8	20.0	20.5	19.3
Irrigation	18.0	22.8	25.0	29.6	32.5	33.3	34.1	34.8	35.0
Subtotal	124.5	272.0	303.4	328.6	356.3	373.9	440.5	503.0	526.1
					Processing industry				
Food processing industry	147.0	177.5	192.0	211.5	212.6	224.0	249.0	295.0	308.0
Food processing machinery	0.7	5.7	5.0	4.9	4.9	5.0	6.0	6.0	6.0
Paper packaging	8.5	14.8	17.0	20.0	26.0	28.0	31.0	35.7	38.0
Glass containers	14.0	25.7	26.0	27.0	30.2	31.0	34.0	41.9	47.0
Steel cans and aluminum	38.0	55.8	62.0	73.7	85.4	86.0	91.0	112.2	122.0
Transport (fuel)	49.6	86.1	102.0	122.3	140.2	153.3	184.0	226.6	246.9
Trucks and trailors (manufacture)	28.0	42.0	49.5	47.0	43.0	44.2	61.0	70.2	74.0
Subtotal	285.8	407.6	453.5	506.4	542.3	571.5	656.0	787.6	841.9
					Commercial and home				
Commercial refrigeration and cooking	121.0	141.0	150.0	161.0	176.0	186.2	209.0	241.0	263.0
Refrigeration machinery (home and commercial)	10.0	24.0	25.0	27.5	29.4	32.0	40.0	56.0	61.0
Home refrigeration and cooking	144.2	184.0	202.3	228.0	257.0	276.6	345.0	433.9	480.0
Subtotal	275.2	349.0	377.3	416.5	462.4	494.8	594.0	730.9	804.0
Grand total	685.5	1028.6	1134.2	1251.5	1361.0	1440.2	1690.5	2021.5	2172.0

Source: John S. Steinhart and Carol E. Steinhart, "Energy Use in the U.S. Food System," *Science*, Vol. 184 (1974), p. 309.

packaged than ever before. These changes can be seen in many areas. For example, since 1950, there has been an almost fivefold increase in the per capita production of frozen food in this country. The introduction of these foods raises overall energy requirements because their distribution requires preparation, packaging, and transportation and storage facilities. Certain new food products, such as potato chips, may be vastly more costly to transport and store because of their increased bulk and fragileness compared to their less processed counterparts. Trends in packaging over the past 20 years which have raised energy costs have included not only a general increase in the use of packaging solely to increase the consumer appeal of foodstuffs, but there has been a switch to more energy-expensive materials. Wood, paper, and reusable glass bottles have been steadily replaced by plastic, nonreturnable bottles and aluminum cans. The latter require approximately twice as much energy to manufacture than the steel cans which they replace! Cultural changes in patterns of food consumption must also account for part of this increase. The most striking change since 1940 is the fact that consumption of beef has more than doubled. This is especially significant because cattle are relatively inefficient converters of vegetable protein, requiring approximately 20 pounds of protein to produce one pound for human consumption. This would not be a critical factor if cattle were grazed on rangeland that would not produce other food crops, but a high proportion of America's beef cattle are fed high-quality grains in feedlots before being slaughtered. It has been estimated that in 1968 as much as 78 percent of the American grain crop was used as animal feed.

Modern marketing practices in the American food system were investigated in detail in an important study carried out for the National Commission on Food Marketing at the request of President Lyndon B. Johnson and published in 1968 (Marple and Wissman 1968). This study was based on the work of 19 academicians and seven private researchers and considered the cost structure of food from farmer to consumer, product innovation and competition, and consumer "needs." Their findings are of particular interest because

they help pinpoint factors in the processing and distribution component of the food system which seem to promote increased energy
costs.

It is a striking fact that productivity in the food-marketing
industry is not measured in terms of how efficiently human need-
satisfying nutrients can be distributed to the population; rather, it is
computed in terms of dollar output per man-hour of labor or return
on investment. In this accounting, staple foods such as meat, flour,
and sugar, which require little processing, are considered to be less
productive because they have a relatively low "value added" in
comparison with soft drinks and cold cereals or other highly
processed food "products." If the population is growing very slowly
and is already satisfying its basic food needs, then logically the only
way for food companies to increase their domestic profits is through
increased competition between companies or through the production of increasingly more expensive new food products. Food
markets may also be increased through exports in a world market
system. Limited increases have also been obtained by raising the
nutritional standard for domestic pets. It is well known that
Americans have recently begun purchasing more high-quality protein for their dogs and cats than families in poor countries can provide for themselves. New food products in general have become one
of the most important means of conducting competition between
giant food corporations struggling for a larger share of the relatively
fixed market. The importance of new food products is underscored
by the comments of a president of the Campbell Soup Company,
cited in the National Commission study, to the effect that a company
without new products would see a 50 percent drop in profits within a
year and would be losing money within five years.

Thus the introduction of new food items and a corresponding
continual upgrading of the energy intensity of subsistence seem to be
a logical outgrowth of an expanding economy in a culture of
consumption. However, it can be assumed that the food habits of any
culture, including a culture of consumption, will be relatively
conservative and will be changed only with difficulty, regardless of

how necessary it may be for manufacturers continually to create and market new food products. The findings of the National Commission clearly bear out this generalization; manipulating American tastes in food—introducing totally new foods or even permutations on existing products—has not been easily accomplished. It is instructive that ideas for new products do not normally originate with the consumer. Only 3 percent of the suggestions for 127 new products in a sample examined by the National Commission study actually came from future consumers. Consumers simply are not clamoring for new products. New product development is in fact a very expensive, very lengthy, and uncertain process of trial and error, in which most ideas prove unmarketable. In the mid-1960s a typical new cold breakfast cereal product required 4½ years of development activity, and nearly $4 million invested in physical design, market research, and advertising before full distribution could be achieved. Only some 5 percent of new product ideas ever reached full distribution, and only about 10 percent of these ever became well established. Even of products that made it all the way to the test market stage, 22 percent were withdrawn short of full development. Beyond that point, another 17 percent were quickly withdrawn. Manufacturers assumed that a product "life cycle" existed, and that every new product would experience a very slow rise in sales or consumer acceptance until it reached a saturation point. A gradual decline would set in as customers dropped the product entirely or shifted to rival brands.

The amounts of money which must be spent on advertising and promotion of new products totally dwarf expenditures for research and development. Only the largest food corporations could afford to develop new products, but the heavy advertising expenses were made less burdensome because they were also tax deductions. Enormous advertising expenditures are an accepted part of the process, as the National Commission study explains, because of the "inertia" of consumers, "arising primarily from reluctance to change established behavior patterns which delays customer acceptance of the new product" (Marple and Wissman 1968:40). The entire process bears a disturbing resemblance to the work of culture-change experts attempting to convince reluctant self-sufficient villagers that they should adopt expensive factory farm techniques. It is happily concluded by the food manufacturers that those products which survive the risky promotion procedure do so because they satisfy a "real" consumer "need."

The nonrandom pattern of advertising expenditures clearly demonstrates that reluctance to change established food habits is strongest where such habits already adequately satisfy basic nutritional needs. Products which appear to be of little nutritional value, or which are at least not a clear nutritional gain over the foods they would replace, often require the most intensive advertising campaigns. The study found this to be true for cold cereals but considered it to be merely the reflection of "higher-than-average uncertainty as to consumer acceptance . . ." (Marple and Wissman 1968:185). In general, staple foods such as fresh fruit, vegetables, meat, and milk, with minimal processing and little added "value," which could form the basis of a nutritionally sound diet, were promoted very little. "Impulse" items such as soft drinks, candy, and other snack foods, and new products generally, were heavily dependent on continual promotion. People must be persuaded to accept food products that are not necessarily good for them, just as peasant farmers must be urged to accept energy-intensive farming practices which in the long run may be highly detrimental.

The "need" for new food products has been supported in an important sociological study by Cyril Sofer (1965) which argues that food habits are not necessarily "rational" from a nutritional viewpoint, anyway, and that food may often serve critical nonfood cultural functions other than nutrition. This generalization is of course true; but it seems to be only in state-level cultures, and particularly in the culture of consumption, that nutritional needs become *secondary* to other cultural functions, such as maintaining food industry profits. This seems to be a very crucial difference between major cultural systems. As was noted in the discussion of potato production on the factory farm, profit was the only reason for growing potatoes; in food marketing the only reason for new food products may also be profit.

As the National Commission study explains: "[The] risky and expensive venture of new product development and introduction is undertaken in hopes of finding a new product which yields a higher gross contribution to overhead and profit on invested assets." (Marple and Wissmann 1968:7)

A further argument in the Sofer study is that people have a basic "need" for new products as an escape from food monotony. Variety is of course also an advantage nutritionally, and it may be that people have a basic need for a varied diet to the extent that it is nutritionally adequate. However, there is no reason to believe that new food products are any advantage in that sense, and there is abundant evidence to the contrary. Sofer indirectly acknowledged the nutritional shortcomings of new food products by stating that people often eat food which they recognize to be harmful, thereby further absolving the food industry from any criticism for actively promoting nutritionally inferior but profitable foods.

Potato Chips and Manioc Cakes

Food processing and varied and nutritious diets were not invented by industrial civilization; they have been with us since the beginnings of culture and man's first use of fire. There is a clear difference, however, between food processing in primitive culture, which is unquestionably "consumer"-oriented, and industrial food processing for a profit. Some of these differences have already been demonstrated, but a brief comparison between manioc cakes and potato chips will heighten the contrasts.

One of the finest examples of food processing in the primitive world can be seen in the manioc complex of South America. Bitter manioc is the staple food crop for many Amazonian Indians. Before the starchy tuber can be eaten, it must be peeled, grated, and squeezed to remove the poisonous juice from the flour. This is accomplished by means of a variety of specialized graters and squeezing devices. The end products may then be further processed into a wide range of foods. The Waiwai of Guyana have developed at least 14 different kinds of bread and 13 beverages based on bitter manioc and its by-products (Yde 1965:28–51). The flour may be sifted in various ways, baked in bread, eaten toasted by itself, or used in soups and stews. The juice is used in soups, and the tapioca extracted from it finds a variety of food uses, sometimes in combination with the flour. All of these processes, of course, take place in the household. They involve no external energy inputs, and no extended shipping or storage. It is erroneous to consider primitive diets dull and monotonous because they do not benefit from supermarkets. There is also no question here of eating potentially harmful food to assure someone else's profit.

In the United States, in 1964, only about half of the potato crop was shipped to consumers as raw tubers to be processed in the household (Talburt and Smith 1967). Even these "unprocessed" potatoes had to be washed mechanically, chemically treated to inhibit sprouting, in some cases colored or waxed, and transported and stored under temperature-controlled conditions. Potatoes destined for chips—and in 1964, this involved about 20 percent of the crop—would go through the washing, sprout inhibition, and temperature control, and in addition might sit in storage for six to eight months. Further chemical treatments included gases or chemical solutions to prevent discoloration of peeled potatoes before cooking and again to avoid after-cooking darkening which occurs as a natural enzymatic process and has no effect on taste or nutritive qualities, but is thought to reduce consumer appeal. Oils, salt, preservatives, and sometimes special artificial flavorings are then added in the final processing, and the end product is packed and shipped in special containers. Then, of course, people must be convinced to eat the product. In 1974 the all-new, vitamin-enriched chip made an experimental appearance on the market to satisfy the "needs" of those who were worried about the nutritional value of the standard chip. The success of the potato chip as a food product is not of course to be found in its nutritional quality, but rather in the fact that it is many times more expensive per pound at the retail level than the ordinary raw potato.

It is obviously, then, an important dimension of industrial food systems, which should not be overlooked, that marketing requirements for food that looks attractive, ships well, and can be stored for extended periods in warehouses and on supermarket shelves mean that many new chemical ingredients are added for strictly economic, nonnutritional reasons. A bewildering array of food additives, estimated in 1972 at some 2,500 different substances, are now being added to food products as coloring agents, synthetic flavors, and preservatives; to prevent caking or separation; to provide body; and for a wide range of other specialized functions (Kermode 1972). Only a few of these additives are used for the purpose of replacing some of the nutrients destroyed in processing. As with pesticide residues, much controversy has arisen over the possible lack of safety of these additives, but few people have questioned the basic marketing system that makes them necessary.

Fishing, Trading, and "Ghost Acreage"

A number of modern nations have so far managed to keep ahead of their food problems by supplementing their own limited food production capability through heavy reliance on fishing and world trade. Fish may be eaten directly or used as a substitute for feed crops for the production of meat, milk, eggs, and poultry. This seems to be a logical step ahead of the Malthusian controls on overpopulation. When the intensification of agriculture has reached the point where further increases can only be achieved if truly prohibitive energy deficits are incurred, then fishing fleets may be expanded and favorable trade agreements reached with nations producing food surpluses. In 1965, food scientist Georg Borgstrom introduced the concept *ghost acres*, referring to the fact that trade and fishing were ways of gaining extraterritorial acres. Ghost acres were calculated in terms of the amount of land a given country would need to put into production to produce an amount of animal protein equivalant to its net food imports and fishery production. According to this reckoning, many nations are shown to have far exceeded the carrying capacity of their farm lands, at least given their present culturally prescribed food patterns, and are now precariously dependent on uncertain international markets and frail marine resources. Japan's ghost acres, for example, exceed its agricultural acreage by more than six times, and the United Kingdom's effective acres are nearly tripled by ghost acres.

World trade is not presently operating as a means of allocating food to countries on the basis of critical nutritional requirements; rather, as with other facets of the industrial market economy, it supports and reflects the world ranking of nations in terms of economic wealth. Scarce protein resources in the form of meat, fish and fish products, nuts, and oilseed cakes move along with bananas, cocoa, coffee, and tea from protein-poor, hungry nations to rich, well-fed nations, propelled by the exigencies of the world cash economy.

Peru, for example, instead of satisfying the obvious needs of the substantial segments of its population that are protein-deficient, finds it more profitable to ship its rich fish meal resource to the United States, where it is fed to chickens to subsidize energy-intensive egg industries. Likewise, Indian oilseed cakes are fed to European cattle, while millions of Indians are starved for protein.

Borgstrom points out that the world's refrigerator ships are at present almost exclusively engaged in moving bananas and frozen meat from Central and South America, Australia, and New Zealand to Western Europe and North America, where they will bring the highest prices. The curious feature of this trade is that in many cases it does not fill a nutritional need in the rich countries that could not be satisfied by simply replacing the imported supplies with domestic equivalents. Brazilian meat and Peruvian fish meal in the United States might be considered an anomaly, but actually it is the logical outgrowth of a system of world market exchanges between nations that have institutionalized inequality.

Not only does this system in many cases quite literally pluck food from the hands of starving people, but it also indirectly deprives them of the ability to produce their own badly needed food. Millions of acres in Africa, Latin America, and Asia which are presently devoted to the satisfaction of the culturally prescribed "need" of the developed nations for chocolate, coffee, and tea might instead by converted to the production of food to satisfy local needs.

Anthropologists Daniel R. Gross and Barbara A. Underwood (1971) have recently shown how such trading patterns may be directly related to malnutrition in Brazil. In recent years, vast areas of the Brazilian northeast were converted from subsistence farms feeding peasants to large-scale sisal plantations on which the peasants became poorly paid laborers. The sisal plantations supplied twine to the United States, where it was used to tie bales of hay, which were in turn used to feed American cattle. Unfortunately, the former subsistence farmers, whose lands were converted from food crops to an export crop, found themselves unable to buy enough food on the market with their meager wages to satisfy the minimal nutritional needs of their families. Systematic malnutrition resulted as the peasants were forced to rely on cheap, high-calorie foods which were low in protein. Different permutations of the same situation have occurred throughout the world where the growing of cash crops for export, either to world or to national markets, has replaced food crops grown to satisfy the nutrional requirements of local peoples.

Such disparity between the nutritional needs of people and the distribution of food has no parallel in primitive culture. In fact, while food may circulate between local households according to need, it is very unusual for cultures not to be totally self-sufficient in their subsistence requirements. In the remarkably few cases where cultures are unable to satisfy their needs either because of periodic misfortunes or because of peculiarly limiting environmental factors, food may indeed be distributed through an "international" trade system that characteristically does *not* operate in terms of normal market principles which determine prices and profits (Sahlins 1972, Chapter 6). The critical aspect of these systems is that exchange rates are socially prescribed and are not set by market competition. The obvious conclusion is that the market rationale is not a logical means of satisfying human nutritional needs.

In primitive chiefdom societies, food consumption patterns may be related to rank. Certain foods may be consumed only by individuals occupying specific ranks as part of a system of sumptuary regulations, but this is not strictly comparable to the present world food distribution system, which reflects the ranking of nations. In a primitive chiefdom, individuals were not systematically deprived of their nutritional needs to support the inequity of the social system, but this is what now happens on a world scale. In 1965, Borgstrom computed agricultural self-sufficiency for various nations on the basis of their reliance on ghost acres and showed that poor Asian nations such as China and India were more than 90 percent self-sufficient, while wealthy Western European nations such as England, Holland, Belgium, and West Germany were only 37 to 60 percent self-sufficient. Clearly, these "developed" nations are being supported by a food system that could not long be sustained if world fisheries declined from overfishing and pollution, or if the world trade network were to collapse or be seriously modified.

There exists, in effect, an international series of trophic levels, in which the nations at the bottom are supported by high-calorie, low-protein diets and supply their high-protein resources to the nations at the upper levels. The upper nations are able to consume the highest quality animal protein and a wide array of very costly sumptuary foods imported from nations where these foods are economically inaccessible to the bulk of the population.

The continued expansion of the world trade and the proliferation of new food products in industrialized nations adds enormously to the energy costs of food, not only because of additional processing, but also because of the further requirements of storage and transportation. There are also diminishing energy returns due to increasing waste and losses. It is normally assumed that at least 10 percent of the food supplies of a given nation is lost annually to spoilage and pests before it even reaches consumers. This may be serious enough in a market system that moves food from one end of the country to the other through complex networks of intermediary wholesalers and retailers. It becomes critical in a system where food may be shipped halfway around the world.

The Limits of Food Production

World leaders seem to be committed to increased food production as the perpetual solution to the Malthusian dilemma and have so far not given sufficient attention to the need to stabilize population growth and to restructure the food distribution system. More intensive subsistence technology has been one of the principal components of international proposals for dealing with the food problem for decades now. The famous "Point Four" program of technical assistance launched by the United States in 1949 made this a prime objective. Since then the United States has been heavily committed to speeding the diffusion of agricultural technology. Private foundations such as the Ford Foundation, the Rockefeller Foundation, and the Kellogg Foundation have devoted millions of dollars since the 1950s to programs of agricultural extension and research designed to raise food production in underdeveloped countries. The United Nations Food and Agriculture Organization has been dedicated to increasing food production throughout the world since its inception, and agricultural development is a key element in UN proposals for the Second Development Decade (1970–80). In 1969 the FAO unveiled its Indicative World Plan for agricultural development, which continues to form the basis for UN food strategy. The plan, as outlined in 1970 by Addeke H. Boerma, now FAO head, calls simply for "increasing productivity through more intensive use of physical resources and modern agricultural technology." Cereal production, because of its crucial dietary role, has been singled out for special attention. The plan also assumes continued economic growth to support the further development of technology and to help poor nations purchase the food imports they will still require even if agricultural development succeeds.

The strategy of intensifying production that has recently taken shape was pioneered by the Rockefeller Foundation and Nobel Prize–winning plant scientist Norman Borlaug. It involves simply exporting the fossil-fuel-subsidized factory farm systems of the highly industrialized nations to the rest of the world. More specifically, it means applying biological engineering to the design of specialized plants that will respond with high yields to the application of large doses of chemical fertilizer, pesticides, and water, in the tropical settings where most of the hungry people are now located. "Miracle" plants have been designed through selective breeding that divert more of their energy into seed production and less into foliage, and that may permit multiple cropping. Such plants may give enormous yields, but in some cases the grain is of markedly reduced nutritional quality or possesses qualities which the target peoples find objectionable. These technical problems, however, are being solved.

This so-called Green Revolution was quickly hailed as an enormous success when per acre yields in many countries soared as these new techniques were applied in the late 1960s, and there were many optimistic statements about rapid doublings in food production and a final conquest over all of nature's limitations. Malthus, it seemed, had been refuted. Some of the most enthusiastic observers felt that the new problem of the disposal of crop *surpluses* would now replace famine as a worry for once-hungry nations:

> It is difficult to remember that only a few years ago there seemed
> to be a very serious prospect of starvation in Asia. Local
> agricultural yields seemed stationary while population was
> rapidly increasing. . . . Now only a decade later, the pendulum

of anxiety has swung considerably. The apparent success of the Green Revolution, at least in cereal production, is beginning to raise doubts not about famine but about disposal of surpluses to national requirements. (Nulty 1972)

Many agricultural success stories have been cited as justification for renewed faith in the unlimited power of technology. Mexico, for example, was able to triple its wheat production and double its corn output within roughly 20 years after agricultural scientists financed by the Rockefeller Foundation began applying modern technology toward the development of miracle plants in 1944 (Fabun 1970).

Regardless of the outstanding successes, many problems have arisen in specific countries that have made implementation of the new technology difficult. Many agricultural extension workers have been frustrated by stubborn peasants, who refused to believe that the new crops would really be an advantage for them because of their obvious vulnerability and the increased dependency on outsiders that they implied. There have also been serious problems in financing the new technology at both national and local levels. Small farmers cannot afford the investment in expensive seeds and chemicals, and neither can poor nations. As was noted earlier, this system ultimately depends on a vast fossil fuel subsidy which has seldom been readily available to poor countries. With recent price increases in petroleum on the world market, and energy crises even in the developed nations, these energy sources are now almost out of reach, and the Green Revolution may simply wither. Even if financing and the energy base were not a limiting factor, water availability and unfavorable weather conditions may be. Even unlimited energy would not solve all the problems involved in getting enough water to enough acres to support an unlimited Green Revolution. Some of the new technology may require so little labor that unemployment results and rural people are forced to move to the cities. It may also prove more successful if practiced on large land-holdings, and small farmers may be driven out. In some cases, transportation and storage facilities have not been adequate to handle either the increased crops or the needed fertilizer. High production may reduce prices below the profit margin, but the prices may still be higher than the poor can pay. Indeed, the social and economic barriers to intensification of food production may be so critical that the actual physical limits may never become a problem.

Many experts fear that the successes registered so far in the Green Revolution may be only temporary, and that serious reversals may occur as the biological liabilities of the new experimental crops begin to surface. It must be assumed that these plants will turn out to be highly susceptible to many new pests and blights or to minor fluctuations in weather. A further unknown is the extent of the ecological impact of industrial farming on a global scale. It is almost certain that further eutrophication will clog inland waters as fertilizer use increases and that pesticides will threaten marine food resources. With the full application of fossil-fuel-powered, factory farm food production, mankind may be taking an irreversible step with implications fully as grave as when primitive hunters first turned to simple farming. Now, however, the price may be much higher.

6

the population problem

The explosive growth of the human population is the most significant terrestrial event of the past million millennia. . . . No geological event in a billion years—not the emergence of mighty mountain ranges, nor the submergence of entire subcontinents, nor the occurrence of periodic glacial ages—has posed a threat to terrestrial life comparable to that of human overpopulation. (Ehrlich & Ehrlich 1972:1)

It has been relatively easy for Americans and other members of the comfortably wealthy industrial nations to see overpopulation as the "root" of all of the world's environmental problems, and of many of its other difficulties as well. Resource depletion, food shortages, and environmental deterioration, plus war and poverty, must all be caused by the presence of too many people in the world. Birth control and family planning programs are the obvious solutions. In 1968, biologist Paul Ehrlich presented this viewpoint dramatically in his book, *The Population Bomb,* which popularized the expression "population explosion," and focused wide attention on the problem and this particular cause. Ehrlich emphatically linked "too many people" together with "too little food" as the cause of hunger in underdeveloped countries and environmental troubles worldwide. On the latter issue, he declared: "The causal chain of the deterioration is easily followed to its source. Too many cars, too many factories, too much detergent, too much pesticide, multiplying contrails, inadequate sewage treatment plants, too little water, too much carbon dioxide—all can be traced easily to *too many people* " (Ehrlich 1968:67).

In 1972, Paul and Anne Ehrlich declared, in the first chapter entitled "The Crisis" in their human ecology textbook, that the population explosion was "the most significant terrestrial event of the past million millennia" and warned that it was suddenly bringing all life on earth to the edge of extinction. Many other writers reject the notion that we are really in a *population* crisis and argue that if we simply achieve an equitable world distribution of wealth and full economic development, the earth can comfortably support many billions more people. Colin Clark even suggests that population growth itself will be the means of bringing further progress to under-developed peoples:

> It [population growth] brings economic hardship to communities
> living by traditional methods of agriculture; but it is the only force
> powerful enough to make such communities change their
> methods, and in the long run transforms them into much more

advanced and productive societies. The world has immense
physical resources for agricultural and mineral production still
unused. In industrial communities, the beneficial economic
effects of large and expanding markets are abundantly clear.
(Clark 1968, Preface)

Both of these extreme views are misleading. There can be little
doubt that rapid population growth and the absolute level of population are important aspects of the environmental crisis, but the level of
consumption is in many respects more critical. As we shall see,
quality of life, or standard of living, must be considered in any
attempt to assess carrying capacity for given environments. Population pressure is always relative to particular cultural conditions.
Instead of treating population as the problem, we shall in this chapter
examine it in broad cross-cultural and evolutionary perspective, and
the present uncontrolled population growth will be seen as one
symptom in a world dominated by the culture of consumption.
Given present consumption patterns, it is equally misleading to deny
the reality of the environmental crisis which accelerates with each
increase in population or consumption. Global economic development may well be a false hope, both because it may be unattainable
and because, if attained, it will only elevate consumption and cancel
any environmental gains that may be achieved, even if world population can be stabilized before a collapse.

There is no disagreement on the basic fact that world population
has grown enormously since the beginning of the industrial era, and
that virtually uncontrolled growth continues in much of the world. It
is also generally recognized that present growth patterns cannot
continue indefinitely. Paul Ehrlich calculated in 1968 that, given a
doubling time of 37 years, which was the estimated world rate at that
time, there would be 60 million billion people, or 100 persons per
square yard over the entire surface of the earth within just 900 years.
Isaac Asimov estimated in 1971 that at growth rates prevailing at that
time, the human population would equal the mass of the globe
within 1,560 years; and within 4,856 years, it would equal the mass

of the universe. The real question is obviously not whether growth will continue, but rather when and how it will stop. Estimates of the maximum feasible global population range from below to double the present level of approximately four billion, while some super-optimists feel that we might accommodate well over 100 billion. If present rates of growth do continue, we shall reach eight billion by A.D. 2000, and will pass 100 billion shortly after A.D. 2100. Given the stresses and strains that are now developing in the food production system, it seems unlikely that the eight-billion mark will be surpassed or even reached within the framework of the present world order.

A major assumption concerning the origin of the population problem, which is at the base of much current policymaking, is that the rapid growth now experienced by the underdeveloped world is simply the result of the combination of traditionally high fertility rates with a sudden lowering of traditionally high mortality rates which has accompanied incomplete modernization. It is usually felt that a value lag relating to family size has somehow not caught up with the drop in mortality, and that further economic development and education will correct the situation, as they have in the developed nations. This interpretation is based on a number of conclusions about primitive demographic conditions which have been shown to be untenable by recent anthropological research, as will be shown directly.

Population Pressure, Carrying Capacity, and Optimum Population

It makes little sense to speak of overpopulation and the need to halt growth if there is no discussion of carrying capacity, optimum population size, and what constitutes population pressure. Surprisingly, these topics are often completely ignored in population programs, even though they must be at least implicit in any attempt to regulate population or set demographic goals. This failure to deal adequately with these aspects of the population problem is perhaps understandable when it is realized that they are culturally and environmentally *relative* concepts and directly involve the most basic characteristics of any culture.

Population pressure has been a widely discussed component of the population problem and is assumed to be some readily apparent, absolute quality; but on closer analysis, it proves to be neither easily recognized nor absolute. In fact, population pressure is culturally defined and can only be relative to particular technological systems, environments, and per capita consumption levels. In traditional New Guinea cultures, population pressure has been found to occur only rarely in an absolute sense, but may be frequently manifest as a *local* imbalance between people and land experienced by particular local clans (Kelly 1968). This may be the case even when the total population is stable simply because random demographic processes, including variation in the sex ratio, birthrates, and mortality, may, under different cultural circumstances, have widely varying impacts on local groups of different size. As a result, certain clans may outgrow their land base while neighboring clans dwindle to extinction. Many cultural devices are employed to relieve this pressure of population on land resources, including transfers of land and people between clans through gifts, adoption, and warfare. Where population pressure is not compensated for by normal redistributive measures, it may be felt as a steady reduction in the culturally defined standard of living, in which people are forced to work longer hours to increase food production. Eventually, there may be a switch to less desirable food sources (Bayless-Smith 1974), or a move to marginal ecological zones (Zubrow 1975). Thus, "absolute" population pressure might be relieved by simply redefining what the members of a culture consider an acceptable standard of living, by technological innovation, or by a reduction in population.

Population redistribution has sometimes been developed to a high degree, particularly in island cultures where adoption is widely used, but it can only be a temporary solution. Resource distribution may help raise regional carrying capacity by evening out local surpluses or seasonal fluctuations; but in many cases, elaborate redistribution systems are dependent on formal political offices and thus can only occur at certain levels of social integration. Migration to relieve population pressure is probably a normal response which occurs automatically whenever ecologically similar territory is readily available for occupation.*

The final option, population control, has been followed by virtually all primitive cultures to some degree. Primitive hunting cultures have followed this course almost exclusively and achieved remarkably stable populations. Cultivators have often established equilibrium systems as well balanced as those of the hunters, but have far more often slipped into subsistence intensification and predatory expansion against their neighbors as their populations have gradually increased.

Population Control Among Primitive Hunters

While many demographers believe that the human population has grown at a slow and steady rate from the very beginning to the origins of agriculture, recent anthropological research suggests that the thousands of years before domestication were characterized by population *equilibrium,* punctuated by only occasional and unusual growth phases. By the eve of the transition to settled farm life, the human population had grown to an estimated five million—an increase of perhaps fivefold over a time span of nearly half a million years.** Much of this increase represented expansion into empty lands. Only

---

*See Dumond (1972) for discussion of responses to population growth.
**See Deevy (1960) and Coale (1974) for general discussion of global population history.

very slight increases in density occurred prior to the introduction of
agriculture. As a general principle, it can be assumed that primitive
cultures quickly established a culturally regulated equilibrium as soon
as their populations had grown to a culturally defined carrying
capacity within specific territories.

It is apparent that *cultural* factors, and not food shortages or high
mortality rates, were the primary factors in setting limits to population
growth in primitive cultures.* This is a particularly significant point,
because it is still widely believed that primitive or traditional cultures
were characterized by uniform high fertility and high mortality rates
and a precarious food supply, but such was decidedly not the case.
Primitive cultures were generally stabilized at a level considerably
below the maximum population densities that their technology and
environment might potentially have sustained. Even Paleolithic
hunters, if they had chosen to work harder and had adjusted their food
preferences away from big game toward a concentration on small
mammals, might have increased their population densities many
times over. It is also likely that famines were very rare during the
Paleolithic period; and while the availability of game certainly did
influence population densities, food shortages per se definitely appear
not to have been the primary factor limiting population growth.

There is overwhelming evidence to suggest that mortality was
also not a significant limiting factor for hunters. Deaths due to disease
were apparently far lower before the establishment of permanent
villages than at any time thereafter. Primitive hunting peoples were
consistently well nourished, they led physically very active lives, and
they apparently avoided most infectious epidemic diseases by
maintaining their populations dispersed so that these diseases could
not become established and spread. Hunters may also have
developed high levels of natural immunity thanks to strong selective
pressure enforced by relatively high infant mortality rates and constant

---

*I have drawn heavily on the survey of Polgar (1972) for supportive data. It should
be borne in mind that all estimates of prehistoric population levels are subject to
considerable error.

exposure to endemic pathogens. Deaths due to warfare were probably very infrequent during the many thousands of years that man lived as a hunter, and homicide and suicide are both decidedly uncommon among undisturbed hunting peoples. The probable occurrence of accidental deaths is more difficult to evaluate, but it seems reasonable that they were never a very significant demographic factor.

Primitive cultures held in reserve an enormous potential for rapid population growth which was activated only under special conditions. Even if mortality rates as high as 50 percent to age 15 are assumed to have been typical for hunting and gathering peoples (half of the population dying before reaching reproductive age)—and this is by no means easily demonstrated—it still would have been easily possible for the population to have doubled each generation if high fertility was culturally encouraged. Such rapid growth probably did occur at times, but was only a regular pattern when previously unoccupied territory was first entered or when a population was recovering from some natural disaster. In the New World, for example, the earliest firm dates for the arrival of man in North America by about 10,000 B.C. are closely followed by his appearance in the far south of South America by 9,000 B.C. Such rapid spread could hardly have been achieved by cultures that were barely keeping ahead of extinction.

The full significance of this new picture of the demography of early hunters can perhaps best be appreciated if it is contrasted with the grim view presented by modern demographers in their attempts to describe the history of population growth and the origin of our present dilemma. Paul Ehrlich, for example, in *The Population Bomb,* states that "our ancestors were fighting a continual battle to keep the birth rate ahead of the death rate." The distinguished demographer Donald T. Bogue summarizes this period in his major textbook, *Principles of Demography,* as follows:

> During the many thousands of years of man's existence on the
> earth before the beginning of civilization, the population problem
> facing most communities was that of survival—to offset
> successfully the terrible attrition of death on their

> numbers. . . . When population did manage to grow, there was
> always the threat of famine, war, and epidemics. Such a situation
> is the only conjecture that is consistent with the facts. . . . We
> are forced, therefore, to conclude that the human race has been
> required by circumstances of high mortality to reproduce at
> near-biological capacity and that a whole system of
> fertility-promoting practices has evolved as an integral part of
> every culture. (Bogue 1969:53–54)

In fact, precisely the opposite situation now appears to have been the case, and the problem that remains is to outline precisely what fertility-*dampening* practices maintained primitive populations in equilibrium.

Among hunters, density limits seem to have been set by the availability of culturally recognized food sources and by the lack of formal political structures to deal with conflict. Expansion of subsistence through intensified collecting or domestication was apparently rejected as a solution far more often than not, and seems to have been a course that was only reluctantly followed in the face of environmental changes. Migration certainly occurred among hunters, but only rarely at the expense of other groups already firmly in possession of their territories. Perhaps most critical was the fact that there was no culturally encouraged reason for increasing population density beyond a certain level. Birth spacing by means of abortion and infanticide seem to have been the primary mechanisms of fertility regulation. It has been assumed that women in nomadic hunting societies were forced to space their children approximately four years apart because of the difficulty of carrying two dependent children on daily foraging expeditions and on the frequent moves to new camps (Sussman 1972). This may be a critical consideration motivating, or at least rationalizing, the family planning decisions of individual women; but if it were an absolute necessity, it would be difficult to explain the rapid growth known to have occurred when virgin territories were occupied. Whatever the motivation for such spacing, and regardless of the methods employed, it will yield a stationary, no-growth population, assuming that an average woman attempts to raise four children and that half of them survive to reproduce.

Population Equilibrium in Aboriginal Australia

One of the most outstanding and best-documented examples of the maintenance of population balance by primitive hunting cultures is presented in J. B. Birdsell's analysis of Australian aborigines, based on 25 years of intensive research. According to Birdsell's findings, Australia supported a constant population of 300,000 aborigines, the maximum that could be supported by a hunting and gathering technology, for perhaps 30,000 years, with only minor fluctuations related to overall changes in the environment. They were not constantly tottering on the edge of disaster, with their numbers held in check by high mortality rates, and they did not continually outstrip their meager resources only to crash precipitously and later rebound. In contrast, the industrial culture now controlling Australia has grown to 13 million in barely 200 years, and shows no indication of being in equilibrium.

The forces that maintained constant population levels involved not only environmental factors, but also included culturally defined territorial spacing mechanisms. Australian cultures were organized into linguistically distinct tribal groups averaging 500 people, which were in turn divided into bands of 25 people composed of families of five persons. Tribal territories were large enough to provide a reliable subsistence base for the population roughly 98 percent of the time, while individual band territories might be somewhat less self-sufficient so that resources from neighboring bands might be needed in 10 or 15 out of every 100 years. Band territories were carefully laid out to ensure that they allowed access to all critical food resources in sufficient quantity for long-range survival. In some coastal regions where a tribal territory included several diverse ecological zones with different resource potentials, each band territory would include portions of each zone. Interband and intertribal ceremonies normally occurred in times of plenty and helped distribute seasonal or random concentrations of food and equalized resources, and thus helped bring population densities closer to the maximum carrying capacity. Bands in drought-stricken areas might be temporarily taken in by more comfortably situated neighbors. Individuals were so emotionally attached to the sacred sites within their traditional territories which represented their totemic origin points that there was no danger that they would ever choose to remain permanently in their refuge. Boundaries were also clearly defined by the wanderings of spirit beings which were recorded in myths and commemorated in intergroup ceremonies. The religious and ceremonial system played a vital role in supporting population balances through boundary maintenance and resource redistribution.

The upper limit for tribal population was set by the density of the communication network which could be supported by hunters and gatherers restricted to foot travel. As tribes grew larger, it became more difficult for the bands within them to remain in contact. When more bands appeared, the frequency, intensity, and length of interactions such as joint ceremonies and intermarriage declined, and linguistic diversity increased, making further communication more difficult. Tribes that grew too small, that lost bands, until they numbered under 500, would automatically interact more with bands in neighboring tribes until they were absorbed into them. Bands needed to include at least 25 people in order to maximize the availability of food, given random variations in hunting success; to provide task groups of optimum size; to ensure demographic viability, given sex fluctuations in births; to defend themselves; and to ensure a large enough pool of marriageable individuals to meet the cultural requirements of band exogamy. Upper limits to band size were apparently set by the lack of strong political controls, which meant that the increased conflicts arising with denser population could only be adequately controlled by fissioning, and by the need to minimize the strain on local ecosystems. Random fluctuation in local band size was regulated through selective infanticide, adoption, and transfers of people in "violation" of normal residence and exogamic norms. Local boundaries were also adjusted by means of occasional duels and skirmishes.

Actual tribal densities varied from lows of perhaps 80 square miles per person in the interior deserts, where rainfall might drop to a mean of only 4 inches per year, to densities as high as two square miles per person in rich coastal or riverine environments. Optimum carrying capacity for tribal territories remained within 10 to 20 percent of the maximum density that could be supported in the best years, thanks to the cultural mechanisms that helped level out the long-range fluctuations in resources due to droughts and other unpredictable events.

It is uncertain what means of birth spacing were most common, but it is clear that selective female infanticide was often practiced by Australians, judging by their unbalanced sex ratios. Abortion and contraception may also have been important spacing mechanisms. It is important to note in this context that the distinction between abortion and infanticide may not be culturally meaningful. Some tribes may induce labor in the third trimester of pregnancy and then kill the fetus if it survives. "Birth" itself, and "humanness," may be culturally defined at a quite different point than that normally recognized by state legal systems (Neel 1968).

That a system of density equilibrium was indeed operating among Australian tribes and bands is apparent from the data which Birdsell presents. The primary density determinant seems to have been environmental, as reflected by a statistically significant inverse relationship between rainfall and size of tribal territory. Deviation from this relationship can be accounted for by the presence of extra water and consequently greater biological productivity in riverine or coastal regions, where carrying capacity is higher than would be expected otherwise. Further evidence can be seen in the fact that large tribes were in the process of splitting into smaller tribes of 500 members when they were first contacted by Europeans. It has also been shown that tribes which were initially fragmented by the acquisition of new initiation ceremonies quickly returned to their original size after the diffusion wave had passed.

The Neolithic Population Explosion

The relatively rapid growth in population which accompanied and perhaps contributed to the adoption of farming is one of the most significant demographic events in human history. It marked the end of the long period of successful population equilibrium that hunting peoples established and initiated a period of almost continuous population growth and a rapid series of interrelated changes which led successively to urbanization, the state, and industrial civilization. It has been estimated that world population suddenly jumped from approximately five million in 8000 B.C. to 86 million by 4000 B.C., a 17-fold increase (Deevy 1960, Coale 1974, Polgar 1972). The four-fold increase related to industrialization between 1650 and 1950 seems relatively minor in comparison, although this later increase did of course occur over a much shorter time period. The scale of the Neolithic expansion is even more dramatic in specific countries. France, for example (Nougier 1954), experienced a hundredfold population increase by 3000 B.C. over densities obtaining during the Upper Paleolithic period, and only a tenfold increase between 3000 B.C. and the 20th century.

Explaining the breakdown of "Paleolithic" population equilib-rium mechanisms must surely be one of the most critical theoretical problems in anthropology. Unfortunately, this question has only recently been posed. Some writers see it as a result of sedentary living which reduced the need to space births; others see the increase in the food supply made possible by argiculture as a key factor. Both of these explanations have serious problems, however.

It is quite reasonable that hunters spaced births in order to pro-tect the health of mother and child as well as because of the mobility problem, and thus the practice may have been continued even after sedentarization. It is well known that many settled village peoples space births four years apart, or even longer, for precisely this reason. Particularly where protein is not widely available, prolonged nursing may be very important to the health of the infant; and where women are heavily involved in agricultural labor, continual pregnancies would be an increased burden.

Increases in food supply, as discussed earlier, are perhaps more likely to be considered *results* rather than *causes* of increased population pressure. Randal A. Sengel (1973) has recently suggested a rather novel solution to this vexing problem. He argues that in the Near East an increased reliance on wild grains, ultimatly caused by climatic changes which increased their prevalence, may well have resulted in a significant augmentation of the protein intake of the population, which in turn lowered the age of menarche and increased the reproductive span of the women. Empirical evidence from Europe indicates that nutritional improvement has apparently had that effect in modern times, and it is by no means certain that the age of menarche is a constant in all human populations. Some writers, however, suggest that the domestication process resulted in the displacement of wild plant foods which were richer in protein, so the question is by no means settled (Flannery 1969).

It *is* clear that even a slight increase in the reproductive span could result in gradual population growth even if the original pattern of birth spacing were retained. It might be assumed that such increased growth would quickly be recognized and the birth-spacing mechanism would be adjusted to restore equilibrium. However, it does not appear that population control in primitive cultures was really carried out with long-range social goals in mind; rather, individual women made "family planning" decisions which were for their immediate self-interest, and in the aggregate these decisions proved to be highly adaptive for the entire culture.

While these demographic changes, whatever their causes, were in the long run revolutionary in impact, they were so slow that, like the domestication process, they would have been imperceptible to the actors. In the Near East, for example, the population may have grown from 100,000 in 8000 B.C. to 2.5 to 12 million by 4000 B.C., with an annual growth rate of only 0.08–0.12 percent (Carneiro and Hilse 1966). At such gradual rates a tribe of 500 people would add only about 12 people in a generation.

Population Control Among Primitive Village Farmers

Population growth was a much more difficult force to contain for sedentary or semisedentary cultures based on domesticated, and thus inherently more elastic, food sources. Primitive farmers certainly have in many cases achieved remarkable population equilibrium, as will be shown in the following sections. But in general, domestication touched off a period of great cultural instability in the world. Suddenly, expanding cultures pushed hunters out of the most fertile lands only in turn to be themselves incorporated into expanding conquest states, and ultimately into an expanding industrial civilization. Hunters, newly transformed into farmers, found their resource bases increasingly inadequate for the support of their growing populations and were forced into more difficult environments or into cultural transformations which they might not otherwise have chosen. In some cases, growing populations simply expanded beyond the carrying capacity of their environments and collapsed without the development of complex political systems or "advanced" technology.

The American Southwest affords an example of this latter outcome. From approximately 7000 B.C. to A.D. 100, that area was occupied by hunters and seed collectors of the so-called "desert tradition," which must have constituted a relatively stable adaptation. Toward the end of that period, domesticated plants from Mesoamerica were gradually adopted; and by A.D. 400, farming villages were becoming established.

Through intensive analysis of the archaeological record in one small valley in Arizona, Ezra B. Zubrow (1975) has reconstructed 1,400 years of population history from the beginnings of domestication up to A.D. 1400. His study shows a steady increase in population within the valley and a continual expansion into more marginal environments as the carrying capacity in the most favorable zones was reached. The population peaked shortly after irrigation was introduced in approximately A.D. 1000, and then began to decline as pressure on the resource base and a change in the rainfall pattern beginning in A.D. 1150 drastically lowered the carrying capacity of the valley. Population densities plunged rapidly between 1100 and 1200 to a small fraction of the peak, and by A.D. 1400 the valley was abandoned completely. Thus a culture of village farmers that was unable to establish a population equilibrium expanded for perhaps 700 years and then totally collapsed. This record stands in striking contrast to the 7,000 years of success that hunters and gatherers enjoyed in the same general environment.

There are many other examples in the archaeological and ethnographic record of village farmers who were able to support their population growth by pushing out their neighbors. Neolithic farmers moved steadily out of the Middle East and spread throughout Europe from 8000 B.C. to 5000 B.C. The fate of the prior hunting peoples is uncertain. While some may have adopted farming or been incorporated into the invading culture, it seems more reasonable to guess that they resisted the change and simply moved into marginal environments and gradually declined. In East and South Africa, Bantu farmers and herders were still expanding into territory occupied by the Bushmen and other hunters when the Dutch began to settle South Africa in the 17th century. Their growth was not halted until the militaristic Zulu empire was finally overwhelmed by the British army in the late 19th century. Marshall Sahlins (1961) has shown how growing African tribal cultures such as the Nuer and Tiv have utilized their segmentary lineage systems as a means of mobilizing on their boundaries, in the absence of formal political leadership, to expand their territory against weak neighbors.

In South America, it is assumed by some investigators that village farmers were well established in the central Amazon Basin, utilizing manioc as their primary staple, by 3000 B.C. (Lathrap 1970). Almost from that point on, the evidence indicates that a continuous period of population growth, migration, displacement, and differentiation of cultures began that continued into modern times. Equilibrium cultures, or those with relatively small, slow-growing populations, were simply pushed up the smaller tributaries, and finally into the interfluvial hinterlands, by successive migration waves from the expanding centers. Among the best known historically of these expanding Amazonian village farmers were the Tupi. They, like the Zulus in Africa, were still spreading south and east up the Amazon and even down the Brazilian coast, pushing aside prior hunters and more stable farmers, when the Spanish and Portuguese arrived in the 16th century.

Chronic warfare and head-hunting recorded for shifting cultivators in many other parts of the world, including New Zealand and Southeast Asia, may also be viewed as responses to a failure to maintain population equilibrium. The Ibans in Borneo were actively expanding against their neighbors, some of whom were hunters, in the late 19th and well into the 20th century. Traditionally oriented hill tribes in northwestern Thailand in the 1960s were growing rapidly, but maintained their cultures intact without warfare by crowding out neighbors and through high rates of migration into lowland areas, where excess population was absorbed into other ethnic groups (Kunstadter 1971).

In spite of these examples of population growth among village farmers, considering the time periods involved, it is apparent that very few such cultures reproduced at the maximum rate for more than a very brief time. Cultural regulation of population growth certainly continued to be a very significant factor even after domestication began. As with hunters, fertility control was probably the most important regulating mechanism for village farmers, although increased mortality through warfare was sometimes an additional control. Abortion, infanticide, contraception, and birth spacing remained the primary means of limiting fertility, although many specific cultural practices which limited the frequency of coitus, or shortened the fertile period by delaying marriage, also became important.

One of the most common birth-spacing practices is the long postpartum taboo on sexual intercourse which occurs very widely among shifting cultivators in tropical climates. The taboo often extends for more than a year after the birth of each child and has been shown to be related to reduced fertility rates in cultures which practice it. The taboo correlates with a number of other cultural practices, and elaborate causal explanations for its occurrence have been proposed (Saucier 1972). It is quite possible that it is not always practiced as an intentional means of birth spacing; but whatever its "cause," it does serve as a critical check on fertility.

The Tsembaga Equilibrium Model

The Tsembaga of New Guinea offer a well-researched example of a primitive horticultural tribe that has developed a complex system of cultural regulation which prevents population pressure on the land from increasing to the point at which famine, technological innovation, or migration would become necessary. The Tsembaga system has been described in detail by anthropologist Roy Rappaport in his monograph, *Pigs for the Ancestors,* and his data have been reduced to a computer simulation model by systems researchers Steven B. Shantzis and William W. Behrens III of the Massachusetts Institute of Technology. The critical component of the system is the growth of the pig herd to a point that triggers a ritual cycle involving warfare and pig slaughters which balance both human and animal populations.*

---

*The Tsembaga model is of course highly idealized, and there are no empirical data to suggest that it has operated as described for any length of time in the past. What is important, however, is how the system *could* operate.

A growing pig herd is highly desirable because pigs are important as status symbols and as sources of high-quality animal protein; but a pig consumes as much of the cultivated crops as an average adult, and the herd quickly becomes more bother than it is worth. A growing pig herd means that people must devote a larger and larger proportion of the cultivated land to raising pig feed, and greater labor efforts must be expended per capita to tending pigs and gardens. Increases in both the human and the pig populations cause a sharp rise in internal conflicts, not only as competition for resources increases, but also because the pigs themselves are a perpetual source of disputes. When these disturbances become intolerable, a ceremonial pig slaughter is held.

In a pig feast, which Rappaport observed in 1963, the Tsembaga pig herd was reduced from 169 animals to 60, and new garden plots were reduced by more than a third below what had been required earlier to support the full herd.

In the simulation model constructed by Shantzis and Behrens, the human population maintains itself indefinitely, fluctuating in 11-year cycles between approximately 220 and 230 persons, while the pig herd fluctuates between 60 and 145 (see Figure 11). Both populations remain in dynamic balance well below the point at which destructive shortening of the fallow cycle would become necessary. The slight increase in normal human fertility rates that might result from the intervention of modern medicine would, if not compensated for by other cultural controls, reduce the ritual cycle to 10 years and shift population levels much closer to the critical carrying capacity. If new health programs were to raise the annual population growth rate from 1.3 to 2.0 percent a year, the control mechanisms would quickly break down, and the human population would peak at over 400 within 120 years and would then quickly plunge to nearly zero. A permanent peace would have a very similar catastrophic impact. It seems clear that as government control is extended over the area, bringing both peace and new medical technology, the Tsembaga will sacrifice long-run stability for short-run gains and will face very serious problem in only two or three generations.

FIGURE 11   The Tsembaga Model.   (Source: Steven B. Shantzis and William W. Behrens III, "Population Control Mechanisms in a Primitive Agricultural Society," in *Toward Global Equilibrium,* edited by D. H. Meadows and D. L. Meadows (Cambridge, Mass.: Wright-Allen Press, 1973), p. 275.)

    If we were to assume that the Tsembaga kept no pig herds, held no festivals or wars, practiced no population control through infanticide or contraception, and experienced no migration, the dynamics of their population might be expected to be far different from that described above. Shantzis and Behrens have constructed a computer simulation of just such a case which dramatically illustrates the inherent imbalances that would arise. Under such conditions, population growth would be constrained only by the availability of land and its productivity per acre. Given a slow rate of uncontrolled population growth based on average fertility and life expectancy rates drawn from United Nations estimates for similar peoples, and starting with only 196 people and 972 acres of potentially arable land, it quickly becomes necessary to shorten the 15-year fallow period in order to put more land into production to feed the growing population. Within less than 60 years, this intensification of food production surpasses the carrying capacity and initiates a continuous decline in yields per acre, reflecting a progressive degradation of the land. Within approximately 80 years, the population would peak and then suddenly plunge to near zero as a result of famines and an almost total decline in soil fertility. This, of course, assumes no technological innovation to increase per acre yields. It seems obvious that under these conditions the Tsembaga would recognize the declining yields within two or three years and would be confronted with the choice of either reducing population growth or technological innovation to prevent the collapse which would be barely three generations away.

The Havasupai Indians

Well-documented cases demonstrating population equilibrium in primitive populations and the mechanisms involved are not common because normally historical depth is absent from the anthropological record. However, the Havasupai Indians of Arizona have been shown historically to have maintained a relative population equilibrium for at least 200 years (Alvarado 1970). Since the first census of this small tribe of farmers and hunters in their Grand Canyon home in 1776 up to the present, their population has fluctuated between a low of 166 (due to a measles epidemic) to a high of 300. The present rise to 350 has only occurred as outside intervention has increased over the past 40 years.

Such stability, in spite of abundant food resources, led anthropologist Anita L. Alvarado to investigate possible explanations, and it was determined that cultural factors limiting fertility have been largely responsible. Among these cultural factors are an imbalanced sex ratio with a preponderance of males, probably due to selective female infanticide, and a significant delay in first marriages. Women traditionally did not marry until age 25–30, and men not until 35–40. The combined effect of these customs is to reduce fertility by not only reducing the number of years when a given woman would be a pregnancy risk, but also by structuring it so that men would be married during their least fertile adult years. The Havasupai also tolerated a rather high proportion of unmarried, widowed, and divorced individuals, who would otherwise have been marriageable. Furthermore, they made use of herbal contraceptives and abortion, and nursed their babies for approximately two years, thereby undoubtedly delaying the resumption of ovulation. Extensive use of the steam bath by the males, followed by a dip in very cold water, may well have been an important spermicide. It is known that the testes produce viable sperm only within a very narrow temperature range, and that extremes may produce temporary sterility. Mortality rates do not appear to have been significantly high aboriginally. Warfare was virtually unknown, and the people appear to have been exceptionally healthy.

Island Population Problems

Perhaps the severest test of their ability to regulate population growth that primitive cultures have faced has been the problem of maintaining equilibrium on the small islands and coral atolls of the Pacific. Certainly, cultures with such restricted land bases would run up against physical limits to population expansion much more quickly than would cultures in continental areas.

The general adjustment process to island environments has been outlined in a theoretical model by Tim Bayliss-Smith (1974) which recognizes three phases of population growth and cultural response. Following the initial settling of an island, there may be rapid expansion and an extensive—i.e., low labor input—subsistence system, which continues until the available land base is filled. Intensification of the food production system may then follow, with greater labor inputs and new technology, or "lower" dietary standards may be introduced. Finally, emigration and direct cultural controls on population growth become necessary. Many of these islands have been settled for a very long time; much of Micronesia, for example, may have been occupied for a thousand years, and the maximum practical limits of technological intensification in food production must have been reached very early, so that this solution would have been quickly exhausted. Actually, many of the coral atolls required an extremely high degree of technological development before *any* kind of gardening could have been established because of the absence of soil and the shortage of fresh water.

In practice, various cultural controls helped maintain population well below any theoretical maximum carrying capacity based on the ultimate limits of food production. In the Polynesian outlier atolls the critical population ceiling seems to have been set by the environmental limits to taro production. Taro was a daily element in the diet and a prime measure of the overall adequacy of the food supply. If cultural preferences were not a factor, then presumably these cultures might have simply switched to crops which provided more calories per acre or per unit of labor such as coconuts, and supported even denser populations. However, it appears that the ideal was for taro to supply approximately 50 percent of the caloric intake, and it was culturally intolerable for it to drop below 25 percent. Coconuts were not expected to constitute more than 25 percent of the diet. Population pressure was clearly present to the extent that the proportions of these critical foods deviated from the cultural ideals. A further form of cultural control of carrying capacity was the planting of nonsubsistence crops, such as ritually important turmeric, which displaced food crops, and the social and ceremonial stress placed on certain marine resources.

Various social and political adjustments helped maximize available resources while minimizing possible ecological stresses to the food systems from overuse. For example, higher levels of social stratification, in which political leaders were given authority to regulate production and distribution of food, seem to have arisen in both Micronesia and Polynesia wherever resources were sufficient to support such developments. Shortages of food and "overpopulation" here, as in the New Guinea example, were in effect treated as problems of allocation; but in this case, they were critical enough that political authority was needed to solve them. Other social mechanisms for allocating people to land, and vice versa, were also widely employed. For example, cognatic descent systems, which were common in the Pacific, were easily manipulated to relieve local pressures. Adoption was also widely practiced; in some Micronesian islands, as many as half of all the children were actually adopted (Knudson 1970).

At the inter-island level, various cultural practices helped relieve local problems and permitted larger densities than might have otherwise been possible, in much the same manner as intertribal relations in aboriginal Australia. For example, if typhoons temporarily destroyed the food resources of a particular atoll, the residents might be temporarily taken in by the residents of unaffected high islands, or they might be sent emergency food. Likewise, if a critical imbalance in the sex ratio developed, individuals might be exported or imported as needed.

Virtually the entire range of fertility control mechanisms were practiced by Pacific island cultures. In Micronesia a woman was often restricted to no more than three children; and abortion, infanticide, coitus interruptus, and frequent periods of ritual celibacy all occurred. In Tikopia (Firth 1957), in addition to these controls, complete celibacy was sometimes required of the younger males in a family if productive land was not available. These unmarried men often set out on overseas voyages and never returned, although if they remained, extramarital access to women was not denied them. When population pressures became intolerable on Tikopia, an entire clan or other social segment was simply driven away, although that was a very rare event. Raymond Firth's conclusion for Tikopia is probably generally applicable for the Pacific as a whole before European intervention: "It can be safely said that until recent years the population of Tikopia was normally in a state of equilibrium with its food supply." (Firth 1957:414)

The State Intervenes

When tribal populations came under the influence of industrial states, three things drastically modified the demographic picture. In the first place, the traditional population control mechanisms invariably dropped out. This may be due to deliberate pressures aimed at eliminating them, as when missionaries halt abortion and infanticide, or when the government forbids warfare. Many important regulating practices may simply be abandoned as other practices which supported them are modified. For example, the traditional religious system provides essential support for the post-partum taboo and a variety of other ceremonial regulations. If the Tsembaga were converted to Christianity, they might voluntarily abandon pig sacrifices, and many of their control mechanisms would collapse. Even if no other modifications in the culture occurred, the elimination of traditional population controls would be certain to lead to rapid population growth.

The state has also provided positive incentives for population growth with its policies designed to extract as many resources from former tribal areas as possible for the smallest capital investment. Labor-intensive agricultural systems, which provide cash crops for export or to pay taxes, generally created a situation in which a large family was more advantageous for a peasant farmer than a small one. Extra children would contribute more to the labor force than their maintenance cost, at least until the limits of labor intensification were exceeded. Clifford Geertz (1963) provides a well documented case example of such a situation from Java.

The third effect of state intervention—the modification of traditional mortality rates—has received the most attention as the principal cause of the population explosion, but it is unlikely to be the most important factor. During the early phase of state intervention with tribal cultures, mortality rates are typically elevated because of violence and the disruption of culture change. In many cases, tribes have been simply exterminated at this point. Extinction has sometimes actually been accelerated by the retention of traditional fertility checks even in the face of severe depopulation. Good examples of this process can be drawn from South America (Wagley 1951) and the Pacific (Schneider 1955). When it has been advantageous to retain a native labor force, however, the culture change process has usually been regulated to minimize undue increases in mortality; and new health measures reducing infant mortality and controlling endemic diseases such as malaria have in the long run succeeded in lowering overall mortality rates. It is quite possible that if the traditional culture remained intact, and if no new incentives for population growth were introduced, a reduction in mortality rates might be easily countered with an adjustment in fertility control mechanisms and no dramatic population explosion would need to occur. Unfortunately, a real test of this hypothesis may never be possible, because modern medical technology has invariably been accompanied by both a loss in traditional fertility controls and the appearance of new incentives for growth. The main point is clear, however—traditional cultures are not in themselves the primary cause of the present population explosion.

Policy Implications

In view of this evidence, many present policies aimed at reducing population growth in the underdeveloped world are based on faulty premises and thus have doubtful chances of success. Mass education as a solution means assuming that "ignorance" is the problem, when actually people may be making very rational individual decisions under the circumstances and they may be very much aware of the long-range consequences of population growth. Policies aimed at instilling new values on family size may actually be quite irrelevant because many traditional population-limiting practices were not directly related to family planning at all. Even the concept of an ideal family size may not be meaningful cross-culturally. Instead, birth spacing, age at marriage, and cessation of childbearing may be the critical factors. Traditional lineage and extended family systems have often been singled out by demographers as specific incentives for high fertility, but this assumption cannot be supported by ethnographic data. Perhaps most importantly, the belief that economic development will be the key to reduced population growth may be erroneous. This is the fundamental assumption shared by many planners in underdeveloped countries today, who continue to see overpopulation as the result of "backward" cultures. It may be true that as economic prosperity has spread through industrial societies, population growth rates have declined; unfortunately, however, there can be no guarantee that this will occur in the underdeveloped world. An even more serious difficulty is the probability that the present rapid rates of growth, combined with the environmental limitations which are already being met, will preclude the attainment of a sufficient level of industrial prosperity to achieve population stability.

Arguing from what we know about the population policies of primitive cultures, it might make as much sense to recommend *de*development or *de*modernization, and a restoration of primitive equilibrium, as to call for further development which has so far only increased the misery of millions of people. At another level, world planners might pursue the kinds of solutions that primitive cultures have followed when population pressures have arisen. In this light, it would be reasonable to attempt technological intensification; but failing that, a global political system might be in order. Such a system would attempt to redistribute people and resources to obtain some equitable, world-maximum living standard, after the fashion of island cultures. This would be a logical advance in a general evolutionary sense, but would probably be very undesirable in an adaptive sense because a one-world culture would be highly unstable. In the end, demodernization may be the only viable solution, whether it is deliberately chosen or not.

internal order

[V]iolence is dangerous to our society. It is disfiguring our society—making fortresses of portions of our cities and dividing our people into armed camps. It is jeopardizing some of our most precious institutions—poisoning the spirit of trust and cooperation that is essential to their proper functioning. It is corroding the central political processes of our democratic society—substituting force and fear for argument and accommodation. (Final Report of the National Commission on the Causes and Prevention of Violence 1969:xv–xvi)

In addition to establishing a successful adaptation to the natural environment, every human society must maintain a certain minimal level of internal order if it is to survive. Conflict and violence must be carefully regulated. Individuals, households, and other social units must have access to basic resources and sufficient involvement with decision-making processes to protect their self-interests. During the thousands of years before the first states appeared, primitive societies successfully minimized this universal problem because they remained basically egalitarian. Differential access to wealth and power did not occur and was therefore not a potential source of conflict. In small, face-to-face communities, where everyone participated in all basic cultural activities, individuals easily found personal satisfactions and fulfillment. Poverty and alienation simply did not exist. Conflicts did of course arise, but they usually took the form of interpersonal antagonisms and domestic quarrels, and seldom represented serious challenges to the established social order.

With the rise of social stratification and the economic specialization that accompanied the appearance of the first states a mere 6,000 years ago, social order suddenly became a far more difficult and dangerous problem. For the first time in human experience, whole segments of a society were denied direct access to and control over their basic subsistence requirements, and real political power rested with a favored few. Poverty and powerlessness became intrinsic aspects of the new social system, and new institutions with internal police powers were needed to maintain a precarious social order. Since their beginning, states have been subject to frequent collapses of social order, civil wars, peasant revolts, and popular uprisings, which, in combination with foreign invasions, have destroyed many individual states. Indeed, seldom have any states survived more than a few hundred years. In view of their obvious instabilities, and considering the relatively recent appearance of state organization, we might be justified in viewing it as a cultural experiment which may yet prove maladaptive.

The modern industrial state, if we consider any of its major variants, is quite clearly not immune to the threat of social disorder in spite of all our efforts at creating stability. This is true even though high levels of productivity have made more material wealth available to more people, and democratic political processes have distributed decision-making powers more equitably. Relative and absolute poverty and powerlessness, and many other problems seemingly inherent in any complex political system, continue to threaten the internal security and domestic tranquility of virtually all states.

The collapse of democratic political systems and their replacement by overwhelmingly powerful and oppressive totalitarian forces represent the ultimate domestic political crisis. Such an event would mean the curtailment of many of the individual freedoms now enjoyed in most industrial nations and might be followed by a period of intensifying civil strife that could effectively destroy civilization as we know it. Such an outcome might occur quite independently of international conflict. Disastrous internal disorders could be precipitated by a major downturn or collapse of our precarious consumption-based economic system; by unresolved urban, ethnic, or racial stresses; and by unresponsive political processes. Terrorist acts and civil disturbances on the part of dissident political groups, racial conflict, spontaneous urban riots and looting, labor strife, organized crime, corruption among high political officials and illegal use of power, rising rates of violent crime and juvenile delinquency, drug abuse—all are symptoms of serious underlying conflicts and contradictions within industrial states.

Anthropologists have traditionally been concerned with a variety of problems relating to social order which are directly relevant to a better understanding of our present crisis. However, before considering the anthropological perspective in detail, a brief review of the social order crisis in America will be presented in order to clarify both the nature of the crisis and current attempts at its solution. The United States provides an excellent starting point for any treatment of this topic because it is widely considered to be the most "advanced" of the industrial nations; yet its violent crime rate is far higher than that of any other modern nation. Perhaps even more importantly, in recent years the American government has supported several massive studies of the problem in an attempt to pinpoint its causes and to work toward the prevention or at least the reduction of violence and disorder.

Violence in America

Violent crime, political terrorism, assassinations, riots, and various other forms of social disorder have always been part of the American scene. It was not until the assassination of President John F. Kennedy in 1963 and the outbreak of widespread urban rioting in 1967, followed in 1968 by violent political demonstrations, campus disturbances, and the assassination of Martin Luther King and Senator Robert F. Kennedy, that the government began to ask serious questions. Several national commissions were called together in the late 1960s to examine various aspects of the crisis. Perhaps the most comprehensive of these commissions was the National Commission on the Causes and Prevention of Violence, established in June of 1968 by President Lyndon B. Johnson. He directed it to "go as far as man's knowledge" could take it in the search for the causes and prevention of violence.

The 13-man commission, headed by Milton S. Eisenhower, worked for a year and a half with a research staff that numbered 100 persons at its peak and was divided into eight major task groups. A total of more than 200 leading scholars assisted the commission with the preparation of 150 separate papers and projects. The latter were published in 13 volumes of task force reports, five investigative reports, and a commission final report. Thirty days of public hearings, in which 150 witnesses testified, were also held. This massive project surely represents the single most ambitious attempt to understand the problem of violence and social disorder undertaken in any modern industrial nation, and its conclusions merit careful consideration.

The final report of the National Commission concluded that while the United States has always been a relatively violent nation, during the 1960s the occurrence of virtually all types of violence increased dramatically over the levels of recent decades. This increase was not a mere reflection of population growth, changes in the demographic structure, or changes in detection and reporting procedures. Between 1958 and 1968 the rate of reported violent crimes (homicide, forcible rape, robbery, and aggravated assault) per 100,000 people doubled. Between mid-1963 and mid-1968, nearly two million people were involved in group protests, urban riots, and demonstrations of various sorts which resulted in an estimated 9,000 casualties, including nearly 200 deaths. This relatively sudden increase in *group* disorders caused widespread alarm and spawned several special commission studies, but such group disorders were not unique in American history. For example, during labor violence between 1902 and 1904, 200 persons were killed and 2,000 injured.

In view of this undisputed general increase in overall violence in America, the commissioners felt that the basic foundations of our society were clearly being threatened and urged that immediate action be taken to control the problem. The dangers of internal disorder were considered to be fully as serious as any external threats, and a reassessment of national priorities, along with a scaling-down of military expenditures for national defense, was called for. As the commissioners stated: "We solemnly declare our conviction that this nation is entering a period in which our people need to be as concerned by the internal dangers to our free society as by any probable combination of external threats."

They called for a doubling of expenditures on the criminal justice process, and greater coordination and efficiency in law enforcement activities in general. They also felt that firearms should be regulated and the availability of handguns restricted. If drastic action was not taken quickly, they foresaw a bleak future for Americans. There would be isolated "safe" areas occupied by upper income families protected by armed guards and electronic surveillance equipment in central city areas, where crime and terror would prevail for the poor at night, when there would be no possible security. Public facilities such as schools, libraries, and playgrounds would also require armed guards. Commuters from safe suburban compounds would travel carefully patroled and "sanitized" corridors in armored cars, while guards would "ride shotgun" on public transportation. All of these defensive measures would lead to further intensification of terror and violence.

The commissioners recognized that merely increasing the efficiency of law enforcement was not sufficient if the underlying *causes* of violence were not corrected. In their view, violence was a *sickness,* a social pathology: "Necessary as measures of control are, they are only a part of the answer. They do not cure the basic causes of violence. Violence is like a fever in the body politic: it is but the symptom of some more basic pathology which must be cured before the fever will disappear."

In order to discover the underlying causes, the report attempted, first of all, to pinpoint where crimes occurred most often and who committed them. It was confirmed that violent crimes were most prevalent in cities of over 50,000 people, where crime rates were 11 times greater than in rural areas. They were most often committed by young, low-income males living under urban slum conditions. An earlier National Commission (United States, National Advisory Commission on Civil Disorders 1968) had declared that this association between crime and slum living conditions was "one of the most fully documented facts about crime." The present report agreed with this assessment and specifically listed poverty, poor housing, and unemployment among the most important factors in an interrelated combination of "powerful criminogenic forces" present in urban slums. The general conclusion was that the urban poor were trapped in a situation from which they could not easily escape because of their inability to earn adequate income. This situation generated frustration and violence because the dominant culture measured success in terms of material wealth, which, in the popular ideology, was considered to be equally available to all who put forth the individual effort to achieve it. The final commission report summarized some of these factors as follows:

> To be a young, poor male; to be undereducated and without means of escape from an oppressive urban environment; to want what the society claims is available (but mostly to others); to see around oneself illegitimate and often violent methods being used to achieve material success; and to observe others using these means with impunity—all this is to be burdened with an enormous set of influences that pull many toward crime and delinquency.

These basic causes were listed as follows:
1.   Revolution of rising expectations
2.   Inadequate law enforcement
3.   Loss of institutional legitimacy
It was argued that economic progress brought rapid social change and greatly increased wealth for some persons while denying it to others. At the same time, it weakened traditional mechanisms of social control and led to frustrations due to inequities in wealth distribution. Inadequate law enforcement and reduced respect for elected authority and established institutions were thought to encourage further crime. All of these causes were seen to be concentrated in urban centers.

Considering all of these "criminogenic" forces, the commissioners felt that it was almost remarkable that more crime did not occur. Since 1968, however, crime rates did of course increase. Within four years, by 1972, the rate had risen a further 30 percent over the already high 1968 level. In 1974, as the unemployment rate and prices began to rise generally, the crime rate reached new heights, rising 17 percent over 1973 levels.

Other studies on violence and disorder in America have often emphasized the "deviant" aspect of this behavior, and have explained it as—at least in part—a problem of faulty socialization or inappropriate values fostered by a subculture of poverty. From this viewpoint, causes are seen to lie largely with the poor people themselves, and the recommended solution becomes "education" in the broadest sense. This view represents a misunderstanding of the adaptive value of deviant behavior under poverty conditions and seriously overemphasizes the role of values in initiating such behavior. It also mistakenly equates such behavior with criminality. Cross-cultural research reveals a common pattern of behavioral coping responses to material deprivation throughout the underdeveloped world and in urban slums in developed nations that is strikingly similar to patterns followed by the urban poor in early industrial England (Eames 1973). Deviant marriage arrangements, the "matrifocal" family, various forms of petty marketing practices, and many other patterns are simply ways of making the best of a difficult situation. Poverty behavior, indeed, presents a consistent picture, but it is because people are adapting to the same problems and not because they are locked in their own self-replicating culture of poverty.

In order to eradicate the basic causes of violence and disorder, the National Commission recommended a major restructuring of urban life, greater expenditures on welfare and improved housing, and so on. Unfortunately, as promising as these recommendations sound, they still leave unchallenged the fundamental problem of stratification itself, which may be the real cause of the social order crisis.

Social Order in Egalitarian Societies

Solving our social order crisis is indeed a formidable task, particularly when it is realized that man's most basic social patterns are perhaps best suited to conditions far different from the highly stratified urban societies to which he is now attempting to adjust. It may be that our most critical social problems can only be treated symptomatically. A certain uncomfortable level of crime and violence and periodic social upheaval may simply be the price that must be paid for the apparent advantages of life in a densely populated, intensely heirarchical society based on differential access to wealth and power. It is certain that most of the criminogenic factors identified by the National Commission are absent in primitive egalitarian societies. With low population densities, with no emphasis on material wealth as a source of status, and with free access to basic resources guaranteed to all, primitive societies face a very different problem of social order, and it is solved in very different, but highly effective ways.

Data on the actual frequency of violence in primitive societies which could be compared with data from our own society are not readily available, but anthropologists who have observed the most traditional hunting and gathering egalitarian societies have generally been impressed with their relatively low levels of internal violence. Some societies, such as the Bushmen of southern Africa and the Semai of Malaysia,* have been characterized as almost totally non-violent, and it would be easy to assume that all primitive peoples led perpetually harmonious social lives. Such, however, is not the case. Some primitive societies, such as the Yanomamo of the Orinoco rain forests, have been described as highly violent (Chagnon 1968). Whatever the actual levels of violence, it is important to note that they generally managed to keep such problems within safe limits. The basic survival of society as a whole was seldom threatened by internal conflict. It could hardly have been otherwise, considering the thousands of years primitive societies endured. There was no "war of all against all" that Thomas Hobbes envisioned, nor was there total harmony. What is of special importance for our purposes

---

*This emphasis is illustrated by the title of Dentan's (1968) book: *The Semai: A Non-violent People of Malaya.*

is that these societies maintained internal order without formal legal codes and specialized law enforcement institutions, and even without formal political offices invested with coercive authority. Primitive societies are dramatic. proof that the expensive law and order machinery that we now require is not the only route to social order.

Any superiority of primitive cultures in the maintenance of social order is unlikely to result from an innate moral superiority of the "noble savage"; rather, it must be due to differences in cultural conditions. Crime and disorder simply could not flourish in a primitive culture. Perhaps one of the most important overall characteristics of primitive cultures likely to predispose them to lower crime rates was the fact that individual self-interest seldom conflicted with the long-range interests of society. Excessive conflict, theft, use of force, or hoarding of resources for exclusive use would all be self-defeating in a primitive society where everyone's survival ultimately depended on mutual trust and cooperation. As was noted in earlier chapters, this same correspondence of interests has also contributed to the ecological success of primitive societies and to the maintenance of population equilibrium.

In low-density primitive societies, conflict is unquestionably further minimized by extreme flexibility in group membership and by the small size of the local, face-to-face residential group. A typical hunting band averaged only approximately 25 people, including children; thus, relatively few adults were ever forced into close interaction. Camps shifted location every few days or weeks, and such moves were often used as an excuse for changing band personnel. Careful studies of modern hunting bands such as the Bushmen have revealed that individuals and families constantly shuffled between bands and that many of these shifts were simply a means of resolving interpersonal conflict without violence (Woodburn 1968:103–110, Turnbull 1968:132–137).

The Importance of Equality
The concept *equality* is critical for an understanding of the differences between primitive societies and states on the question of

social order. No one is of course ever totally equal with anyone else in any society; but in primitive societies the differences that separate people are age, sex, and unique personal qualities exclusively. Positions of prestige and influence are open to all persons qualified to occupy them. For example, anyone with sufficient skill may become a respected hunter or a band leader. Morton Fried has defined an egalitarian society very neatly as follows:

> An egalitarian society is one in which there are as many positions of prestige in any given age-sex grade as there are persons capable of filling them. Let it be put even more strongly. An egalitarian society does not have any means of fixing or limiting the number of persons capable of exerting power. As many persons as can wield power—whether through personal strength, influence authority, or whatever means—can do so, and there is no necessity to draw them together to establish an order of dominance and paramountcy. (Fried 1967:33)

Of equal importance is the situation with regard to basic physical necessities. No one in an egalitarian society is denied access to the means of production. Fried is emphatic on this point: "In no simple society known to ethnography is there any restriction on access to the raw materials necessary to make tools and weapons. This statement can be made flatly about resources in the habitation area of a given unit. . . ." (Fried 1967:58)

Land, water, and game are always open for use. Although boundaries may be recognized for tribal, band, and occasionally family territories, trespass regulations either do not exist or are not enforced, and group membership fluctuates widely. Among primitive horticulturalists, access to land may be regulated by corporate descent groups, but these are not rigid organizations, and membership changes may commonly occur if land shortages arise. Individual ownership of property certainly does occur, but it is normally restricted to personal weapons and artifacts, game killed, herd animals, and crops—things in which personal labor has been invested. With use-access to basic resources open to all, and particularly when residential shifts are part of the subsistence round, there are no real advantages to be gained by asserting individual title to land. In regard to movable property, one can only make practical use of so many goods; and given both the need for mobility and the cultural emphasis on generosity, there is no incentive either to hoard or to steal property. Furthermore, in a small society a thief would be unable to hide. All of these factors are almost certain to minimize the occasion for interpersonal conflict.

Thus, there exist in primitive societies cultural conditions which reduce the basic causes of violence and disorder, and specific mechanisms to reduce the frequency of otherwise unavoidable problems. There are also direct and effective means of handling any trouble that does arise, and there are specific mechanisms to channel conflicts. Serious breaches of norms could result in expulsion from the society—which would mean the loss of all physical and emotional support for the recalcitrant individual. Survival without kinsmen is virtually impossible, and an exiled troublemaker would have difficulty being accepted by other societies where there is no anonymity. Such a drastic sanction rarely needs to be applied, but the threat is always in the background. In many societies the threat of witchcraft accusation may be an effective means of compelling conformity. Chronic troublemakers may find themselves accused of witchcraft, and they may be blamed for causing a variety of sicknesses and community misfortunes. In extreme cases, accused witches may be publicly executed.

Conflict Resolution
In addition to simply moving away, egalitarian primitive societies often employ highly ritualized methods of conflict resolution. In-group interpersonal violence may even be encouraged by some cultures, but it is usually very carefully regulated. The Yanomamo Indians (Chagron 1968), for example, recognize several distinct levels of violence in a carefully graded series of increasing intensity. Their disputes may be settled by ritual duels, which range in extremes from chest pounding, in which two men exchange bare-fist blows to the chest, to spear-throwing duels. Intermediate duels

involve blows to the side and club fighting. Minor injuries and prominent scars may result from these actions, but deaths are uncommon. More pacific ritual forms of conflict resolution in egalitarian societies include Eskimo song duels, in which the disputants publicly insult each other until the loser is laughed down by the audience. Generally, in these cultures, when disputes are not settled by the individuals most directly involved, they are resolved by community consensus. The objective is merely to restore order, not to punish. Abstract notions of "justice" are quite irrelevant in this situation.

Leadership

While there is no concentration of coercive power in political offices in egalitarian societies, this does not mean that there is no leadership or political organization. Headmen have been described for some of the most simple hunting bands, but their authority is severely limited. For example, among the Nambikuara Indians of Brazil, described by Claude Levi-Strauss (1944), the band headman is delegated primary decision-making responsibility for band subsistence activities, selection of routes and campsites, and interband relations. He is only a leader as long as his followers consent to his leadership, and he must not recommend actions that band members would not agree to. A chief's success is measured by his ability to see that the band is well fed. He is also expected to excel in generosity, and constant demands are made on him for food and small articles.

Thus a Nambikuara headman must be an especially skillful, dedicated, and hardworking individual. He bears a heavy responsibility for band well-being and security, but his position is always tenuous. If his leadership qualities falter, the band may simply disintegrate as disgruntled individuals and households seek out other band leaders with whom to align themselves. A headman was generally allowed a young second wife to ease the burdens of leadership, but the only other rewards appear to have been highly personal, and few persons desired the position. Band headmanship in a primitive society, therefore, is not the kind of political office that occurs at higher levels of sociopolitical integration. In fact, Levi-Strauss had a

difficult time explaining why anyone would even aspire to such a
position in Nambikuara society and concluded that "there are chiefs
because there are, in any human group, men who, unlike most of
their companions, enjoy prestige for its own sake, feel a strong
appeal to responsibility, and to whom the burden of public affairs
brings its own reward." (Levi-Strauss 1944)

Social Order in NonEgalitarian Societies

The simplest nonegalitarian societies are often called chiefdoms
(Service 1962, Chapter 5), and many ethnographic examples are
known from the Pacific, Africa, and the Northwest Coast of North
America. Chiefdom societies restrict the number of individuals who
can occupy important positions within the society, but still permit
relatively free access to basic natural resources. Social control
remains largely a matter of kinship, but true political offices exist.
Ranking within a chiefdom may be highly elaborated, with a
hereditary chief at the top, and each corporate descent group may be
ranked both relative to each other and internally. The authority of the
chief is defined by the position he occupies, and his peculiar
personality and special skills are a relatively minor aspect of his
qualifications. The office of chief is ritually set apart and reinforced
by a variety of sumptuary regulations or taboos, such as the right to
eat special foods or to own certain articles. Conflicts may become
intense as individuals vie for status, and rebellions may occur when
particular chiefs overstep the customary bounds of their office; but in
general, the social order problem is qualitatively much simpler, even
given ranking, than when full stratification exists.

  Stratified societies, most fully represented by states, begin with
all the potential social order problems implied by ranking in
chiefdoms, but they add the critical element of restricted access to
strategic resources. According to Morton Fried's (1967:186) concise

definition, "[a] stratified society is one in which members of the same sex and equivalent age status do not have equal access to the basic resources that sustain life." This involves the arrangement of people into classes according to their degree of access to power and resources. There is also a pervasive division of labor by economic specialization, such that no one except certain rural peasants can directly provide for more than a very small proportion of his basic needs. The ruling elite at the top of the hierarchy can effectively regulate access to and use of both critical natural resources and the technological means of production. Control over water, soil, and air may in this way be denied to large segments of society.

With the development of stratification, for the first time in human history, cultural conditions arose in which internal exploitation of one subgroup by another could exist. Exploitation is an emotional and value-laden concept, which many social scientists prefer not to deal with, but in discussing problems of social order, it cannot be avoided. Webster defines exploitation as "unfair utilization." The catch here is in the meaning of "unfair," because no one would dispute that "utilization" of one class by another exists in a stratified society. Certainly, the ruling class is totally dependent for its well-being on the lower classes because it draws its labor force and all its food, goods, and services from them. The "fairness" of this arrangement may be judged from both an inside and an outside view. From the inside, if the members of the lower class do not feel they are being treated unfairly, exploitation would not exist. From the outside, the system might be labeled exploitative when the lower class is clearly deprived of basic physical necessities, while the upper class basks in costly luxury. This kind of material deprivation can be objectively measured and clearly defined in terms of health status, food supply, clothing, housing, and other indicators, and may relate to both a minimal *survival level* and a culturally defined minimum *comfort level*. Material deprivation of either sort is absolute deprivation and is encompassed by the popular concept *poverty*. Relative deprivation, or the feeling that one is not as "well off" as he would like to be in comparison to the next higher class, may exist whenever there is an inequitable distribution of wealth and power, and can occur above the absolute level. Deprivation of some kind seems to be a universal feature of all stratified societies. Some socialist countries may be more successful in easing the absolute deprivation of different classes, but classes exist in these countries nonetheless, and so does the potential for alienation and disorder. Classical Marxian theory, of course, calls for the ultimate end of social stratification and the state after the dictatorship of the proletariat crushes any counterrevolution, but this utopia has not yet arrived.

It is difficult for anyone viewing a particular stratified society from the outside to understand why the impoverished lower classes so often seem to accept their lot without a struggle; but in fact, such systems could not exist without the threat of physical coercion and the use of powerful forms of thought control (Harris 1971). The use of police force, brutality, and imprisonment in support of the political power, wealth, and property rights of the ruling class is certainly a familiar element in the history of all states. However, in many of the ancient agrarian states, such as those in Egypt, Mesopotamia, Mexico, and Peru, the need for such force was apparently minimized by the force of the great state religions, which encouraged the lower classes to accept their position as part of a divinely established order. An elaborate esoteric priesthood, awesome pyramids, and complex, dramatic ritual would have been highly intimidating for anyone who doubted his place in the divine scheme. In fact, many impoverished peasants may never have considered themselves to have been exploited. In modern industrial societies such as the United States, the recommendation of the National Commission that police forces be strengthened is clear indication of the continuing importance of physical coercion. The mass media and the institutions of formal education may also be interpreted as forms of thought control which perhaps replace the role of a state religion and fully support the established order. Anthropologist Marvin Harris (1971) suggests that television may be a very important new means of minimizing social disorder in highly stratified societies by occupying peoples' minds and providing at least vicarious involvement with all levels of the society. A further stabilizing factor, as was noted earlier, has been continuous economic growth, which has helped convince the people in the lowest strata that they are moving up even though their relative position has remained constant.

Population Density, Stratification, and Conflict

Many of the social order problems in modern society seem to a considerable extent to be density-related phenomena. As we noted, a hunting band is a very successful, egalitarian, and low-friction group, but it includes only about 25 people. Primitive village farmers require more formal means of conflict resolution, but they may still avoid any political centralization. It has been suggested that a truly egalitarian society can only be maintained within a continuously interacting, face-to-face population of no more than approximately 250–500 persons which has common goals to pull it together. As population densities increase, not only do people have a more difficult time keeping track of their relationships simply because there are now too many to sort out, but the probability of conflict over everyday irritations becomes much more likely. Invariably, population densities greater than 500 in a single social unit either break up into antagonistic factions, and/or they become hierarchically ordered (Reynolds 1972). Either of these developments may increase the per capita violence level over that of lower density societies, but still holds it within bounds.

Modern urban centers are thus heavily and perhaps unavoidably predisposed toward conflict. Relative and absolute deprivation usually exist because of stratification; and because of economic specialization, there are numerous mutually competing factions, many of which are not directly represented in the hierarchy of political power. A further problem is that young males in the lowest classes often have little hope of gaining full adult status in the society because they are systematically excluded from culturally approved forms of self-assertion and competition.

The Origin of States and Inequality

> How did vast segments of humanity get cut off from access to the earth's natural resources? Why was control of the soil, water, and even the air yielded up into the hands of a relatively small group of people? (Harris 1971:393)

State organization thus seems to be at the root of many of our social order problems, and if we are to understand the origin of these problems, we must consider the origin of the state itself. In view of the disproportionate cost that the majority paid to support the ruling classes, particularly in the earliest states, the origin of such a system has long presented social science theorists with a very knotty problem. The factors leading to the evolution of states are—like the causes of food production—varied, complex, and interrelated. It seems clear that population growth, increasing control of food production by political authorities, economic specialization, regulation of regional trade and water control systems, and warfare over access to resources in restricted environments have all played a part, but no single theory offers a completely adequate explanation. There does seem to be a distinction between the development of *pristine* states, which could apparently only occur under very special cultural-ecological conditions, and the development of *secondary* states, which result from conquest or the threat of conquest by other states. It was noted earlier that population growth may itself be both encouraged by and result from political development; but whatever its cause, as population density increases, political hierarchies become almost inevitable.

The Disintegration of Social Order

> In a disintegrating society one would tend to find subcultures
> developing along all of these different lines in varying degrees:
> there will be an increase in delinquency violence, and all the
> various forms of retreatism, such as drugs, drink, strange religious
> cults, and mental disease. Such a society will be characterized by
> a general feeling of aimlessness, a frantic, almost pathetic search
> for originality, overpreoccupation with anything capable of
> providing short-term entertainment, and beneath it all a feeling of
> hopelessness of the futility of all effort. (Goldsmith et. al.
> 1972:127)

There are strong reasons for suspecting that many of our most serious
social problems that afflict individuals and families at a very personal
level, such as alcoholism and other forms of drug abuse, child abuse,
mental disorders, alienation, suicide, and the breakdown of families,
may all have a common cultural etiology. They may best be
considered social pathologies symptomatic of industrial civilization's
inability to provide adequately for the emotional needs of
individuals. In some respects, they may indeed represent the
disintegration or at least the failure of social order, but this does not
mean that they foreshadow the imminent collapse of society. Social
pathologies may be highly adaptive under certain cultural
conditions, and like poverty-coping mechanisms, they may allow
people to survive what would otherwise be an intolerable
environment.

All of these problems have much in common. Like crime, they
are often more prevalent in urban centers; and although statistics
may be misleading, many of these pathologies seem to be on the
increase. While supportive data are not always available, anthropologists would generally agree that in undisturbed primitive cultures such conditions are either totally absent or very infrequent.
There is also striking and undisputed evidence that as primitive
cultures are absorbed by industrial states, they quickly begin to suffer

from a wide range of social disintegration pathologies, among which alcoholism is perhaps the most conspicuous.

As in the case of crime, enormous attention has been focused on all of these problems, and vast funds have been spent on discovering their causes and working toward their prevention. Entire "industries" are devoted to the treatment of specific problems, but significant results never seem to be achieved. Perhaps the only way to find the real causes of such problems will be to examine healthy cultures and determine what characteristics they possess that are lacking where psychopathologies are common. Anthropologist Stanley Diamond (1974, Chapter 7) has carried out such an analysis for schizophrenia, a mental disorder that may afflict 60 million Americans. He concludes that schizophrenia is basically a way for individuals to deal with the inadequacies of their culture, and that it is irrelevant in primitive cultures, which consistently satisfy basic human needs.

8

war and international order

[The] one crisis that must be ranked at the top in total danger and imminence is, of course, the danger of large-scale or total annihilation by nuclear escalation or by radiological-chemical-biological warfare (RCBW). (Platt 1969)

The threat of nuclear war is the most critical world crisis in many people's minds, and certainly it is the crisis to which the United States government has devoted its largest share of national resources. John Platt (1969), in his crisis survey, cited in Chapter 1, ranked nuclear and what he called RCBW (radiological-chemical-biological war) as the most urgent and dangerous crisis now faced by mankind. He argued that because such a war could occur at any moment and might mean total annihilation, it deserved the top spot on his crisis intensity chart. In his view, however, this crisis will be short-lived; but he felt that this was no cause for optimism because if it is not solved within the next 20 to 50 years, we may all be dead.

Anthropologists have rarely focused their attention on the specific threat of nuclear war, but they have devoted considerable research effort toward understanding intergroup relations at all levels of culture, the evolution of war, the cultural functions of war, and the nature of human aggression. This work has obvious relevance to the present international crisis and will be examined directly; but first the nature of the nuclear threat, and the current thinking of defense strategists and other specialists on the topic, must be considered.

The Doomsday Machine

> In a recent University of Chicago Round Table broadcast, Leo Szilard made some remarks which have caused something of an uproar. These comments, reprinted in the April *Bulletin* along with a few paragraphs amplifying the technical argument, relate to the possibility of using the hydrogen bomb to destroy the human race. The matter is obviously of some importance, and it seems worth-while to check the technical side of the argument. (Arnold 1950)

A significant phase in the evolution of high-energy culture was entered in 1945 when atomic energy was directed toward military applications. The first atomic bombs released the destructive power of 20,000 tons of TNT (20 kilotons), a thousand times more energy than the largest bombs previously used in war. Subsequent advances in nuclear weaponry have made even these devastating bombs seem puny in comparison. The first hydrogen bomb, exploded just nine years after Hiroshima, was 750 times more powerful again and released energy equivalent of 15 million tons of TNT (15 megatons). It is estimated that this represents more than the total of all explosives used in all previous wars; but even these bombs are dwarfed by the 50- and 100-megaton superbombs which could be employed in future wars. Fortunately, only the relatively lightweight 20-kiloton atomic bomb has seen direct combat use, when two bombs destroyed the Japanese cities of Nagasaki and Hiroshima in 1945, killing nearly 100,000 persons and causing more than 200,000 total casualties.

While they have not been used in war, the superbombs have been extensively tested, and many of their effects can be quite precisely predicted.* It is known, for example, that a single 20-megaton ground burst on New York City would leave a crater 640 feet deep and half a mile across (Stonier 1964). The fireball would instantly consume everything within a circle 4.5 miles wide, or an area of more than 15 square miles. During the first 30 seconds the blast shock would generate 160-mile-an-hour winds and would demolish most buildings within a circle 15 miles across. The shock, together with the cratering effect, would destroy the underground subway systems. An air burst would cause heavy structural damage within a 20-mile circle, and would rip out windows and tear off doors within a 40-mile circle. Windows as far as 100 miles away might be broken. The intense heat would ignite secondary fires on combustible material within a circle 50 miles across. It is almost certain that these fires would create gigantic firestorms which would quickly incinerate all of New York City and its environs, burning

---

*See for example, Glasstone (1962) for basic primary data. Also Martin and Latham (1963), Stonier (1964), York (1972), Wiesner and York (1964).

perhaps 1,000 square miles. Six million people would probably die.

If a single nuclear weapon can obliterate one of the world's largest cities, what about entire nations? Or all of humanity? Defense planners may publicly deal with the fate of nations and cities, but the larger question is left for science fiction writers, and most people prefer not to trouble their conscious minds with any of these matters. The ultimate survival of the human race is, of course, the principal topic of this book, and it would be absurd not to deal seriously with what must be the ultimate threat, regardless of how unthinkable or unpleasant it may be. The possibility of the extinction of mankind through its own actions was of course mentioned earlier in relation to ecocatastrophes touched off by the day-to-day pursuit of economic progress, but what we consider here is the destruction of humanity as a direct or indirect outcome of war.

Apart from science fiction, *the* basic question was asked of physicists as early as 1950, even before the hydrogen bomb was successfully exploded. In the radio discussion referred to in the opening quotation of this section (Arnold 1950), nuclear physicist Leo Szilard commented that it would probably be possible to construct a hydrogen-cobalt bomb that would generate enough radioactive global fallout to expose everyone on earth to 10,000 rems, many times over the 500 rems required for a fatal dose, and enough to kill most people protected by standard fallout shelters. He speculated that while this exposure would kill virtually all of mankind, a handful of people might survive, because accidents of local weather patterns and topography might create safe pockets. Such intense radioactivity would of course also wipe out most other life forms, and would so disturb global ecosystems that even isolated pockets would have difficulty surviving very long.

The cobalt bomb is the factual basis for the so-called "doomsday machines" of science fiction writers, but there has been remarkably little discussion of the implications of such devices. Surely, if man does actually now possess the technological capacity to construct an instrument of war that will exterminate the entire human race, this is significant.

The technical side of Szilard's theory has of course been examined by other physicists, and there seems little doubt that such bombs are indeed possible. Szilard himself felt that the only technical uncertainty concerned the success of the hydrogen bomb itself, and that problem was quickly overcome. The only real barrier to the construction of such a doomsday weapon is simply that of time and money, and this could easily be overcome by a "dedicated" nation. In 1950, Szilard estimated that collecting the necessary ingredients and assembling the bomb would require $40 billion and 5–10 years' work, and he concluded that humanity was in no immediate danger. That cost might have seemed prohibitively expensive in 1950; but today, $40 billion represents less than 50 percent of the annual defense budget of the United States, and this is precisely a recent estimate for the price tag on a minor refinement of an existing weapon system—the introduction of ULMs (undersea long-range missile systems). Even more alarming than the technological feasibility of a doomsday device is the ease with which it could be fitted into the "arms culture" of a modern industrial nation. In view of current military logic, a doomsday machine could easily become the ultimate cornerstone of the policy of "nuclear deterrence," and it could be further justified as a certain employment boost for the economy. It represents an obvious evolutionary progression in both military technology and strategic concepts.

Apart from deliberate doomsday machines, the likelihood that worldwide fallout from a massive nuclear exchange between the United States and Russia would destroy the entire human race has fortunately been somewhat overdrawn. The *On the Beach* theme is apparently not well founded. A massive exchange designed to maximize civilian casualties due to fallout might succeed in killing almost everyone in the northern hemisphere between latitudes 30° and 60° north, but this would still leave some 40 percent of humanity relatively unaffected. The long-range effects of such a war would, however, almost certainly be global and incalculable.

Anthropologist Leslie A. White, writing in 1949 as the full implications of the possible military use of nuclear energy were just beginning to be assessed, clearly foresaw the threat to both humanity and civilization posed by this new technology. He felt that total nuclear destruction was possible but not inevitable, and speculated that a world order might eventually emerge from the radioactive ruins. In any event, he was philosophically prepared to accept the worst:

> The belief and faith that civilization, won at such great cost in pain and labor, simply cannot go down in destruction because such an end would be too monstrous and senseless, is but a naïve and anthropocentric whimper. The cosmos does little know nor will it long remember what man has done here on this tiny planet. The eventual extinction of the human race—for come it will sometime—will not be the first time that a species has died out. Nor will it be an event of very great terrestrial significance. (White 1949:391)

Mad: Mutual Assured Destruction

> [We] must be able to absorb the total weight of nuclear attack on our country—on our strike-back forces; on our command and control apparatus; on our industrial capacity; on our cities; and on our population—and still, be fully capable of destroying the aggressor to the point that his society is simply no longer viable in any meaningful twentieth-century sense. (Secretary of Defense Robert S. McNamara public address, Sept. 18, 1967)

The fundamental basis of military strategy between the nuclear superpowers has been their mutual ability to "deter" aggression by threatening the total destruction of a would-be aggressor. Critics have dubbed this concept of nuclear deterrence MAD—an acronym for *mutual assured destruction* (Carter 1974). This has been the basic strategic concept which has propelled the arms race and has resulted in the concentration by the Soviet Union and the United States of far more weapons than would ever be needed to execute their own mutual destruction. Since 1949, when the Soviet Union exploded its own atomic bomb, the world has witnessed a staggering increase in the destructive power of weapons, and a parallel increase in the speed and efficiency with which these weapons can be delivered to their targets. The Hiroshima bomb was delivered by a propeller-driven B–29 bomber flying at a speed of 300 miles per hour. Such a plane required 20 hours to reach a target on the other side of the globe. Today, missiles can do the job very precisely within 30 minutes (Weisner and York 1964). An incredible redundancy and overkill characterize the arsenals of both superpowers. For example, in 1968, it was estimated that the United States required a mere 400 warheads to destroy the Soviet Union, but it then possessed 2,000 (Garwin and Bethe 1968); and now, with the deployment of multiple warheads, the figure has jumped to 10,000, while there has been no appreciable change in the defense capability of the Soviet Union. Each side possesses at least three independent weapons systems, consisting of bombers, ICBMs (intercontinental ballistic missiles), and SLBMs (submarine-launched ballistic missiles), and any of these could destroy the other side even after taking major losses. These systems have rapidly diversified as the arms race has progressed, but most experts now feel that no dramatically new surprises are in store. ICBMs have perhaps reached their effective practical size limits, and there seems little point in building larger bombs, but pinpoint accuracy can still be perfected. The MIRV (multiple independently targeted reentry vehicle) concept has vastly increased the destruction capability of an individual missile, but has not really altered the ability of either side to destroy the other. New arms developments now being proposed, such as ULMs (undersea long-range missile systems), or air-mobile ballistic missiles, represent only minor refinements of existing technology. The only serious challenge to nuclear deterrence would be the development of an effective "counterforce" program which would allow one side to destroy the retaliatory force of the other, but this is an unlikely possibility.

Counterforce may be avoided by the simple expedient of launching the retaliation before the attacker's weapons hit, and serious attempts to develop a counterforce strike merely increase the likelihood of an accidental nuclear exchange.

The defense side of the arms race has always been at a disadvantage because it must be geared to a particular type of attack, and given the lead time required for the development and deployment of any military system, even the most elaborate defense system may be obsolete before it is in place. The most critical problem for defense against nuclear attack is that the defense system must be virtually 100 percent effective or the nation would still be destroyed, because even a handful of warheads penetrating the defenses would be enormously destructive. In the United States, defense systems have expanded from the radar networks, jet interceptors, and fallout shelters of the 1950s, to the ABMs (antiballistic missiles), ASWs (antisubmarine warfare systems), AWACs (airborne warning and control system), underground command centers, soft and hard missile silos, and satellite observation systems of the 1960s and 1970s (Greenwood 1973, Garwin 1972, Scoville 1972, English and Bolef 1973). An attack can now be detected at the instant it is launched, and some of the attacking missiles can be destroyed, but the employment of simple decoys and electronic countermeasures virtually guarantees that some warheads will penetrate even the most sophisticated defense systems. Thus the MAD doctrine seems assured indeed. The final irony of the entire arms race is that as military capabilities have increased, there has been a proportionate *decrease* in national security. Hence the generalization that evolutionary progress may be maladaptive is again confirmed.

Postattack Society:
Will the Survivors Envy the Dead?

The combined assault of radiation, insects, disease, and fire could temporarily strip off the plant cover of vast areas. If the attack is sufficiently widespread, it is conceivable that a few years later almost all the forests would have been destroyed, and most of the countryside would have become converted into marginal grasslands, if not actually stripped, leaving a naked earth to be ravaged by the ever-present forces of erosion. (Stonier 1964:135)

The recovery of nature is by no means a foregone conclusion. There is a very real possibility that if the United States were hit hard enough by a nuclear attack most of the country would be converted into a barren desert. (Stonier 1964:141)

It might seem that the mere existence of overwhelmingly destructive nuclear weapons would make the entire concept of war both obsolete and unthinkable, but this is unfortunately not the case. As a logical extension of the policy of nuclear deterrence, government planners and their research contractors have for more than two decades been busily exploring the feasibility of nuclear war. Their work describes "postattack society" in intricate detail, on the optimistic assumption that the country will indeed survive a nuclear war intact, and will then quickly proceed to restore itself to its prior condition. The theme underlying all of these studies, and perhaps best exemplified in the title of Herman Kahn's book, *Thinking About the Unthinkable,* is that nuclear war is not madness at all; rather, it is something that we had better go ahead and prepare for. This conclusion is based on research methods and value judgments that most anthropologists would find incredibly narrow and short-sighted—and even dangerous, considering that such work merely increases the probability of nuclear war by making it seem "feasible." It is also an ironic twist that demonstrating the feasibility of nuclear war of course actually undermines the mutual suicide basis of the deterrence policy, but few experts acknowledge this paradox.

Numerous computer simulations have been run as a basis for estimating total casualties, property damage, and projected rates of economic recovery for a wide variety of nuclear attacks on the country. For example, the so-called "Holifield Attack," run in 1959 for a congressional committee, assumed that 1,466 megatons would be ground-burst on military bases and on all major population and industrial centers. The "Spadefork Attack," run in 1962 for the U.S. Office of Emergency Planning, aimed 1,779 megatons primarily at military targets, and air-burst half of the weapons. The "UNCLEX Attack," published by the Office of Emergency Planning in 1964, assumed that 1,600 weapons were launched against the United States, and half reached their targets with a yield of 3,583 megatons. In this attack, half of the weapons were deployed against military installations, and the remainder were divided between industry and population. It should be obvious that data-skewing imponderables are numerous even at this point (not only the number of weapons employed and the targets selected, but the time of year and precise hour of attack are among the critical variables that must be specified), but the planners still present distressingly precise profiles of "postattack society."

On the basis of such simulations (Heer 1965), estimates have been made of the exact age and sex composition of "survivors," along with their marital status, political affiliation, religion, ethnic identity, occupation, educational background, and even their attitudes on welfare and tolerance for nonconformists. One such study concluded that a nuclear attack would slightly increase the proportions of Republicans, Protestants, and conservatives in the total population—as if such considerations would even be relevant concerns after the bomb!

Casualties vary tremendously according to which simulation is used; but of course, none even approach total destruction, because that would mean that there would be no "postattack society" to write about. The Spadefork Attack claims only 18 percent of the population, the Holifield Attack accounts for 30 percent killed, and the UNCLEX Attack for 50 percent killed (approximately 100 million people) and an additional 15 percent injured but surviving. After these attacks the surviving members of the work force immediately go back to their jobs. After UNCLEX, the planners project that 20 percent of our production capacity will be restored within 10 days, 30 percent within a year; and the factories will be up to 60 percent of their preattack output after longer repairs. Optimists will be happy to know that, given the enormous population reduction, there will actually be a net increase in the per capita dollar value added in manufacturing. Kahn (1961) predicts that after a moderate nuclear war, if everything goes well, we shall have our gross national product and overall consumption levels back to normal within 10 years or less.

Of course, none of these studies attempt to make nuclear war seem desirable, but they are very concerned with improving its bad public image and deemphasizing the horror it would bring. At the Third Interdisciplinary Conference on Selected Aspects of a General War held at Princeton in 1968, biophysicist Stafford Warren stressed the importance of making people believe that they would personally survive a nuclear attack: "[When] we talk about shocking conditions we've got to emphasize too the escape elements in this picture, since we can protect an awful lot of people. Each one must have the hope that he will escape unhurt or unirradiated. While the situation is admittedly grim we've got to do something better in order to break down this log jam of apathy." (DASA 1971:315)

Herman Kahn, in his major study *On Thermonuclear War,* minimizes the social cost of the genetic damage and other injuries that fallout might cause by stressing that these are problems that will be spread thinly and far into the future. For example, he estimates that even though the results of nuclear war are "long-lasting and somewhat incalculable," they *might* add only one percentage point to our present rate of serious birth defects, and he concludes optimistically that: "Most people will be able to live with such increased risks." (1961:47) He cautions that "we should not magnify our view of the costs of the war inordinately because such postwar risks are added to the wartime casualties (1961:42). With incredibly shallow regard for the future, he affirms that "if you spread the genetic damage over tens of thousands of years you have done something very useful." (1961:48)

In fact, in spite of all the thousands of pages of special studies on the feasibility of nuclear war, no single definitive sociocultural and environmental impact statement has yet been written on the subject—or, indeed, ever could be written because, properly speaking, the impact of such a war is incalculable. The specialized studies undertaken so far serve only to give planners a false sense of security. By focusing on fragments of the total picture, researchers can very easily reach comfortable conclusions. A study of food availability in postattack society conducted by Stanford Research Institute, for example, concluded that while Thelma Lu's Candies would be a total loss when the bomb falls on Albuquerque, Pepsi-Cola and 7-Up bottlers would be back in business within a few weeks, and there would be plenty of potato chips to go around (Rappaport 1971:95–105). At the Third Interdisciplinary Conference, cited earlier, it was pointed out that in general the food problem wouldn't be as bad as some might imagine because "you'll have fewer people to feed. . . ." (DASA 1971:311)

Surprisingly, the basic question of whether or not American society as a whole would survive is not usually even faced by most of the planners in their feasibility studies. This point became glaringly obvious at the Third Interdisciplinary Conference, and is well illustrated by the following comment by one of the participants: "[There] is a big difference between laying out the physical possibilities that you've got to work with and trying to answer the question of the extent to which you will have a viable functioning social system in the post-attack period. They're not trying to answer that question; they haven't yet." (Peter Nordlie, Human Sciences Research, Inc. DASA 1971:410)

These studies focus on isolated, short-term effects, and lack a real overview. They share the critical weakness of their failure to consider adequately the frailty of the highly specialized and interdependent industrial economic system and the total dependence of this system, in turn, on equally fragile and interdependent ecological systems. Not only will the energy systems be destroyed, but so will the transportation systems that must move the energy which fuels the transportation system. The factories will be destroyed, and so will the machines that make other machines. One study noted as an aside that all the conifers in the entire Northeast would be killed (DASA

1971:303). This would in itself be an ecological disaster that would dwarf any catastrophe in recent experience, and would set off a chain reaction of other totally unpredictable events. There would be staggering problems of social disorder, disease, insect infestations, and radiation contamination. Some researchers even warn that a large war could lead to a drastic reduction in temperature and could even touch off an ice age. Certainly, no one can predict the precise outcome of a nuclear war, but it would be foolish to assume that industrial society would simply rebuild. There might well be no reconstruction.

Cross-Cultural Perspectives on War

A knowledge of how and why primitive peoples made war may shed light on the prospects for war or peace in our own time. (Naroll 1966:14)

Perhaps the single most important perspective that anthropologists can bring to the study of war is the contrast between primitive and modern war. In fact, depending on the definition of war, it may be said to be totally nonexistent among many of the simplest cultures; and even where it does occur in primitive cultures, there are significant qualitative differences which make primitive war profoundly different from its modern counterpart. These points are critical, because they bear directly on the central question of whether or not modern war can be prevented. The evidence strongly suggests that war may in fact be an inherent feature of civilization to such an extent that we cannot have one without the other.

The most widely accepted definitions of war would automatically exclude much of the intergroup conflict that typically occurs between primitive communities. War is generally considered to be an organized armed conflict between political units in pursuit of a group goal. To the extent that *organization* and *group objectives* are emphasized, this kind of war is absent at the lowest levels of culture. Bronislaw Malinowski was emphatic on this point: "[We] do not find among these lowest primitives any organized clash of armed forces aiming at the enforcement of tribal policy. War does not exist among them." (1944:277)

Many writers would further restrict the definition of war to armed conflict between nation-states carried out for national objectives. Quincy Wright, unquestionably the world's leading authority on war, used the term in its widest meaning to include violent intergroup conflict or armed aggression in any form; but in his monumental work, *A Study of War*, he strongly emphasized the qualitative differences between primitive and civilized war: "War in the sense of a legal situation equally permitting groups to expand wealth and power by violence began with civilization. . . . Only among civilized people has war been an institution serving political and economic interests of the community, defined by a body of law which states the circumstances justifying its use, the procedures whereby it is begun and ended, and the methods by which it is conducted." (1942:39)

Certainly, the major conclusion of any evolutionary study of intergroup conflict, whatever we choose to call it, is that its form is strongly related to the form of political organization of a given culture. As an empirical generalization, it can be stated that as a culture's political system becomes more centralized, its military organization becomes more complex, its weapons and tactics become more effective, and individual engagements become more costly in terms of casualties (Otterbein 1970). There is also a predictable shift in the immediate goals for fighting and in the supporting ideology. The nature of the interrelationship between political centralization and war cannot yet be precisely explained, but they have evolved together. The state makes war, and war helped to create states.

If the immediate objectives that commonly motivate political communities to fight with their neighbors are analyzed, they can be grouped into four major categories, following the work of several researchers (Wright 1942:278–283, Naroll 1966, Otterbein 1970). These categories are *defense, plunder, prestige,* and *political control;* and it is assumed that they reflect considerations that both military decision makers and the combatants have in mind when they go to war. Anthropologists also recognize many other "functions" of war; these four categories do not pretend to include all the psychological factors that may motivate particular individuals to fight. What is significant about these categories is that they do not occur in different cultures in a random, unpredictable manner; rather, they tend to be distributed in an orderly arrangement that reveals a great deal about the nature of war and its relationship to political organization. There are cultures where no organized fighting occurs for any of these reasons, and such societies may justifiably be said to lack war. In general, the motives for war tend to be cumulative, so that, for example, if a culture goes to war in order to extend political control over a neighbor, it will probably also fight for defense, plunder, and prestige. However, if a culture fights for plunder, it may not fight for political control, and those cultures that do not fight for defense do not fight at all. This property of related variables is called *scalability* and is demonstrated for a few selected cultures in Table 7. It will be noted that those cultures with the highest scores on the scale, or the most motives for war, are politically centralized and usually states, while those with the fewest motives are politically uncentralized. Figure 12 illustrates this relationship more accurately, drawing on data from a worldwide sample of 46 cultures examined by Keith Otterbein in his cross-cultural study of the evolution of war. It is significant that none of the politically decentralized cultures in his sample used war for purposes of political control, and that while all states fought for defense and economic advantage, many uncentralized cultures did not.

. Otterbein also worked with a composite scale of military sophistication which reflected the general military effectiveness of cultures. For example, cultures with standing armies or age-grade warrior societies were considered to be militarily more effective than those lacking such organization. Likewise, more flexible tactics,

TABLE 7 Political organization and war motives

	defense	plunder	prestige	control
Uncentralized:				
Bands:				
Copper Eskimo	0	0	0	0
Tiwi	+	0	0	0
Tribes:				
Somali	+	+	0	0
Wondi	+	+	+	0
Centralized:				
Chiefdoms:				
Sema	+	+	+	0
Mutair	+	+	+	0
States:				
Thai	+	+	+	+
Aztec	+	+	+	+

Source: Data are from a worldwide sample of 46 cultures examined by Keith Otterbein (*The Evolution of War: A Cross Cultural Study* [New Haven: Human Relations Area Files Press, 1970]).

more deadly weapons, the presence of fortifications, negotiations, and war for political domination were all treated as indicative of greater military sophistication. Here again, the split between decentralized primitive cultures and centralized chiefdom and state cultures was striking. Table 8 presents the data from the cross-

TABLE 8 Political organization and military sophistication

political organization	military sophistication		
	low	high	total
Centralized	3	13	16
Uncentralized	24	6	30
Total	27	19	46

Source: Keith Otterbein, *The Evolution of War: A Cross Cultural Study* (New Haven: Human Relations Area Files Press, 1970).

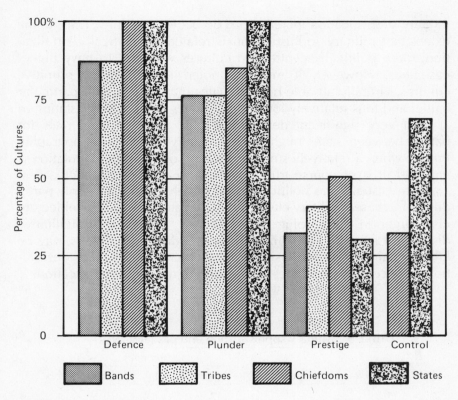

FIGURE 12   Motives for War.   (Source: Data are from a worldwide sample of 46 cultures examined by Keith Otterbein (*The Evolution of War: A Cross Cultural Study* [Human Relations Area Files Press, 1970]).)

cultural sample which confirms the generalization that more politically centralized societies tend to be more sophisticated militarily.

Attempts to estimate and compare casualty rates are difficult and often misleading, but some trends are obvious (see Table 9). Otterbein rated casualty rates as high if a third or more of the forces engaged in given battles are killed, and was able to show that as military sophistication increases, so do battle casualties. Thus, to the extent that military sophistication is related to political centraliza-tion, more politically centralized cultures will tend to have higher casualties. However, it must be noted that in many primitive cultures, virtually all able-bodied males may engage in a particular battle, and thus relatively low casualty rates could be devastating or at least very significant demographically. High casualty rates for battles between states might have a relatively minor demographic impact when a relatively small proportion of the male population is engaged. It is of course true that there is a staggering increase in *absolute* casualties as political systems evolve, but this is only partly due to increased military effectiveness because the forces fielded are also larger in an absolute sense. Surely, however, a qualitative distinction must be recognized when hundreds of millions may be killed within minutes in a single engagement. This level of destruc-tion is, of course, the highest expression of military sophistication.

TABLE 9   Military sophistication and casualty rates

military sophistication	casualty rates		
	low	high	total
High	7	8	15
Low	13	5	18
Total	20	13	33

Source: Data from Keith Otterbein, *The Evolution of War: A Cross Cultural Study* (New Haven: Human Relations Area Files Press, 1970).

Cross-cultural comparisons rating the frequency of war have also been used to test the validity of the argument that a high degree of military sophistication acts as a deterrent to war. The evidence suggests that this generalization does not hold true for primitive cultures and preindustrial states. Actually, quite the opposite situation is more likely.* The more sophisticated a community is militarily, the more frequently it engages in aggressive war and is itself attacked in turn. Thus, we may cautiously generalize that as cultures become more politically centralized, they become more militaristic, fight more often, and have higher casualty rates.

Otterbein also noted a strong positive correlation between a high degree of military sophistication and military "success" measured in terms of expanding territorial boundaries. Approximately half of the militarily sophisticated societies in his sample were expanding their territories, while only 15 percent of the "unsophisticated" cultures were expanding. Thus, it would be easy to conclude that a more effective military capability is a selective advantage for a culture in competition with its neighbors. However, nuclear weapons, even though they may represent the highest degree of sophistication, would appear to be a distinct disadvantage. Cultures engaging in nuclear war are very unlikely to emerge victorious.

War can also be viewed in terms of the technological systems which support it. W. W. Newcomb, Jr., (1960) presents a four-part typology placing the simplest hunter-gatherers in type 1, and arguing that their technology simply could not support large armies on extended campaigns and gave them nothing special to fight for, anyway. Type 2 war includes what is usually considered "primitive war." Here again, there is little economic incentive for prolonged fighting, but technological productivity is high enough to support more elaborate campaigns than previously. Type 3 war includes "civilized war" based on a developed agriculture and a complex division of labor. Type 4 includes modern war based on fossil fuels, and is vastly larger in scope and more destructive than any previous wars. A fifth type, "nuclear war," might obviously be added. This typology does not of course explain the existence of war, but it does help to specify some of the limitations and possibilities inherent in particular technological systems.

---

*Both Otterbein (1970) and Naroll (1966) make this point.

War and Human Nature

> [It] is meaningless to say that war is inevitable because of the
> pugnacity of man as an animal. While man has original drives that
> make war possible, that possibility has only been realized in
> appropriate social and political conditions. (Wright 1942:5)

The issue of the relationship between war and human nature has
been argued and reargued for many years. Quincy Wright's above-
quoted response to the debate represents the careful conclusion of a
scholar who directed the University of Chicago's Social Science
Research Committee project on the causes of war from 1926 to
1941. Prominent anthropologists such as Bronislaw Malinowski
(1941) and Margaret Mead (1940), who joined the debate during
World War II, took much the same position; and this view remains
the general consensus among anthropologists today. Man may
indeed possess an innate capacity for aggression, but this capacity
must be culturally shaped.

Unfortunately, the basic question has apparently not been
settled to everyone's satisfaction. In recent years the issue has been
revived by popular writers such as Robert Ardrey (1966) and Konrad
Lorenz (1966), and the whole question continues to have important
implications for the current debate on alternatives to war. Ardrey, for
example, argues that man's innate agressiveness and territoriality are
a basic foundation for war. This has practical implications because
those who emphasize the instinctive argument would have us study
our biological background to learn the causes of war and,
presumably, methods of preventing it. This approach diverts
attention from the critical *cultural* factors that are the real causes of
war, and leads to the conclusion that war either is inevitable or can
be prevented if man's innate aggression is channeled from war into
harmless sporting events. Meanwhile, the fundamental cultural basis
for war goes unchallenged.

Much of this debate has not been very fruitful and is certainly
misleading. Aggression must be clearly distinguished from war
because, while aggression per se may be understandable to some

extent in biological terms, warfare is a *cultural* phenomenon carried on between cultural groups. From the foregoing discussion of the evolution of war, it should be clear that during most of man's existence, war, as usually defined, simply did not exist until the evolution of centralized political organization, even though man's biological inheritance must have remained constant. War very often does have an obvious boundary-maintaining aspect, but if "territoriality" is instinctive, this instinct, like the "instinct" for violence, is almost infinitely variable because many human groups do not fight over territory. It certainly does not seem very illuminating to view the present arms race as either a result of instinctive territoriality or aggression between the United States and the Soviet Union.

Another side of the human nature approach which is equally misleading is the view that we must understand individual psychology if we are to explain war. It is of course true that individuals must be psychologically prepared for war, and that soldiers may be motivated to fight by factors originating within their own personalities; but the fact remains that these "causes" of war are overshadowed by more basic cultural variables. The dynamics of individual psychology, like man's capacity for violence, can be culturally expressed in a variety of ways, which may or may not include war.

The Causes of War

> From an anthropological perspective any kind of war is generally a symptom of the absence, inadequacy, or breakdown of other procedures for resolving conflicts. (Koch 1970:43)

Anthropological research supports the conclusion that war is caused by many interacting variables, and it seems doubtful that any fully adequate single explanation for its existence will ever be found.

However, the general factors predisposing a given culture to war, and some of war's probable effects or functions, can be outlined. At the broadest level, as the above quotation suggests, war is simply one way of dealing with conflict, but it must be stressed that the sources of conflict are largely culturally determined, as is the form the conflict will actually take.

Perhaps more anthropological attention has been devoted to developing functional analyses of war than to any other aspect of the problem.* Functionalist research merely attempts to answer the question: "What does war do in a given society?" It does not provide a complete explanation of why war exists or how it came to be. The assumption is simply being made that it must have had survival value for certain cultures under certain adaptive conditions. This should not, however, be construed as a defense of the status quo or a rationalization for war. When an anthropologist states that war in a particular society performs some critical adaptive function, that is not to say that something else might not do the job as well or even better. Critics (Hallpike 1973) correctly point out that war may be beneficial for certain groups at certain levels of analysis, while it may be very disadvantageous in other respects. It should also be stressed that functionalists do not assume that individuals waging war are necessarily aware of the "functions" they may be serving.

Many of the most convincing and interesting functional explanations of war deal with its role in maintaining ecological balances. Warfare serves the obvious function of helping to adjust local imbalances that may develop between land or other resources and people. There is ample evidence that even in primitive cultures, local groups may sometimes be wiped out and their territory confiscated by their neighbors, but such events are relatively infrequent. Chronic warfare may also have a significant demographic impact. Raiding for the express purpose of acquiring wives, and thereby redistributing women, is also not uncommon. It has been suggested that at least

---

*See Vayda (1968) for example.

one effect of stock raiding in herding societies is to help maintain herd size at optimum levels (Sweet 1965). Groups with especially large herds might logically be more vulnerable to raiding parties than those with very small, easily defended herds. Empirical evidence to support this hypothesis is scanty, but it is an interesting possibility. War is certainly one possible outcome of "pressure" on resources; but, as was noted in a previous chapter, this kind of pressure is not easily defined, and there are many other cultural solutions to the problem. In view of the extraordinary resource consumption rates that have come to characterize industrial civilization, however, resource competition may well be one of the most important causes of modern war. Furthermore, the incredible global imbalances that now exist in consumption may become the basis for "wars of redistribution."

War may have many not so obvious side effects that merit consideration. For example, in the Tsembaga example cited earlier, war was apparently a critical element in a delicately balanced equilibrium system. An intriguing side effect of the warfare between the Chippewa and Sioux Indians from 1780 to 1850 was the con- version of their vast battleground into a de facto game preserve for their most important game animal—the Virginia deer (Hickerson 1965). Perpetual hostility between the two groups made hunting a very risky affair over a large area of prime deer habitat in western Wisconsin and central Minnesota. It is assumed that this buffer zone provided a steady stock to replenish the more heavily hunted areas and served as a strategic reserve in times of unusual scarcity when hunters might disregard the dangers of ambush and hunt within the contested zone itself. Similar buffer zones seem to be a common characteristic along the frontiers separating many tribal cultures, and in many of these cases a resource conservation effect may also be important.

At the lowest levels of sociopolitical organization, conflict arising from interpersonal relations involving individuals from different sovereign groups often resulted in chronic intergroup feuding and perpetual hostility. In many societies that lacked centralized political authority strong enough to punish offenders, personal revenge seeking through armed retaliation was the only way for dealing with intergroup crimes such as murder, theft, rape, and trespass. As political organization and economic productivity become more developed, intergroup competition for important resources replaces personal revenge as the most obvious cause of conflict. In fact, some authorities argue convincingly that conflict over restricted prime agricultural land between expanding societies was a principal cause of war and the evolution of the state itself (Carneiro 1970). This "environmental circumscription" theory does seem to explain neatly why most of the first states developed where they did and why states never evolved independently in many areas where basic resources were unbounded. It does not, however, explain the conflict-generating growth itself; but as was discussed in earlier chapters, this is one of the key problems for anthropology, and the "circumscription" theory cannot be faulted for not answering it. There are undoubtedly other intervening variables involved in state formation, but it is clear that war does become a basic factor in the continued growth and maintenance of states once they appear.

Perhaps the most important point to consider is that states possess unique features, absent in primitive cultures, that must increase the likelihood of war, and that industrialization makes these features even more pronounced. The intensification of economic production and consumption is an obvious feature of state systems that places great additional stress on natural resources and must make competition over resources much more likely. Social stratification by wealth must further intensify this major disequilibrium factor. Another critical aspect of the class system is that it creates politically powerful groups with vested interests in promoting wars for their own advantage and places them in a position to manipulate the lower classes to this end.

With industrialization, the development of world markets has added a new dimension to the potential for conflict, and global wars have made their appearance. While many authorities may debate the role that resource competition played in the two world wars recorded in our history books, there can be little doubt that it was the principal cause for the long war between civilization and primitive cultures. During the final phase of this war, between approximately 1780 and 1930, as many as 50 million tribal people may have died and approximately half of the globe was wrested from their control (Bodley 1975:38–41). The terminal skirmishes of this conflict for resources are still taking place, but remarkably little note has been made of these events, even though in scale and importance they must dwarf our own world wars.

There is really no reason to separate war from the total world crisis because wars, like urban violence, overpopulation, and environmental deterioration, are merely symptoms of the underlying adaptive shortcomings of industrial civilization. The present sources of intergroup conflict may be sought in the imbalances of wealth and power that exist at both national and international levels, and in the rising stresses of population and increasing resource consumption. These destabilizing factors, together with the absence of effective alternatives to war as a means of conflict resolution, are at the root of our present crisis.

Preventing War

The most popular and obvious means of preventing war call for the establishment of some form of world political structure. Indeed, cultural evolutionist Leslie A. White argued more than 20 years ago that such a step would be a logical evolutionary development and the *only* way to bring world peace: "World peace will come, if it ever does, not because we shall have bred out the pugnacious instinct, or sublimated it in mass athletic contests, but because cultural development, social evolution, will have reached the ultimate conclusion of the age-old process of merging smaller social groups into larger ones, eventually forming a single political organization that will embrace the entire planet and the whole human race." (1949:134)

The United Nations is of course a step in that direction, and many other ingenious world political mechanisms have been proposed, but it seems unlikely that these efforts will be really successful unless the more basic causes of conflict and the deeper problems of industrial civilization are also dealt with. There is a clear need to increase research efforts toward understanding the causes and the extent of our present ecological imbalances, as well as the nature of stratification and the cultural foundation of the military system. We may also gain many useful ideas for the establishment of a viable world order by examining conflict-reducing mechanisms built into many primitive cultures.

9

the future

Obviously, we stand on the threshold of postcivilization.
When we reach solutions to today's problems, the society
and culture that we will have built for the purpose will be of
a sort the world has never seen before. It may be more, or
less, civilized than what we have, but it will not be
civilization as we know it. (Bohannan 1971)

The future cannot of course be precisely predicted, but no view of the future will be satisfactory if it does not consider the pervasive nature of the present crisis and the many separate risks it poses. The future will almost certainly be a "solution," either planned or unplanned, to the diverse problems created by industrial civilization. In this final chapter, it is argued that all of the crises discussed so far are manifestations of what is in fact a single world crisis that will only be solved by a complete cultural transformation. This is perhaps the most important conclusion to be drawn from the present work, and provides a basis both for assessing the effectiveness of the many planning programs now being developed to shape the future and for evaluating the many alternative futures that futurist researchers are exploring.

The Diagnosis: "Terminal Civilization"*

Our problems are all extremely complex, interrelated, and in a general sense multicausal, but many of the most critical are obvious correlates of evolutionary progress. Over and over in the preceeding chapters, it has been shown that a specific crisis was either totally absent or at least not a serious problem before the evolution of civilization. Many crises have also not arisen or not become critical until the appearance of industrial civilization. However, it would be misleading to state that civilization has itself been the direct cause of our most serious problems, because many of the conditions that we are here calling problems enjoy a peculiar cause-and-effect relationship with cultural progress. For example, war, population growth, and technological advance are all causes of and results of general evolutionary progress. Any attempt to single out causes is

---

*This phrase was used in a cartoon by Ron Cobb published in 1970.

further complicated by the fact that individual crises are themselves interrelated in similar feedback mechanisms—population growth may lead to war, which accelerates technological advances, which promote population growth, and so forth.

This multicausality and complex interrelationship between problems has important implications for any attempt to identify causes and find solutions. In many cases, it is apparent that current problem-solving efforts are inadequate because they treat isolated symptoms and avoid basic underlying factors. An example from the medical field may illustrate this point. Twenty years ago, Dr. T. L. Cleave (1974), Surgeon-Captain of the British Royal Navy, linked together a whole list of seemingly diverse diseases, including dental decay, peptic ulcers, obesity, diabetes, constipation, and varicose veins, into a single category which he called the "saccharine disease." Using historical data and research on primitive peoples, he argued that all of these conditions are caused at least in part by the extensive use of concentrated carbohydrates such as sugar and white flour by modern industrialized populations. This radical change in diet over the patterns that man had evolved during many thousands of years altered body chemistry and greatly slowed transit times in the digestive tract by reducing dietary bulk, thereby creating many pathogenic conditions. Other researchers had simply not seen the problems as related, perhaps because they did not examine populations where these pathologies were absent, and they did not seek basic cultural causes. At higher levels of analysis, it may be that virtually all of the easily recognized crises—including war, pollution, poverty, overpopulation, overconsumption, hunger, and alcoholism—are, like the saccharine disease, really different manifestations of a single interrelated cultural "disease" that might be labeled "civilization." Industrialization may be simply the terminal phase that has developed after a 5,000-year incubation period.

To be convincing, this "cultural pathology" approach must not only identify primitive cultures as the major cultural type that does not suffer from the disease, it must also sort out the specific cultural conditions that seem to be most directly responsible for the symptoms. In a general sense, it appears that the closely interrelated variables, *social stratification* and extreme *specialization of labor,* are perhaps the most fundamental characteristics of civilization, from which other critical problem-causing features are ultimately derived. Stratification and specialization are the foundation of the market economy, wealth concentration, political centralization, and the frequent conflict between individual and subgroup self-interest, on the one hand, and societal interest, on the other. All of these cultural arrangements, while they are not in themselves crises, do tend to promote overpopulation, overconsumption, and other symptoms of the environmental crisis, and are clearly linked to poverty, war, crime, and many personal crises.

At this phase of the disease, continued specialization may be a fatal flaw. Specialists are now busily treating symptoms as causes; and in many cases, certain groups even have a special stake in—and indeed may profit by treating—specific symptoms. The defense establishment, for example, "treats" war, the police and legal professions treat crime, and various health professionals and social workers handle personal crises. The very specialization of these fields makes it unlikely that researchers will perceive connections between deliberately isolated and apparently unrelated symptoms. In many cases, even if a definitive solution were discovered, it would almost certainly be resisted by specialist groups because it might be a clear threat to their job security. Real peace would cause enormous dislocation for the military, and numerous studies indicate that even disarmament would have far-reaching economic repercussions within the military-industrial complex and throughout the entire economy. It should be no surprise that the discovery of the saccharine disease and its simple cure has had relatively little impact on either the health or the food industries. In this case the investigation has not been carried far enough. The concentrated carbohydrates which seem to be the immediate cause of so many of our current health problems are produced and distributed by a massive food industry, which in turn is merely one expression of extreme stratification and specialization.

If this analysis is correct, radical surgery may be the only certain way to save the patient. Extreme forms of social stratification and economic specialization may simply be maladaptive. The kind of drastic cultural transformation that eliminating, or at least detoxicating, stratification and specialization would involve is so profound that it might seem sheer madness even to propose it. However, such a transformation and its full implications should be explored. It may be some comfort to realize that the kinds of cultural changes that might be required to effect a cure are no more sweeping than the kinds of changes that have been thrust upon much of the so-called "developing world" in recent decades. In fact, economist Robert L. Heilbroner's prescription for development may describe precisely the scope of the change that will be needed to solve the world crisis: "Nothing short of a pervasive social transformation will suffice: a wholesale metamorphosis of habits, a wrenching reorientation of values concerning time, status, money, work; an unweaving and reweaving of the fabric of daily existence itself." (1963:53)

Impact Assessment and Regional Planning

Large-scale regional planning projects and environmental impact studies are new efforts to identify and alleviate at least some of the adverse side effects of progress before they occur. While this work does represent a very promising attempt to shape the future along more desirable lines, and even though it is wide in scope and interdisciplinary in nature, it still lacks the anthropological perspectives that would provide a broad sense of the problem and a clear definition of future goals.

In the United States the National Environmental Policy Act of

1969 (United States, Environmental Protection Agency 1973) provides the legal charter for a sweeping evaluation of the immediate and long-run impact of industrial expansion on both man and the environment. The broad purpose of the act is to make it official policy to encourage harmony between man and nature, to prevent damage to the biosphere, and to stimulate human health and welfare. This purpose is to be accomplished without sacrificing a "high standard of living"; but it is clear that "progress," as it has been measured in the past, will not continue to be the sole standard of national welfare. There is explicit recognition of the fact that unchecked population growth, industrialization, urbanization, and resource exploitation represent serious threats to the well-being of the nation. The act specifically declares that "all practical means" be used to carry out the policy, and requires that all federal agencies use a "systematic, interdisciplinary approach," including the social sciences, in environmental decision making. Most importantly, the act requires that for every federal action "significantly affecting the quality of the human environment" an environmental impact statement must be prepared, detailing:

(i) the environmental impact of the proposed action,

(ii) any adverse environmental effects which cannot be avoided should the proposal be implemented,

(iii) alternatives to the proposed action,

(iv) the relationship between local short-term uses of man's environment and the maintenance and enhancement of long-term productivity, and

(v) any irreversible and irretrievable commitments of resources which would be involved in the proposed action should it be implemented.

If these questions were raised for all major cultural activities in modern industrial states and were then systematically investigated, the underlying causes of the world crisis would almost certainly be uncovered, and basic remedial action might be possible. This is clearly an area of research where anthropologists can make a profound contribution toward guiding our future cultural development. Assessing the impact of cultural practices on man, nature, and culture has long been a concern of anthropology; but in the past, this activity has not been directed toward specific goals, such as providing solutions to the world crisis.

Impact assessment is still in an experimental stage, but a number of weaknesses in the present procedure are already apparent. In the first place, future "needs" that proposed actions are designed to satisfy are characteristically identified on the basis of current cultural conditions and past trends. Thus an inherently conservative element is built in, and projections for future growth in population and consumption become self-fulfilling prophesies. There has also been a tendency to deemphasize the cultural implications of proposed actions in favor of detailed treatment of the immediate impact on nature, and a concomitant failure to explore fully the "no-action" or "no-growth" alternative.

In many cases, impact statements also suffer from the limitations of specialization. Problems are seen in isolation, and even though they may be explored individually in great detail, their aggregate consequences and implications may be overlooked. The construction of an electric transmission line in a particular county, the Alaska oil pipeline, and coal stripping in the West are treated in separate statements, while the real question of energy use in the culture may be either completely avoided or else it is handled by other specialists. Radically different solutions to the problems posed are simply not being adequately explored. Really fundamental questions regarding human needs, the long-range viability of our system of cultural adaptation, and the assessment of human costs and benefits in a highly stratified society are still not being addressed. These are anthropological questions; unfortunately, however, not even anthropologists have yet shown sufficient interest in them. Perhaps anthropologists should prepare an environmental impact statement for civilization as a whole and seriously attempt to detail the full consequences of this profound cultural transformation.

Planning Progress for the Pacific Northwest

The shortcomings of present planning processes and the possibilities for anthropological input may be explored further by a brief consideration of a concrete example. Among the most ambitious attempts at regional planning have been the massive studies of future land and water development in the United States that were authorized by the Water Resources Planning Act of 1965. Here, we shall examine the Columbia–North Pacific Region Comprehensive Framework Study (Pacific Northwest River Basins Commission 1971–1973) that was conducted over a five-year period by 20 federal agencies in cooperation with seven western state governments. The main report covering the entire region consists of a summary volume and an 18-volume Appendix that runs into thousands of pages covering such topics as energy, flood control, wildlife, the economic base, and so on. In addition, there are subregional studies that are equally impressive. The overall purpose of the project was outlined as follows: ". . . to provide a broad guide to the best use, or combination of uses, of water and related land resources of a region to meet foreseeable short- and long-term needs. This involves broad scaled analyses of the region's water and related land resource problems, both present and future, and general appraisals of the probable nature, extent, and timing of measures for their solution."

By A.D. 2020, the planners project that the population of the region will more than double its 1970 base population of 6.3 million, per capita incomes will triple or quadruple, requirements for electrical energy will increase tenfold, water requirements will triple, the potential for flood damage will quadruple, and there will be enormous unsatisfied demands for recreation, fish, and game. A vast, multibillion-dollar proposal was made for the development of new reservoirs, thermal power plants, and numerous special projects and programs, all designed to meet future "demands" and still preserve environmental "quality" and retain "flexibility" for future contingencies.

Some of the limitations of this immense planning project are immediately apparent when it is realized that economic efficiency and regional economic development are ranked among the primary objectives and that future needs are only projected for 50 years. There is no systematic treatment of the basic fossil fuel energy base and the implications of shortages. Likewise, there is no detailed consideration of radical alternatives to the need for electric energy such as the reduction of demand or the development of decentralized low-output domestic generators. Also overlooked is the basic question of what kind of regional culture might be developed if the billions of dollars slated for further expansion along the lines already laid down were to be diverted to the development of an essentially low-energy means of satisfying basic human needs. The anthropological record provides countless other solutions to the problem of developing land and water resources that simply have not been considered.

Views of the Future

In recent decades, there has been an enormous outpouring of future-oriented literature. While no attempt at a full survey of this work will be attempted here, it is possible to examine some of the alternatives that futurists envision in terms of the anthropological perspectives on the world crisis developed in preceding chapters. For convenience, futurist writers may be grouped into three categories:
1. Biological evolutionists and consciousness transformationists
2. Scientific technocrats
3. Paraprimitivists

Biological evolutionists and consciousness transformationists such as Teilhard de Chardin are concerned with drastic transformations of man's present biological and/or psychic makeup. Possibilities here are almost endless, but if any should materialize, man's basic nature might totally change. However, such changes must either lie in the remote future or will be unaffected by deliberate planning, and need not concern us here.

Scientific technocrats such as Buckminster Fuller and Herman Kahn seem to have captured most of the attention of government planners. These futurists emphasize continual technological changes as the solution for all problems. Kahn and Anthony J. Wiener, perhaps the most influential of the futurists, present a detailed projection for the next few decades in their major work, *The Year 2000,* published in 1967. This work grew out of attempts to explore alternative futures supported by the Commission on the Year 2000 of the American Academy of Arts and Sciences and the Hudson Institute, a private research organization. Much of the book is built around the basic assumption that there will be a continuation at least to A.D. 2000 of what the authors call the *basic, long-term multifold trend* of industrialization, modernization, urbanization, population growth, and technological advance. While it is recognized that "surprising" deviations (such as war and natural disasters) from this "standard world" are possible, no serious internal problems are expected to prevent the arrival of a "postindustrial society" of mass leisure and affluence. There is no sense of an obvious world crisis in this projection. Five years later, in *Things to Come* (Kahn and Bruce-Briggs 1972), the "unlikely" possibility of a technological collapse, economic crises, and disillusionment with progress is given somewhat more credence, but the basic multifold trends still seem assured.

The Best of Both Worlds: A Paraprimitive Solution

[If] we are aware of our own best interests, we should try to restore to some extent to our own technological society the structured

character of a pre-industrial society. Can we not combine the
advantages of the former with those of the latter? Or, if we cannot
have the best of both worlds, should we not find some
compromise solution? (Taylor 1972:154)

For our purposes, the most important and promising group of futurist
writers and planners are those who demonstrate a clear appreciation
of the gravity and complexity of the world crisis and explore truly
radical alternatives designed to solve the basic problems. One of the
most thorough outlines for a national-level cultural transformation
was published in 1972 by the editors of the British science journal
The Ecologist, under the title *Blueprint for Survival.* This work begins
with the assumption that the continuation of present trends—or in
Kahn's terms, the "long-term multiform trend"—will mean certain
collapse for industrial civilization within the lifetime of many persons
living today. The authors feel that radical change of some type is
inevitable, and rest their argument primarily on the environmental
crisis and related social system disruptions. The goal set for their
planning is the creation of a truly stable and sustainable society that
will "give the fullest possible satisfaction to its members."
(Goldsmith 1972:21–23) Such a society would display the following
characteristics:
1.   Minimum disruption of ecological processes
2.   Maximum conservation of materials and energy
3.   A population in which recruitment equals loss
4.   A social system in which the individual can enjoy, rather
     than feel restricted by, the first three conditions (Goldsmith
     1972:23)
The specific means by which this goal may be achieved do
indeed represent a sweeping transformation of industrial culture and
are so clearly spelled out that they deserve to be presented in full:
1.   A control operation whereby environmental disruption is
     reduced as much as possible by technical means
2.   A freeze operation, in which present trends are halted
3.   A systematic substitution, by which the most dangerous
     components of these trends are replaced by technological

substitutes whose effect is less deleterious in the short term
but over the long term will be increasingly ineffective
4. Systematic substitution, by which these technological
    substitutes are replaced by "natural" or self-regulating ones
5. The invention, promotion, and application of alternative
    technologies that are energy- and materials-conservative
6. Decentralization of polity and economy at all levels, and
    the formation of communities small enough to be reason-
    ably self-regulating and self-supporting
7. Education for such communities (Goldsmith 1972:23–24)

At the heart of the proposals to reduce ecological disruption is
basically a reestablishment of natural as opposed to technological
regulation of ecological processes. In agriculture, for example, the
Blueprint envisions heavy reliance on biological control of insect
pests and on organic fertilizers. Resource management would be
accomplished by a tax system that would punish wasteful use of
energy and raw materials, and reward long-lived, labor-intensive
products. Pressure on the natural environment would also be
reduced by the establishment of a stationary population. In Britain,
where population already exceeds the carrying capacity in terms of
local food production, the plan calls for a reduction in population by
50 percent over the next 150 to 200 years.

Significantly, the key to the entire transformation lies in the
social system, which of course should be no surprise to anthropologists. The *Blueprint* points out that within a small, relatively
face-to-face and highly self-sufficient community, individuals would
be much more likely to organize and accept the cultural restraints
that would be needed to maintain long-term stability. Borrowing
freely on anthropological views of primitive communities, the authors emphasize that such small-scale societies would also provide
abundant personal satisfactions and stimulation that would more
than compensate for the reduction in consumption that stability
would require. Decentralization, self-sufficiency, and self-regulation would greatly reduce the need for transportation, and many
of the obvious costs of urbanization and massive centralized po-

litical systems. What they recommend is not a total abandonment of the nation-state concept, but rather the establishment of a new political system based on neighborhoods of 500 people as minimal units organized into communities of 5,000 and regions of 500,000 with national representation. The selection of 500 as the size of the minimal unit is surely no accident because, as has been indicated earlier, this is the mean size for many primitive societies and may represent the operation of some fundamentally human character- istics. Their plans call for well-integrated, carefully timed imple- mentation stretching over many years.

Biologist Paul Ehrlich has developed an alternative future along similar lines (Ehrlich 1974, Ehrlich and Harriman 1971). He argues that the most developed nations (*overdeveloped* in his terms) must undergo dedevelopment, and proposes a new constitution and complete political reorganization for the United States to help achieve such a goal. The presently underdeveloped areas must settle for semidevelopment emphasizing agrarian self-sufficiency, and a total restructuring of the world trade system will be required.

These proposals are drastic, of course, and they will be criticized as totally unreasonable and politically impossible to implement. The authors of the *Blueprint* have a very direct response to such criticisms: "If we plan remedial action with our eyes on political rather than ecological reality, then very reasonably, very practicably, and very surely we shall muddle our way to extinction." (1972:18)

What Ehrlich and the *Blueprint* propose is basically what Taylor calls the *paraprimitive solution.* It is an attempt to combine the best elements of industrial civilization with the obviously superior components of primitive cultures in order to establish a stable, utopian society. The notion of such a synthesis has very strong appeal, as a brief glance at the strength of the so-called counter- culture indicates. It was recently estimated (Conover 1973) that there are some 2,000 communes of various types, 200 underground newspapers, 50 journals, and 500 free schools actively exploring alternatives to the dominant consumption culture in the United

States. There is, of course, great diversity in the degree to which these groups reject industrial technology, but their pervasive disenchantment with progress and their frequent use of primitive models is striking. Very few, if any, of these experimental communities are totally self-sufficient, or really primitive in the strict sense. They are still dependent on the larger culture for many of their basic needs and can exist only with its sufferance. Furthermore, as Gordon Rattray Taylor (1972) points out, for a paraprimitive community to prove really successful, it must involve a larger number of people than most present communes are working with. A model paraprimitive society would theoretically include several local communities of 500 people and would need to sustain a minimum level of "soft" industrial technology, presumably including medicine, engineering, electronics, and assorted other specialties. We do not know what the minimum size of such a society would be, but this is a question that could certainly be investigated. There could be wide differences in the technological mix, population density, and other cultural features that individual societies might opt for, depending on local environmental conditions and other considerations.

The most critical question, however, is whether or not industrial technology could be supported by a society that rejected stratification and extreme specialization. As long as these two fundamental elements of civilization are retained, it seems unlikely that the very real advantages of primitive culture can be secured. In a sense, the experiment has already failed. There have been countless well-intended efforts to guide the "acculturation" of primitive societies coming into contact with the industrial world to allow them to enjoy "the best of both worlds"; but invariably, they have been destroyed in the process. Elsewhere, I have argued that primitive cultures and industrial civilization are simply incompatible—no fruitful merging can ever be achieved. However, the concept of deliberately planned synthetic cultures may well be a different matter, and until such cultures have been seriously experimented with from an anthro-

pologically solid base, the possibility of a truly successful paraprimitive solution should not be completely rejected.

The real barrier to the success of such a solution may well be the
very existence of social stratification and the special interest groups
of the dominant industrial culture. Any paraprimitive solution would
mean phasing out much of the existing cultural establishment, but it
is a fundamental anthropological principle that cultures resist
change. Short of a total collapse of the system due to some major
catastrophe, it seems unlikely that existing power structures will
voluntarily relinquish their power. It has been suggested by some
writers (Heilbroner 1974) that quite the opposite situation might
actually occur as the world crisis deepens—there may be much
greater political centralization to cope with the new problems. That
would of course be a move toward greater evolutionary complexity.
Cultural evolution may indeed be irreversible—until it has run its
course and primitive cultures reestablish themselves.

bibliography

ALVARADO, ANITA L. "Determinants of Population Stability in the Havasupai Indians." *American Journal of Physical Anthropology*, Vol. 33, No. 1 (1970), pp. 9–14.

ANDERSON, E. N., JR. "The Life and Culture of Ecotopia." In *Reinventing Anthropology*, edited by Dell Hymes, pp. 264–83. New York: Pantheon Books, Inc., 1969.

ANONYMOUS LETTER. *Current Anthropology*, Vol. 12, No. 2 (1971), p. 245.

ARDREY, ROBERT *The Territorial Imperative*. New York: Atheneum Publishers, 1966.

ARNOLD, JAMES R. "The Hydrogen-Cobalt Bomb." *Bulletin of the Atomic Scientists*, Vol. 6, No. 10 (1950), pp. 290–92.

ASIMOV, ISAAC "The End." *Penthouse*, January, 1971.

BARNETT, HAROLD, AND MORSE, CHANDLER *Scarcity and Growth: The Economics of Natural Resource Availability*. Baltimore: Johns Hopkins University Press, 1963.

BARNETT, HOMER G. *Anthropology in Administration*. New York: Row, Peterson, 1956.

BARTLETT, H. H. "Fire, Primitive Agriculture, and Grazing in the Tropics." In *Man's Role in Changing the Face of the Earth*, edited by William L. Thomas, Jr., pp. 692–720. Chicago: University of Chicago Press, 1956.

BAYLISS-SMITH, TIM "Constraints on Population Growth: The Case of the Polynesian Outlier Atolls in the Precontact Period." *Human Ecology*, Vol. 2, No. 4 (1974), pp. 259–95.

BENEDICT, RUTH *Patterns of Culture*. New York: Mentor Books, 1959.

BIRDSELL, J. B. "Some Environmental and Cultural Factors Influencing the Structure of Australian Aboriginal Populations." *American Naturalist*, Vol. 87, No. 834 (1953), pp. 171–207.

"Some Population Problems Involving Pleistocene Man." In *Population Studies: Animal Ecology and Demography*, Vol. 22, pp. 47–69. Cold Springs Harbor Symposia in Quantitative Biology, 1957.

"On Population Structure in Generalized Hunting and Collecting Populations." *Evolution*, Vol. 12, No. 2 (1958), pp. 189–205.

"Some Predictions for the Pleistocene Based on Equilibrium Systems among

Recent Hunter-Gatherers." In *Man the Hunter,* edited by Richard B. Lee and Irven DeVore, pp. 229–40. Chicago: Aldine Publishing Co., 1968.

"Ecology, Spacing Mechanisms, and Adaptive Behavior in Aboriginal Land Tenure." In *Land Tenure in the Pacific,* edited by Ron Crocombe, pp. 334–61. Melbourne: Oxford University Press, 1971.

"A Basic Demographic Unit." *Current Anthropology,* Vol. 14, No. 4 (1973), pp. 337–50.

BOAS, FRANZ *Anthropology and Modern Life.* New York: W. W. Norton & Co., Inc., 1928.

BODLEY, JOHN H. *Victims of Progress.* Menlo Park, Calif.: Cummings Publishing Co., Inc., 1975.

BOERMA, ADDEKE H. "A World Agricultural Plan." *Scientific American,* Vol. 223, No. 2 (1970), pp. 54–69.

BOGUE, DONALD T. *Principles of Demography.* New York: John Wiley & Sons, Inc., 1969.

BOHANNAN, PAUL "Beyond Civilization." *Natural History,* Vol. 80, No. 2 (1971), pp. 50–67.

BORGSTROM, GEORG *The Hungry Planet.* New York: Macmillan, Inc., 1965.

The Hungry Planet. 2d ed. New York: Macmillan, Inc., 1967.

BOSERUP, ESTER *The Conditions of Economic Growth.* Chicago: Aldine Publishing Co., 1965.

BOULDING, KENNETH "The Economics of the Coming Spaceship Earth." In *Environmental Quality in a Growing Economy: Essays from the Sixth Resources for the Future Forum,* edited by Henry Jarrett. Baltimore: Johns Hopkins University Press, 1966.

BROWN, HARRISON *The Challenge of Man's Future.* New York: Viking Press, Inc., 1954.

"Technological Denudation." In *Man's Role in Changing the Face of the Earth,* edited by William L. Thomas, Jr., pp. 1023–32. Chicago: University of Chicago Press, 1956.

BROWN, LESTER R. *Man, Land and Food.* United States Department of Agriculture FAE Report No. 11. (Washington, D.C.: U.S. Government Printing Office, 1963).

BROWN, PAULA, AND BROOKFIELD, H. C. *Struggle for Land.* Melbourne: Oxford University Press, 1963.

CARNEIRO, ROBERT L. "A Theory of the Origin of the State." *Science,* Vol. 169 (3947) (1970), pp. 733–38.

"Slash-and-Burn Agriculture: A Closer Look at Its Implications for Settlement Patterns." In *Men and Cultures,* edited by A. F. C. Wallace. Philadelphia: University of Pennsylvania Press, 1960.

"The Transition from Hunting to Horticulture in the Amazon Basin." *Proceedings of the Eighth International Congress of Anthropological and Ethnological Sciences,* pp. 244–48. Tokyo and Kyoto, 1968.

CARNEIRO, ROBERT L., AND HILSE, D. F. "On Determining the Probable Rate of Population Growth during the Neolithic." *American Anthropologist,* Vol. 68 (1966), pp. 177–81.

CARTER, BARRY "Nuclear Strategy and Nuclear Weapons." *Scientific American,* Vol. 230, No. 5 (1974), pp. 20–31.

CHAGNON, NAPOLEON *Yanomamo: The Fierce People.* New York: Holt, Rinehart and Winston, Inc., 1968.

CHARBONNIER, G. *Conversations with Claude Levi-Strauss.* London: Jonathan Cape, Ltd., 1969.

CHAYANOV, A. V. *The Theory of Peasant Economy.* Homewood, Ill.: Richard D. Irwin, Inc., for the American Economic Association, 1966.

CLARK, COLIN *Population Growth and Land Use.* London and New York: Macmillan Co., 1968.

CLARK J. G. D. *Prehistoric Europe: The Economic Base.* New York: Philosophical Library, Inc., 1952.

CLEAVE, T. L. *The Saccharine Disease.* Bristol: John Wright & Sons, 1974.

COALE, ANSLEY J. "The History of the Human Population." *Scientific American,* Vol. 231, No. 3 (1974), pp. 40–51.

COHEN, YEHUDI (ED.) *Man in Adaptation.* 2d ed. Chicago: Aldine Publishing Co., 1974.

COMMONER, BARRY *The Closing Circle.* New York: Alfred A. Knopf, Inc., 1971.

CONOVER, PATRICK W. "The Potential for an Alternate Society." *The Futurist,* June, 1973, pp. 111–16.

COOK, EARL "The Flow of Energy in an Industrial Society." *Scientific American,* Vol. 224, No. 3 (1971), pp. 134–44.

COOKE, G. W. "The Carrying Capacity of the Land in the Year 2000." In *The Optimum Population for Britain,* edited by L. R. Taylor, pp. 15–42. London and New York: Academic Press, Inc., 1970.

COON, CARLETON S. *The Hunting Peoples.* Boston: Little, Brown and Co., 1971.

COTTON, STEVE (ED.) *Earth Day—The Beginning.* New York: Arno Press, Inc. (Bantam), 1970.

DAKEYNE, R. B. "Conflicting Interests on Bougainville." *Pacific Viewpoint,* Vol. 8, No. 2 (1967), pp. 186–87.

DALTON, GEORGE *Economic Development and Social Change: The Modernization of Village Communities.* Garden City, N.Y.: Natural History Press, 1971.

DE BELL, GARRET (ED.) *The Environmental Handbook.* New York: Ballantine Books, Inc., 1970.

DEEVY, EDWARD S. "The Human Population." *Scientific American,* Vol. 203 (1960), pp. 195–204, 1969.

DASA. DEFENSE ATOMIC SUPPORT AGENCY *Proceedings of the Third Interdisciplinary Conference on Selected Effects of a General War.* DASIAC Special Report 120, Vol. 3 (DASA 2019–3). 1971.

DENTAN, ROBERT K. *The Semai: A Nonviolent People of Malaya.* New York: Holt, Rinehart and Winston, Inc., 1968.

DEWHURST, J. FREDERIC, AND ASSOCIATES *America's Needs and Resources: A New Survey.* New York: Twentieth Century Fund, 1955.
 America's Needs and Resources: A Twentieth Century Fund Survey Which Includes Estimates for 1950 and 1960. New York: Twentieth Century Fund, 1947.

DIAMOND, STANLEY *In Search of the Primitive*. New Brunswick, N.J.: Transaction Books, 1974.
"The Search for the Primitive." In *The Concept of the Primitive*, edited by Ashley Montagu, pp. 96–147. New York: Free Press, 1968.

DUMOND, DON E. "Population Growth and Political Centralization," In *Population Growth: Anthropological Implications*, edited by Brian Spooner, pp. 286–310. Cambridge: M.I.T. Press, 1972.

EAMES, EDWIN, AND GOODE, JUDITH G. *Urban Poverty in a Cross Cultural Context*. New York: Free Press, 1973.

EHRLICH, PAUL "Eco-Catastrophe." *Ramparts*, September, 1969, pp. 24–28.
The Population Bomb. New York: Ballantine Books, Inc., 1968.

EHRLICH, PAUL, AND EHRLICH, ANNE *Population, Resources, Environment*. San Francisco: W. H. Freeman and Co., 1972.
The End of Affluence. New York: Ballantine Books, Inc., 1974.

EHRLICH, PAUL, AND HARRIMAN, RICHARD L. *How to Be a Survivor: A Plan to Save Spaceship Earth*. New York: Ballantine Books, Inc., 1971.

ENGLISH, RICHARD D., AND BOLEF, DAN I. "Defense against Bomber Attack." *Scientific American*, Vol. 229, No. 2(1973), pp. 11–19.

FABUN, DON *Food: An Energy Exchange System*. Beverly Hills, Calif.: Glencoe Press, 1970.

FAIRCHILD, HOXIE NEALE *The Noble Savage: A Study in Romantic Naturalism*. New York: Columbia University Press, 1928.

FINKEL, A. (ED.) *Energy, the Environment, and Human Health*. Acton, Mass.: Publishing Sciences Group Inc., 1974.

FIRTH, RAYMOND *We the Tikopia*. New York: Barnes and Noble Books, 1957.

FLANNERY, KENT V. "Origins and Ecological Effects of Early Domestication in Iran and the Near East." In *The Domestication and Exploitation of Plants and Animals*, edited by Peter J. Ucko and G. W. Dimbleby. London: Gerald Duckworth and Co. Ltd., 1969.

FOSTER, GEORGE *Applied Anthropology*. Boston: Little, Brown and Co., 1969.

FRIED, MORTON *The Evolution of Political Society*. New York: Random House, Inc., 1967.

GARWIN, RICHARD L. "Anti-Submarine Warfare and National Security." *Scientific American*, Vol. 227, No. 1 (1972), pp. 14–25.

GARWIN, RICHARD L., AND BETHE, HANS A. "Anti-Ballistic Missile Systems." *Scientific American*, Vol. 218, No. 3 (1968), pp. 21–31.

GEERTZ, CLIFFORD *Agricultural Involution: The Process of Ecological Change in Indonesia*. Berkeley and Los Angeles: University of California Press, 1963.

GLASSTONE, SAMUEL (ED.) *The Effects of Nuclear Weapons*. Atomic Energy Commission. Washington, D.C.: U.S. Government Printing Office, 1962.

GOLDSMITH, EDWARD, ET AL. *Blueprint for Survival*. Boston: Houghton Mifflin Co., 1972.

GOODENOUGH, WARD H. *Cooperation in Change*. New York: John Wiley & Sons, Inc., 1963.

GOULET, DENIS *The Cruel Choice: A New Concept in the Theory of Development*. New York: Atheneum Publishers, 1971.

GREENWOOD, TED "Reconnaissance and Arms Control." *Scientific American*, Vol. 228, No. 2 (1973), pp. 14–25.

GROSS, DANIEL R., AND UNDERWOOD, BARBARA A. "Technological Change and Caloric Costs: Sisal Agriculture." *American Anthropologist*, Vol. 73, No. 2 (1971), pp. 725–40.

GUSTAFSON, A. F., ET AL. *Conservation in the United States*. Ithaca, N.Y.: Comstock, 1939.

GUTKIND, E. A. "Our World From the Air: Conflict and Adaptation." In *Man's Role in Changing the Face of the Earth*, edited by William L. Thomas, Jr., pp. 1–44. Chicago: University of Chicago Press, 1956.

HAGOOD, MEL A. "Which Irrigation System?" *11th Annual Proceedings, Washington Potato Conference*, pp. 83–86. Moses Lake, Washington, 1972.

HALLPIKE, C. R. "Functionalist Interpretations of Primitive Warfare." *Man*, Vol. 8, No. 3 (1973), pp. 451–70.

HARDIN, GARRETT "The Tragedy of the Commons." *Science*, Vol. 162 (1968), pp. 1243–48.

HARRIS, DAVID R. "The Origins of Agriculture in the Tropics." *American Scientist*, Vol. 60, No. 2 (1972), pp. 180–93.

HARRIS, MARVIN *Culture, Man and Nature*. New York: Thomas Y. Crowell Co., Inc., 1971.
Culture, People and Nature. New York: Thomas Y. Crowell Co., Inc., 1975.

HEER, DAVID M. *After Nuclear Attack: A Demographic Inquiry*. New York: Praeger Publishers, Inc., 1965.

HEILBRONER, ROBERT L. *The Great Ascent: The Struggle for Economic Development in Our Time*. New York: Harper & Row Torchbooks, 1963.
An Inquiry Into the Human Prospect. New York: W. W. Norton & Co., Inc., 1974.

HELFRICH, HAROLD W., JR. (ED.) *The Environmental Crisis*. New Haven and London: Yale University Press, 1970.

HENRY, JULES *Culture against Man*. New York: Random House, Inc., 1963.

HERSKOVITS, MELVILLE J. *Economic Anthropology*. New York: Alfred A. Knopf, Inc., 1952.

HICKERSON, HAROLD "The Virginia Deer and Intertribal Buffer Zones in the Upper Mississippi Valley." In *Man, Culture and Animals: The Role of Animals in Human Ecological Adjustments*, edited by Anthony Leeds and Andrew P. Vayda. Publication No. 78. Washington, D.C.: American Association for the Advancement of Science, pp. 43–65. 1965.

HOCKETT, CHARLES F., AND ASCHER, ROBERT "The Human Revolution." In *The Subversive Science: Essays toward an Ecology of Man*, edited by Paul Shephard and Daniel McKinley, pp. 13–42. Boston: Houghton Mifflin Co., 1969.

HOLDREN, JOHN P., EHRLICH, PAUL R. (EDS.) *Global Ecology*. New York: Harcourt Brace Jovanovich, Inc., 1971.

HSU, FRANCIS "Rethinking the Concept 'Primitive.'" *Current Anthropology*, Vol. 5, No. 3 (1964), pp. 169–78.

HUBERT, M. KING "Energy Resources." In *Resources and Man*, National Academy of Sciences, pp. 157–242. San Francisco: W. H. Freeman and Co., 1969.

ISAAC, ERICH "On the Domestication of Cattle." In *The Subversive Science: Essays toward an Ecology of Man,* edited by Paul Shephard and Daniel McKinley, pp. 190–209. Boston: Houghton Mifflin Co., 1969.

JACOBSEN, THORKILD, AND ADAMS, ROBERT M. "Salt and Silt in Ancient Mesopotamian Agriculture." *Science,* Vol. 128 (1958), pp. 125–58.

KAHN, HERMAN *On Thermonuclear War.* Princeton: Princeton University Press, 1961.

Thinking about the Unthinkable. New York: Horizon Press, 1962.

KAHN, HERMAN, AND WIENER, ANTHONY J. *The Year 2000: A Framework for Speculation on the Next Thirty-three Years.* New York: Macmillan, Inc., 1967.

KAHN, HERMAN, AND BRUCE-BRIGGS, B. *Things to Come: Thinking about the 70's and 80's.* New York: Macmillan, Inc., 1972.

KELLY, RAYMOND C. "Demographic Pressure and Descent Group Structure in the New Guinea Highlands." *Oceania,* Vol. 38 (1968), pp. 36–63.

KEENLEYSIDE, H. L. "Critical Mineral Shortages." In *Proceedings of the United Nations Scientific Conference on the Conservation and Utilization of Resources, 17 August–6 September 1949,* pp. 38–46. Lake Success, N.Y.: United Nations, 1950.

KERMODE, G. O. "Food Additives." *Scientific American,* Vol. 226, No. 3 (1972), pp. 15–21.

KNUDSON, BOB "Time Management—It Pays." *11th Annual Proceedings, Washington Potato Conference,* pp. 71–76. Moses Lake, Wash., 1972.

KNUDSON, KENNETH E. "Resource Fluctuation, Productivity, and Social Organization on Micronesian Coral Islands." Doctoral dissertation, University of Oregon, 1970.

KOCH, KLAUS-FRIEDRICH "Cannibalistic Revenge in Jalé Warfare." *Natural History,* Vol. 79, No. 2 (1970), pp. 41–50.

KUNSTADTER, PETER "Natality, Mortality and Migration in Upland and Lowland Populations in Northwestern Thailand." In *Culture and Population,* edited by Steven Polgar, pp. 46–60. Cambridge, Mass., and London: Schenkman Publishing Co., Inc., 1971.

LANDSBERG, HANS H. *Natural Resources in America's Future: A Look Ahead to the Year 2000.* Baltimore: Johns Hopkins University Press, 1964.

LANDSBERG, HANS H.; FISCHMAN, LEONARD L.; AND FISHER, JOSEPH L. *Resources in America's Future: Patterns of Requirements and Availabilities 1960–2000.* Baltimore: Johns Hopkins University Press, 1963.

LATHRAP, DON W. *The Upper Amazon.* New York: Praeger Publishers, Inc., 1970.

LEE, RICHARD B. "Kung Bushman Subsistence: An Input-Output Analysis." *Contributions to Anthropology: Ecological Essays.* National Museums of Canada Bulletin 230 (1969), pp. 73–94.

"What Hunters Do for a Living, or, How to Make Out on Scarce Resources." In *Man the Hunter,* edited by Richard B. Lee and Irven De Vore, pp. 30–48. Chicago: Aldine Publishing Co., 1968.

LEE, RICHARD B., AND DEVORE, IRVEN *Man the Hunter.* Chicago: Aldine Publishing Co., 1968.

LEVIN, M. G., AND POTAPOV, L. P. *The Peoples of Siberia.* Chicago: University of Chicago Press, 1964.

LEVI-STRAUSS, CLAUDE "The Social and Psychological Aspects of Chieftainship in a Primitive Tribe." *Transactions of the New York Academy of Sciences,* Series 2, Vol. 7 (1944), pp. 16–32.

LORENZ, KONRAD *On Aggression.* New York: Harcourt, Brace and World, 1966.

LOVERING, T. S. "Non-Fuel Mineral Resources in the Next Century." *Texas Quarterly,* Summer, 1968, pp. 127–47.

LUTEN, DANIEL B. "United States Requirements." In *Energy, the Environment, and Human Health,* edited by A. Finkel, pp. 17–33. Acton, Mass.: Publishing Sciences Group Inc., 1974.

McCARTHY, FREDERICK D., AND McARTHUR, MARGARET "The Food Quest and the Time Factor in Aboriginal Economic Life." In *Records of the Australian-American Scientific Expedition to Arnhem Land,* Vol. 2: *Anthropology and Nutrition.* Edited by Charles P. Mountford, pp. 145–194. Melbourne: Melbourne University Press, 1960.

McHALE, JOHN *World Facts and Trends.* New York: Macmillan, Inc., 1972.

MacNEISH, RICHARD S. "Speculation about How and Why Food Production and Village Life Developed in the Tehuacan Valley, Mexico." *Archaeology,* Vol. 24, No. 4 (1971), pp. 307–15.

MALINOWSKI, BRONISLAW "An Anthropological Analysis of War." *American Journal of Sociology,* Vol. 46 (1941), pp. 521–50.
Freedom and Civilization. New York: Roy Publishers, Inc., 1944.

MALTHUS, THOMAS R. *An Essay on the Principle of Population* (parallel chapters from the [1st] and [2d] editions). New York and London: Macmillan Co., 1895.

MARPLE, GARY A., AND WISSMANN, HARRY B. (EDS.) *Grocery Manufacturing in the United States.* New York: Praeger Publishers, Inc., 1968.

MARSH, GEORGE P. *Man and Nature.* New York: Charles Scribner's Sons, 1864.

MARTIN, THOMAS L., JR., AND LATHAM, DONALD C. *Strategy for Survival.* Tuscon: University of Arizona Press, 1963.

MAZUR, ALLAN, AND ROSA, EUGENE "Energy and Life Style." *Science,* Vol. 186 (4164) (1974), pp. 607–10.

MEAD, MARGARET "Earth People." In *Earth Day—The Beginning,* edited by Steve Cotton, pp. 222–23. New York: Arno Press, Inc. [Bantam], 1970.
"Warfare Is Only an Invention—Not a Biological Necessity." *Asia,* Vol. 40 (1940), pp. 402–5.

MEADOWS, DONELLA H., ET AL. *The Limits to Growth.* New York: Universe Books, 1972.

MEGGERS, BETTY J. *Amazonia: Man and Culture in a Counterfeit Paradise.* Chicago: Aldine Publishing Co., 1971.

MEGGERS, BETTY J., AND EVANS, CLIFFORD *Archeological Investigations at the Mouth of the Amazon.* Bulletin 167. Washington, D.C.: Bureau of American Ethnology, Smithsonian Institution, 1957.

MINING MAGAZINE "Bougainville Project Nearing Completion." *Mining Magazine,* Vol. 124, No. 5 (1971) pp. 377–381.

MONTAGU, ASHLEY "Sociogenic Brain Damage." *American Anthropologist,* Vol. 74,
    No. 5 (1972), pp. 1045–61.
MORGAN, LEWIS HENRY *Ancient Society.* New York: Henry Holt and Co., 1878.
MOSELY, MICHAEL EDWARD *The Maritime Foundations of Andean Civilization.* Menlo
    Park, Calif.: Cummings Publishing Co., Inc., 1975.
MURDOCK, GEORGE P. "Human Influences on Ecosystems of High Islands." In *Man's
    Place in the Island Ecosystem,* edited by F. R. Fosberg, pp. 145–52. Bishop
    Museum Press, 1963.
NAROLL, R. "Does Military Deterrence Deter?" *Trans-Action,* Vol. 3, No. 2 (1966),
    pp. 14–20.
NASH, MANNING *Primitive and Peasant Economic Systems.* San Francisco: Chandler
    Publishing Co., 1966.
NATIONAL ACADEMY OF SCIENCES. *Resources and Man.* San Francisco: W. H. Freeman
    and Co., 1969.
NEEL, JAMES V. "Lessons from a Primitive People." *Science,* Vol. 170 (1970), pp.
    815–21.
    "Some Aspects of Differential Fertility in Two American Indian Tribes."
    *Proceedings of the Eighth International Congress of Anthropological and
    Ethnological Sciences,* Vol. 1 (1968), pp. 356–61. Tokyo and Kyoto, 1968.
NEWCOMB, W. W., JR. "Toward an Understanding of War." In *Essays in the Science
    of Culture,* edited by Gertrude Dole and Robert L. Carneiro, pp. 317–36. New
    York: Thomas Y. Crowell Co., Inc., 1960.
NIETSCHMANN, BERNARD *Between Land and Water: The Subsistence Ecology of the
    Miskito Indians, Eastern Nicaragua.* New York and London: Seminar Press,
    1973.
NOUGIER, LOUIS-RENÉ, Essai sur le peuplement prehistorique de la France. *Population*
    (Paris) Vol. 9, pp. 241–273, 1954.
NULTY, LESLIE *The Green Revolution in West Pakistan.* New York: Praeger Publishers,
    Inc., 1972.
ODUM, HOWARD T. *Environment, Power, and Society.* New York: John Wiley &
    Sons, Inc., Inter-Science, 1971.
OTTERBEIN, KEITH *The Evolution of War: A Cross Cultural Study.* New Haven, Conn.:
    Human Relations Area Files Press, 1970.
PACIFIC NORTHWEST RIVER BASINS COMMISSION *Columbia–North Pacific Region
    Comprehensive Framework Study.* 18 Vols. 1971–1973.
PADDOCK, WILLIAM, AND PADDOCK, PAUL *Famine—1975!* Boston and Toronto: Little,
    Brown and Co., 1967.
PAYNE, ROGER "Among Wild Whales." *New York Zoological Society Newsletter,*
    November, 1968, pp. 1–6.
PIMENTEL, DAVID, ET AL. "Food Production and the Energy Crisis." *Science,* Vol. 182
    (4110) (1973), pp. 443–49.
PLATT, JOHN "What We Must Do." *Science,* Vol. 166 (1969), pp. 1115–21.
POLGAR, STEVEN "Population History and Population Policies from an
    Anthropological Perspective." *Current Anthropology,* Vol. 13, No. 2 (1972), pp.
    203–11.
PORTER, BERNARD *Critics of Empire.* London: Macmillan Co., 1968.

RAPOPORT, ROGER *The Great American Bomb Machine*. New York: E. P. Dutton & Co., Inc., 1971.

RAPPAPORT, ROY "The Flow of Energy in an Agricultural Society." *Scientific American*, Vol. 224, No. 3 (1971), pp. 117–32.

Pigs for the Ancestors: Ritual in the Ecology of a New Guinea People. New Haven: Yale University Press, 1968.

REDFIELD, ROBERT *The Primitive World and Its Transformations*. Ithaca, N.Y.: Cornell University Press, 1953.

REED, STEPHEN W. *The Making of Modern New Guinea*. Philadelphia: American Philosophical Society, 1943.

REICHEL-DOLMATOFF, GERARDO *Amazonian Cosmos: The Sexual and Religious Symbolism of the Tukano Indians*. Chicago and London: University of Chicago Press, 1971.

REINING, PRISCILLA "Report of the Working Group at the Tokyo Congress." *Current Anthropology*, Vol. 10, No. 4 (1969), pp. 371–74.

REYNOLDS, VERNON "Ethology of Urban Life." In *Man, Settlement, and Urbanism*, edited by Peter J. Ucko, R. A. Tringham, and G. W. Dimbleby, pp. 401–8. London: Gerald Duckworth and Co. Ltd., 1972.

RIBEIRO, DARCY *The Civilizational Process*. Translated by Betty J. Meggers. Washington, D.C.: Smithsonian Institution Press, 1968.

RICHARDS, PAUL W. "The Tropical Rain Forest." *Scientific American*, Vol. 229, No. 6 (1973), pp. 58–67.

RYAN, PETER (ED.) "Bougainville Copper Project." In *Encyclopedia of Papua New Guinea*, Vol. 1, pp. 92–102. Melbourne: Melbourne University Press, 1972.

SAHLINS, MARSHALL "Evolution: Specific and General." In *Evolution and Culture*, edited by Marshall Sahlins and Elman R. Service, pp. 12–44. Ann Arbor: University of Michigan Press, 1960.

"Notes on the Original Affluent Society." In *Man the Hunter*, edited by Richard B. Lee and Irven DeVore, pp. 85–89. Chicago: Aldine Publishing Co., 1968.

"The Segmentary Lineage: An Organization of Predatory Expansion." *American Anthropologist*, Vol. 63, No. 2 Pt. 1, pp. 322–45.

Stone Age Economics. Chicago: Aldine Publishing Co., 1972.

SAHLINS, MARSHALL, AND SERVICE, ELMAN R. (EDS.) *Evolution and Culture*. Ann Arbor: University of Michigan Press, 1960.

SAPIR, EDWARD "Culture, Genuine and Spurious." In *Culture, Language and Personality*, edited by David G. Mandelbaum, pp. 78–119. Berkeley and Los Angeles: University of California Press, 1964.

SAUCIER, JEAN-FRANÇOIS "Correlates of the Long Postpartum Taboo: A Cross-Cultural Study." *Current Anthropology*, Vol. 13, No. 2 (1972), pp. 238–49.

SCHNEIDER, DAVID "Abortion and Depopulation on a Pacific Island: Yap." In *Health, Culture, and Community*, edited by B. D. Paul, pp. 211–35. New York: Russell Sage Foundation, 1955.

SCOVILLE, HERBERT, JR. "Missile Submarines and National Security." *Scientific American*, Vol. 226, No. 6 (1972), pp. 15–27.

SENGEL, RANDAL A. "Comments." *Current Anthropology*, Vol. 14, No. 5 (1973), pp. 540–42.

SERVICE, ELMAN R. *Primitive Social Organization.* New York: Random House, Inc., 1962.

SHALER, NATHANIEL S. *Man and the Earth.* New York: Duffield, 1905.

SHANTZIS, STEVEN B., AND BEHRENS, WILLIAM W., III "Population Control Mechanisms in a Primitive Agricultural Society." In *Toward Global Equilibrium,* edited by D. H. Meadows and D. L. Meadows, pp. 257–88. Cambridge, Mass.: Wright-Allen Press, 1973.

SHEPHARD, PAUL, AND MCKINLEY, DANIEL (EDS.) *The Subversive Science: Essays toward an Ecology of Man.* Boston: Houghton Mifflin Co., 1969.

SMITH, PHILIP E. *The Consequences of Food Production.* Module in Anthropology Reading, Mass.: Addison-Wesley Publishing Co., Inc., 1972.

SOFER, CYRIL "Buying and Selling: A Study in the Sociology of Distribution." *Sociological Review,* July, 1965, pp. 183–209.

SOLOW, ROBERT M. "The Economics of Resources or the Resources of Economics." *American Economic Review,* Vol. 64, No. 2 (1974), pp. 1–14.

SOUTHALL, A. "The Illusion of Tribe." In *The Passing of Tribal Man in Africa,* edited by Peter C. Gutkind, pp. 28–50. Leiden: Brill, 1970.

SPAULDING, WILLARD M., JR., AND OGDEN, RONALD D. *Effects of Surface Mining on the Fish and Wildlife Resources of the United States.* Bureau of Sport Fisheries and Wildlife Resources Publication 68. Washington, D.C.: U.S. Government Printing Office, 1968.

SPOEHR, ALEXANDER "Cultural Differences in the Interpretation of Natural Resources." In *Man's Role in Changing the Face of of the Earth,* edited by William L. Thomas, Jr., pp. 93–102. Chicago: University of Chicago Press, 1956.

SPOONER, BRIAN *The Cultural Ecology of Pastoral Nomads.* Module in Anthropology No. 45. Reading, Mass.: Addison-Wesley Publishing Co., Inc., 1973.

STEINHART, JOHN S., AND STEINHART, CAROL E. "Energy Use in the U.S. Food System." *Science,* Vol. 184 (1974), pp. 307–16.

STONIER, TOM *Nuclear Disaster.* Cleveland and New York: World Publishing Co., Meridian Books, 1964.

STURTEVANT, WILLIAM C. "Urgent Anthropology." *Current Anthropology,* Vol. 8, No. 4 (1967), pp. 355–61.

SUSSMAN, ROBERT W. "Child Transport, Family Size, and Increase in Human Population during the Neolithic." *Current Anthropology,* Vol. 13, No. 2 (1972), pp. 258–59.

SWEET, LOUISE "Camel Pastoralism in North Arabia and the Minimal Camping Unit." In *Man, Culture and Animals: The Role of Animals in Human Ecological Adjustments,* edited by Anthony Leeds and Andrew Vayda, pp. 129–152. Publication No. 78. Washington D.C.: American Association for the Advancement of Science, 1965.

TALBURT, WILLIAM F., AND SMITH, ORA *Potato Processing.* Westport, Conn.: Avi Publishing Co., 1967.

TAX, SOL "Discussion." In *Man the Hunter,* edited by Richard B. Lee and Irven De Vore, pp. 345–46. Chicago: Aldine Publishing Co., 1968.

"Letter to Associates." *Current Anthropology,* Vol. 12, No. 2 (1971), pp. 243–54.

" 'Primitive' Peoples." *Current Anthropology,* Vol. 1 (1960), pp. 441–45.

TAYLOR, GORDON RATTRAY *Rethink: A Paraprimitive Solution.* London: Secker & Warburg, 1972.

THOMAS, WILLIAM L., JR. (ED.) *Man's Role in Changing the Face of the Earth.* Chicago: University of Chicago Press, 1956.

TOFFLER, ALVIN *Future Shock.* New York: Bantam Books, Inc., 1971.

TROWELL, HUGH C. "Kwashiorkor." *Scientific American,* Vol. 191, No. 6 (1954), pp. 46–50.

TURNBULL, COLIN "The Importance of Flux in Two Hunting Societies." In *Man the Hunter,* edited by Richard B. Lee and Irven DeVore, pp. 132–37. Chicago: Aldine Publishing Co., 1968.

UNITED NATIONS, DEPARTMENT OF ECONOMIC AFFAIRS *Proceedings of the United Nations Scientific Conference on the Conservation and Utilization of Resources, 17 August–6 September 1949.* Lake Success, N.Y., 1950.

UNITED NATIONS, FOOD AND AGRICULTURE ORGANIZATION *Third World Food Survey.* Freedom from Hunger Basic Study No. 11. Rome, 1963.

UNITED NATIONS, TRUSTEESHIP COUNCIL "Report of the United Nations Visiting Mission to the Trust Territory of New Guinea, 1968." *Trusteeship Council Official Records: Thirty-fifth Session (27 May–19 June 1968).* Supplement No. 2. New York, 1968.

"Report of the United Nations Visiting Mission to the Trust Territory of New Guinea, 1971." *Trusteeship Council Official Records: Thirty-eighth Session (25 May–18 June 1971).* Supplement No. 2. New York, 1971.

UNITED STATES, DEPARTMENT OF COMMERCE *Census of Agriculture.* Vol. 1: *Area Reports,* Part 46, "[state of] Washington." Washington D.C.: U.S. Government Printing Office, 1969.

Census of Agriculture. Vol. 5, Part 4, "Sugar Crops, Potatoes, Other Specified Crops." Washington D.C.: U.S. Government Printing Office, 1969.

UNITED STATES, DEPARTMENT OF THE INTERIOR, BUREAU OF LAND MANAGEMENT *Draft Environmental Impact Statement: Proposed Federal Coal Leasing Program.* 2 vols. Washington D.C.: U.S. Government Printing Office, 1974.

UNITED STATES, ENVIRONMENTAL PROTECTION AGENCY *Legal Compilation: Statutes and Legislative History, Executive Orders, Regulations, Guidelines, and Reports (General).* Vol. 1. Washington, D.C.: U.S. Government Printing Office, 1973.

UNITED STATES, NATIONAL ADVISORY COMMISSION ON CIVIL DISORDERS [Kerner Report]. Washington, D.C.: U.S. Government Printing Office, 1968.

UNITED STATES, NATIONAL COMMISSION ON THE CAUSES AND PREVENTION OF VIOLENCE *Justice: To Establish Justice, to Ensure Domestic Tranquility.* Final Report. Washington, D.C.: U.S. Government Printing Office, 1969.

UNITED STATES, PRESIDENT'S MATERIALS POLICY COMMISSION *Resources for Freedom* (Paley Commission Report). Washington, D.C.: U.S. Government Printing Office, 1952.

UNITED STATES, PRESIDENT'S SCIENCE ADVISORY COMMITTEE *The World Food Problem:*

A Report of the Panel on the World Food Supply. 3 vols. Washington, D.C.: U.S. Government Printing Office, 1967.

VANEK, JOANN "Time Spent in Housework." *Scientific American,* Vol. 231, No. 5 (1974), pp. 116–20.

VAYDA, ANDREW P. "Primitive Warfare." In *International Encyclopedia of the Social Sciences.* Macmillan Publishing Co., Inc., and Free Press, 1968.

WAGLEY, CHARLES "Cultural Influences on Population." *Revista do Museu Paulista,* Vol. 5 (1951), pp. 95–104.

WHITE, LESLIE A. *The Evolution of Culture.* New York: McGraw-Hill Book Co., Inc., 1959.

The Science of Culture. New York: Grove Press, Inc., 1949.

WHITE, LYNN, JR. "The Historical Roots of Our Ecological Crisis." *Science,* Vol. 155 (1967), pp. 1203–7.

WIESNER, JEROME B., AND YORK, HERBERT F. "National Security and the Nuclear-Test Ban." *Scientific American,* Vol. 211, No. 4 (1964), pp. 27–35.

WILLEY, GORDON R., AND SHIMKIN, DEMITRIC B. "The Collapse of Classic Maya Civilization in the Southern Lowlands: A Symposium Summary Statement." *Southwestern Journal of Anthropology,* Vol. 27, No. 1 (1971), pp. 1–18.

WOODBURN, JAMES "An Introduction to Hadza Ecology." In *Man the Hunter,* edited by Richard B. Lee and Irven DeVore, pp. 49–55. Chicago: Aldine Publishing Co., 1968.

"Stability and Flexibility in Hadza Residential Groupings." In *Man the Hunter,* edited by Richard B. Lee and Irven DeVore, pp. 103–10. Chicago: Aldine Publishing Co., 1968.

WRIGHT, QUINCY *A Study of War.* 2 vols. Chicago: University of Chicago Press, 1942.

YDE, JENS *Material Culture of the Waiwai.* Nationalmuseets Skrifter. Etnografisk Roekke X. Copenhagen: National Museum, 1965.

YORK, HERBERT F. "The Great Test-Ban Debate." *Scientific American,* Vol. 227, No. 5 (1972), pp. 15–23.

YOUNG, VERNON R., AND SCRIMSHAW, NEVIN S. "The Physiology of Starvation." *Scientific American,* Vol. 225, No. 4 (1971), pp. 14–21.

ZUBROW, EZRA B. *Prehistoric Carrying Capacity.* Menlo Park, Calif.: Cummings Publishing Co., Inc., 1975.

index

SUBJECT INDEX